Statecraft

By David Murdoch

Table of Contents:

XXIX: Racism

Conclusion:

Introduction:

Jesus Christ told Pilate 'my kingdom is not of this world'. Christ is a King, who possesses all power over all things, but when He established His church, He was not establishing a political state. He was building the door by which people would enter His country – a country that was not like the political states of this world, with laws and government.

This kingdom is not of this world, but this kingdom exists. It exists within the hearts of every person who has accepted the gospel and obeyed its teachings in his life. It exists in this physical world here and in heaven above, but it does not belong to this world with its passing ephemerality.

If Christ wanted to establish a political state, it would not have been difficult. He could just have used His divine power to destroy His enemies and make the world bow down before Him as their earthly king.

In the DC comics film 'Batman vs Superman', Batman has a vision of Superman using his alien power for dominating the world; if Christ had been following the human way of establishing His kingdom, rather than God's way, He would have been something like that idea from that movie, but far more powerful. He wouldn't have needed jihadists or zealots to fight to establish His rule, because He actually is God and He doesn't require the strength of human beings to establish His kingdom, as though He could not have done it Himself.

Salvation doesn't come from the political state.

Establishing the rule of Christ on Earth is not accomplished by force of arms or the power of institutions; it is established by the willing reception of His gospel and the taking up of the cross by those who have received His love.

But political states do exist even so. There are governments, there are laws and constitutions, there are police forces and armies, there are bureaucracies and borders. These things exist and they are necessary to exist as well in our sinful world, because by a mercy of God, He has allowed us to have such things so that we can live a better existence, where people can live together in relative peace and order.

People who don't fear being killed or harmed in a lawless world can live together, contribute their talents to building up a civilization and developing their world to improve their material existence. Thus, the state was created and gave this security to people. Otherwise the Neolithic revolution may have never worked, and we would still be living as nomads, foraging and hunting for our own survival, while sleeping in caves. God's mercy gave us the gift of the state.

The call of the gospel is that all people should accept and obey the teachings of Jesus Christ. This includes men and women, people of every race, people of every occupation and job, etc. It includes the street cleaner who sweeps the fallen leaves off the road in autumn, it includes the security guard who checks the passes of employees at an office tower, it includes the farmer who has an orchard of pear trees on his land, it includes the lawyer who deals with real estate issues... and it also includes the leaders of the country and the government itself.

All are called to follow the gospel, including the king and queen, including the president and prime minister,

including the judges and public security officials, including
the generals and officers, including the parliamentary
deputies and the members of the politburo.
The gospel of Jesus Christ is not about establishing a
political state, but political states and those who run them
are obligated to follow the teachings of Jesus Christ. Christ
established a kingdom in the hearts of people, however,
which also includes the hearts of those that run political
states for the public benefit. They who run states must also
obey His teaching and perform their duties according to
His will. From that perspective alone, we can properly
speak of the concept of such a thing as a 'Catholic State'
or a 'Christian state' as a political entity, even though
Christ's true kingdom is something different from them.
Christ didn't establish a political entity, but political entities
are obliged to obey Christ's teachings. A state that obeys
His teachings can be called a 'Catholic state' or a 'Christian
state'. But even if it were called this, the political entity in
itself is not the kingdom that Christ established.

Many in the modern day think that politics and religion
ought to be separate.
It was Gandhi, however, who said that whoever thinks that
politics and religion are separate, understands neither.
Politics is guided by moral codes and values. Religion is
intrinsically connected to moral codes and values. People
who have no morals or have morals completely
independent from religion may not understand the
connection between religion and politics. But in virtually
every society where religion informs the moral codes of
people in anything beyond a purely superficial way, one
cannot look at politics as ever being truly separate from

religion.

Should politics be governed by Truth and morality? If the answer to that question is yes, then how do you determine what Truth and morality is?
That is the central philosophical question underlying all political science. Do you use science to know what Truth and morality is? Do you use religion for it? Do you use some ideology for it? Do you use popular opinion and the will of the electorate to decide what is right and wrong, what is true and what is false?
There is no state that can exist without grappling with that question and trying to give it an answer in its own way. But the question ultimately has to be answered in order for decisions regarding politics to be made.

If religion provides the answers to questions about Truth and morality, then obviously religion should provide guidance to politics.
People fear that if politics and religion are intermixed, then it would pollute religion with worldly power or that it would blind politics by irrational or false teachings.

Those who follow the latter opinion are more likely to be those who would answer 'no' to the question of whether religion provided the answers to questions about Truth and morality. They may believe other things provide such answers, but not religion, and hence they wish to keep politics free from such influence.
I believe that there are many religious ideas that come from human beings and not from God, and that these should not guide politics, but I also know that the answers

to the questions about Truth and morality are not fully answered without religion. And in fact, many of the governments in history that wanted to exclude religion from political decisions simply adopted other ideologies or belief systems to guide their decisions, and these ideologies or belief systems were the practical equivalent of religions, and the decisions they made were often more destructive, more irrational and more misguided than were the decisions of the states that allowed for the possibility that religion had something to say in guiding politics.

Those who follow the former opinion may be fearful of real historical precedent of both modern times and the past when religious authorities and political authorities became intermixed, and the sins of people in politics were done with God's name on them, thus profaning the holy name of the Creator on Earth. Through doing so, they may have caused many people to turn away from God.
I believe that this concern is very valid, but it still doesn't mean that politics should have no connection to religion. As long as there are politics, they will need to be guided by something. There is no political entity in existence that is in fact guided by nothing. The question is not whether or not political decisions need guidance, but rather what it is that should provide that guidance, whether it is religion, ideology or philosophy.
If removing God's name from politics puts an end to the misuse of His name, then we may as well also just wipe out the faith of Jesus Christ from the Earth along with it, because we will thus protect the holy faith from ever being misused sinfully if people can no longer know it or call upon it. But Christ came down to the world to offer

Himself to human abuse and humiliation, so that they
would have the light and not live in darkness any longer.
He came down to let Himself be mistreated, because
through doing so, people would find salvation. His name
will be abused if human beings can know it, but He wills for
human beings to know it even still.

How should states govern in order to obey the gospel and
the teachings of the church?
In pondering this question, I write this book.
Establishing a 'Catholic state', where the government
follows the gospel of Christ as it is taught by the church is
not salvation itself, but it is part of the same obedience to
the gospel that all people are called for, through which we
may find salvation.

As in other things I have written, I will put a prayer at the
end of each chapter that I invite the reader to pray with
me.

Lord, we pray that whatever is in this book that is good will
benefit ourselves and the world. We pray that you help all
governments and rulers of the world to answer the call of
the gospel with obedience. We ask for these things, if it is
your will, in Jesus' name, Amen

Part I: General Principles
I have some general principles that I want to explain first as an underpinning to further topics I am going to address in this book. The first part of this book will deal with these general principles.
I have listed eight in total, which I think are important. These principles are things that I think bear true universally, in all times and places. That is to say, they affect every country, state and civilization, regardless of whether it is in the modern age, whether it is in the Middle Ages, whether it is in the future, whether it is in the West, whether it is in the East, whether it is in Africa, whether it is on a small island, etc.
Later in the book I will deal with more specific topics that may not relate universally, but which still hold lessons that can be learned that can be useful for studying.

Lord, we pray that you help us to have a deeper understanding of these principles and a deeper understanding of your will regarding how states ought to run themselves. We ask for these things, if it is your will, in Jesus' name, Amen

I: Utopia

In a perfect world, there would be no need for
government. In a sinful world, there is a need for
government.
If human beings never committed theft, you would have
no need for locks or security systems to protect something.
If human beings never told lies, you would never need
witnesses or evidence to prove something.
If human beings never engaged in violence and war, you
would never need soldiers and armies for defence.
If no one ever did anything wrong, you would have no
need for laws, for courts, for police, for lawyers or trials.
If people always did what was right, you would have no
need for a state to order them about what to do, for they
would already be doing it.

People don't do what is right, and because they don't do
what is right, the state must exist to limit their freedom.
Thomas Hobbes was correct in his conclusion that the state
was needed because humanity was bad when left to their
own nature. It is not the 'natural state' of human beings
that makes them bad, but it is temptation and corruption
brought on from original sin that makes us like this.
Many political theorists made their most fundamental and
critical flaws in their understanding of statecraft on this
first principle. Marx failed to take into account the problem
of human sinfulness when he assumed that once the
working class ran the world, they would do away with all of
the evils of the previous society. Many revolutionaries
were the same; they assumed that once the oppressors

were done away with, once independence was achieved,
or once a new order was constructed, the problems would
end, while failing to take into account that the same
problems of human sinfulness grow back into new forms of
oppression no matter what way the world is changed.
Human sinfulness isn't cured by statecraft. You don't
reorganize the laws and state institutions and find that
people are now going to act virtuously from now on or the
devil's temptations are somehow stopped by human
institutions and ideas.
Sin obliges law to exist to give limits to it, but law itself is
not the cure for sin.

Sin creates a need for control.
If people could be trusted to be responsible and only drive
a car when they were competent to do so, then you would
never need a system to license them. But because people
can't be trusted to do that, therefore you need to limit
their freedom and only allow them to drive when they pass
a test to get a license.
If people could be trusted to never abuse their children,
then you wouldn't need laws that could take away their
custody of their children if necessary. But because people
can't be trusted to do that, therefore such laws have to be
created.
If people could be trusted to never destroy the natural
environment, then you wouldn't need laws to curtail
businesses in how they operate. But because people and
companies can't be trusted to be so responsible on their
own, therefore you need to put laws on them to limit what
they can do.
If people could be trusted to be fair to their employees and

not to abuse them, then you wouldn't need to pass labour
laws to control them and protect the employees' rights.
But because you can't trust people to do that, therefore
you must pass such laws to limit what employers can
demand from their employees.
If people could be trusted to take care of the poor and
marginalized in their own nation, then you wouldn't need
the government to step in and make legislation to help
these people, because people would have already done
that on their own.

People need laws and governments to rule them, because
they fail to do what they should have done on their own.

If a society built a school out of its own money, and built a
hospital out of its own money or they maintained the
roads out of their own money, then you would never need
a government to collect taxes from them to pay for these
things.
If all the elderly were taken care of by the communities
around them, then the government would have never
needed to create mandatory pension plans. If the poor and
marginalized were looked after by their neighbours, by the
people who lived in the same society with them, who
came from the same first parents and yet refused to
recognize these people as their brothers and sisters, then
the government would never need to institute a social
safety net to make sure that such people would not be left
uncared for.
If everyone contributed freely and selflessly for the
common good so that whatever needed to be built and
completed, was indeed built and completed, then you

would never need a government to tax people to get the funds ready to build these things.

But people won't do that on their own.

If we told the people of a city to make free donations to support the school system, rather than collecting the needed money through taxes, then the city would come up short for the funds needed for the school system. This is because people wouldn't be willing to simply donate the needed money on their own. When you force them through taxation, then they would be willing to give up the money.

And yet, if you tax them, it is less efficient then a mere donation. Since, if you donate, there are no middlemen that need to be paid. It would actually cost people less to just donate the money paid to the school system than for the same money to be forced out of them by taxes; but people will not donate if asked to do it freely. When you use taxation, the taxes must also pay for all the offices of government that deal with the taxes along with the things that the taxes will be used to fund.

People in fact have to pay more through taxes than if they had simply donated everything on their own, but the world would never work if you just asked people to pay for everything out of their own free will, because people are not willing to do that. Thus, it becomes necessary to force them, otherwise the society doesn't work.

The kingdom that Jesus wishes to establish is a kingdom without sin. For this very reason, it can be properly said that the kingdom of God is not a political state. Since, if everyone lived together in harmony, love and justice, out of their own choosing, why would you ever need laws,

governments and police to control them?
His kingdom indeed is not of this world. Once His kingdom is established, all political authority would be entirely unnecessary.
Jesus will succeed, and when He returns, there will be a kingdom on this physical world where those who live within it will obey everything in the gospel out of their own heart and not because they are forced by controls.

But, as long as we live in this time period now, when human beings remain sinful and God is patiently waiting for them, to give them all a chance to return before it is too late, it becomes necessary then to have political states, so that the amount of suffering that human beings must suffer in this sinful world can be less.

If there were no laws, governments and enforcement, then this entire world would break apart from the sins within it. We would live like people in the days of the cavemen, because nothing in civilization would be possible to exist, nor would any of the achievements that can be done when people work together in a society be achieved.

The world can accomplish more when it works together. But many people are not willing to work together in a way where peace can be maintained between them, unless they are forced.
Those who work together under force will accomplish more than those who are not forced and do not work together, but the ones who work together without being forced will accomplish the most of all.
To be a slave in Rome was better than living as a free

person in a cave in the wilderness. To live as a peasant under the hand of a feudal lord who kept the peace was probably a safer existence than living in the days of the cavemen when any person could potentially murder you with impunity.

It is better to eat one's bread under a dictator than to eat grass in the wilderness.

It is from the love of God that He allows for states to exist, to help make it easier for sinful human beings to pass their time in this world, so that their sins do not cause them to suffer more than they need to in this life.

Lord, we pray that you help us to end our sins and to become responsible citizens of the place we live in. We pray that you help us to live by conscience, so that we may not need coercion to make us to do what we should be doing. We ask for these things, if it is your will, in Jesus' name, Amen

II: The Paradox of Politics

Political power is a paradox. It is a paradox that points to
the reason why it has to come to an end.
States must exist because people are sinful.
If you leave people without control, they will hurt each
other, they will not help one another, they will do things
that are wrong. If you control them, you can minimize how
much they hurt each other, you can oblige them to help
those who need it and you can minimize the things that
they do that are wrong.
If people could be counted on to always do what was right,
you would need no authority at all in this world. But it is
because you can't count on them to do that, you do in fact
need such authority, so that the suffering that people must
have in this fallen world can be lessened through the
implementation of such authority.
However, there is a paradox in this.
People are sinful, which is why political power must exist.
But political power is not handled by angels or perfect
beings in heaven. It is handled by people, who are also
sinful.
The people who receive the power over society will also do
things that are wrong. And the evil things that they do will
in fact lead to the corruption, decay and ultimate
destruction of the political systems that they manage.
The paradox is that states must exist because people are
bad, and states also must die because people are bad.
There is no state in history that has been able to
continuously hold power without eventually coming to die
and being replaced with something new. No matter the

political system, whether it be the demise of a dynasty that ruled as monarchs, the collapse of a single-party rule or the corruption and overthrow of democratic institutions. Every state has its own time to die, just like every person has his own time to die.

Human beings invited death into the world by their sins. States, likewise, bring about the inevitable collapse of their institutions by the fact that they do what is wrong. Sin is the reason why states must come to be, and sin is the reason why they cannot continue forever.

If you could create a perfect political system, where the leaders, the judges, the police, the people of authority, all could be trusted to do the right thing with the authority that you gave them... on the day that you did that, you would find that none of their jobs were necessary any longer.

Every state in existence requires at some level that people can be trusted to do the right thing, or else the institutions of the state become dysfunctional. And yet the paradox is that if you actually could trust them to do the right thing, the state would have never been needed to begin with.

You can install checks and balances, you can create oversight, you can design institutions in any number of different ways to try to prevent abuses from happening. But no matter what way that you design the system, the ultimate truth is that it is still human beings that are running it, and you need them to uphold the institutions in the way that they were designed or else the design has no force in it. But their own sinfulness will lead them to corrupt the design, to erode the checks, to pervert the system and overpower whatever supposed wisdom the designers of the state had when they thought that these methods were going to succeed.

Sin creates the need for political power and sin is the thing that destroys political power.

God will destroy all political power in the end. The paradox of political power is a profound truth that points to the reason why the final victory belongs to God's kingdom alone.

God's kingdom is a kingdom without sin. In such a kingdom, all political power would be unnecessary. Everyone would do everything that they ought to do everyday without any need to coerce them into doing it. It is in the sinful world that political power is needed to control people. And the sinful world itself, by its sins, corrupts and destroys every empire, every dynasty, every republic, every constitution, every set of laws imagined and put down by every state in history, without fail. Understanding this paradox is why one can know that Christ's victory over every power in the world separated from Him is absolutely inevitable.

The countries and political order that exists in our day are no exception to this. The sinfulness of human beings will destroy the states and political orders that exist today just as it has done for every other state and political order in prior history.

People in this world are motivated by money, power and the things of this world. States can get people to work and do things in society with the use of worldly rewards. People can be motivated to build and create with money and mammon.

If a state builds its system in a way that it relies upon people doing the right thing out of purely selfless motivations, the state will be disappointed, because people are sinful and this is not what motivates them. The state has to use a love of mammon to motivate people to do what it needs them to do. A business needs to pay people money to get them motivated. A teacher has to award marks to motivate his students. A country's economy produces wealth and prosperity through the enticement of worldly rewards. If the teacher just asks the students to do the assignment out of the goodness of their hearts even though it counts nothing to the final grade, they will not work at it or they will not work as hard at it. If the business asks people to work without any incentive, they will not do the work. If a state asks people to do what needs to be done, but without any reward for them, they will come up short.

This is how people are motivated and the state is governing over both those who are going to end this life in grace and those who are going to end this life in sin. For the latter, mammon is what they serve in life and for the former, temptation to serve mammon will still be a strong force in their lives for most of them even if they end their lives free from its slavery. In this environment, the state usually cannot get people to do what needs to be done without offering worldly rewards.

If people were motivated purely by selfless motivations, the state wouldn't need to pay them to get them to work and the state would have never been needed in the first place.

Sin requires states to utilize a love of mammon to motivate the people to do the work that the state needs done. But it is precisely because people are motivated by mammon and not by goodness that the state becomes dysfunctional and the system corrupts itself until it produces its own end.

Sin creates the need for a monetary system and an economic system based on the pursuit of wealth, but sin will also be the thing that corrupts and leads this system to ruin.

Sin will create economic injustice, poverty and inequality. People will attain wealth and not use it for the good of their neighbour, because their love was for mammon and not for God. This economic injustice will create conflict, like as Marx predicted, which will threaten the state. It will create other problems as well that will threaten the state. Sometimes the threat of conflict may be large, other cases it may be less; depending on the virtue of the people, the society will deal with its injustices in a better way or a worse way and thus avoid or hasten such conflict. But as long as the injustice exists, the possibility of conflict will remain, just as like how as long as the kindling is still smoldering, it remains possible for the fire to reignite. What Marx did not correctly predict, was that even if the forces of conflict succeed in revolution and changing the state with its unjust system, the same sinfulness in human nature will create the exact same injustice, poverty and inequality in the successor of that state, as long as its successor is a state. This in turn will also plant new seeds of conflict.

Marx was right in predicting that the only solution to this dialectic was to end in a society where economic justice was upheld and all were equal. He was mistaken in failing to realize that there is no human state where such can ever be achieved; because human states are built on a premise of imperfection which is the source of the injustice. He was mistaken in failing to realize that to achieve this, it is the human heart that ultimately needs to change, not the state structures and economic system that needed change. He was most of all mistaken for failing to realize that only in Christ's kingdom in a people united with Him in His grace was this dream ever possible.

Everything related to states is like this. They require a need to be instituted because of sin, but it is because of sin that they never work correctly.

Political states will never be utopias because the reasons for their existence require imperfection to be present. Monetary systems will never adequately serve the poor or eliminate unjust inequality, because the reason for they must be created to motivate people presupposes that people are not motivated by justice and goodness. The judicial system will never treat people entirely fairly, because if people were truly fair, a judiciary would never have been needed. Nothing that belongs to a state will ever work the way it was supposed to work, because an assumption of imperfection is inherent in the reason for why it was required.
Sin creates the need for these things, and yet sin is exactly the reason why all these things are ultimately doomed to fail.

Political authority is something of this sinful world. Christ's kingdom is not of this world, however. All political authority must eventually come to die just as this sinful world must come to die. It cannot exist forever because it is corrupted by sin, and if it were not corrupted by sin, it would naturally come to an end anyways since it would then lose the reason for why it was needed in the first place.

Christ will put every authority under His feet and obliterate it. In the end, in His Kingdom, there will no longer be anyone above anyone else, any need for laws or officials, any need for payments for work, any need for courts or police, because everyone will obey the law of the King without the need for any force or motivation to make them to do it other than love for Him and one another.

Only in a world without sin could anything ever function correctly, and a world without sin would be one where Christ was loved and obeyed, since it is because of sin that we refuse to love Him and obey Him.

Christ hangs on the cross, seemingly defeated by the power of the world, and yet His victory is guaranteed, because all the power of this world is mortal, while His kingdom alone is immortal. His kingdom alone has the solution to the paradox, which is why His victory is inevitable.

Lord, we pray that human beings will put an end to their sins, so that political power will become unnecessary and your Son may truly rule over our world. We ask for these things, if it is your will, in Jesus' name, Amen

III: Exorcism

No matter how much power a state accumulates, it never becomes powerful enough to prevent the devil from entering it and corrupting it from the inside. No matter how strong the institutions of the state become, they never become strong enough to undo the evil in the human heart.
There is no system of checks and balances that can ultimately protect a state from the demons that fell from heaven who tempt human beings to sin.

The people of Gerasa tried to tie down the demoniac with chains, but he broke through the chains. Defeating evil is not a matter of human strength and technology.
Many states in history have tried to root out the evil that rotted them from the inside and led to their downfall through many different means, but ultimately failed.
Every state wants to preserve itself and establish peace and prosperity for its people, but the only way to do so is ultimately by curing the sinfulness of human nature. Christ is the only solution to that problem that exists. He is the One that can drive out the spirit of darkness from the world. He is therefore the solution that every state needs to cure itself of evil.

When Christ came to the world, He referred to Himself as the 'son of man'. In Hebrew, 'man' is also 'Adam' (the first man) and Christ perhaps could have also been translated as saying He was the 'son of Adam'.
Christ was the Son of God. But He referred to Himself as

the son of man; as the son of Adam. He was God, but He insisted on referring to Himself as a human being rather than as God. Only when Christ was explaining the Truth to people about His Father would He let them know that He was God, because it was necessary that they understood this. But otherwise, He referred to Himself as the Son of man.

There is a story of the desert mothers of Egypt who spent their lives praying in the Sahara as hermits away from civilization, during the time of the early church, wherein one of the mothers once conversed with a demon and she asked the demon what it was that defeated him.

She asked the demon, 'is it fasting that defeats you?'

The demon replied, 'we do no eat'

She asked the demon, 'is it vigils that defeats you?' (staying awake all night in prayer)

The demon replied, 'we do not sleep'

She asked, 'then what it is that defeats you?'

The demon said, 'nothing other than humility defeats us'

Christ came down to the world and referred to Himself simply as a human being. He did signs and miracles and even said that others would do greater signs and miracles than those that He did.

He could have called Himself the Son of God and walked around demanding that He be treated according to His position, but if He had done that, He would have had no power to drive out the demon that He came into the world to drive out.

It was because Christ had completely 100% rejected the spirit of evil that He let go of all of His identities and titles, and referred to Himself as merely a human being. It was the evil spirits that shouted out that Christ was God, and He silenced them. He called Himself a mere human being and the devil tried to call Him the Son of God.

He was the Son of God and when it became necessary for people to understand this identity, He would explain this in His teaching to them, but otherwise He would always refer to Himself as a human being only.

He did miracles, but He would give the Spirit for others to do miracles too, and He prophesied that others would do even greater miracles than He did. He had the Holy Spirit, but He gave the Spirit in an equal measure to His disciples just the same as He had. He had God as His Father, but He gave Him as a Father to everyone else just as He was first a Father to Jesus. He did not keep anything for Himself to hold onto and then say 'look, because I have this, I am still better than you'.

He considered Himself no more important than any other human being in the world. He was everything, but He insisted on calling Himself simply as a son of Adam, just as we are all sons and daughters of Adam, without the slightest hint of being above anyone else.

Christ's work in the gospel is a kind of exorcism. Just as a priest recites prayers over a possessed person to drive a demon out, Christ was doing everything He did in this world, all as part of prayer of exorcism that began at His incarnation and ended with His death and resurrection. Every action and word that He was saying was part of this exorcism He was carrying out to drive the demon out of this world. Therefore, He referred to Himself as the 'son of man' and put Himself no higher than anyone else, because through doing so, He would completely 100% reject the dragon, leaving not even the tiniest space for the dragon to hold.

In human mythology 'dragon' is a creature that represents great power. The Emperors of China called themselves dragons because they believed that they had divine power over all other beings. The dragon is greater than a lion or a bear, greater than an eagle or a whale, it is the apex creature over all other creatures.
It is the devil who the Bible refers to as the 'dragon'. He is inflated with pride and concerning himself with dominating all other creatures as weaker than himself.
Christ on the other hand is stronger than the devil, and He bends Himself down in humility to put Himself beneath all other creatures and serve them as their slave.
If Christ had taken His own identity as something to stand upon or had pointed at His own divine heritage as a reason for why he was above all other men, like an emperor who believed himself to be the son of a god or the son of heaven, then the devil's influence would remain and the devil's works would remain, because Christ would have adopted the devil's works as His own.
Christ repudiated the pride that the devil had brought into creation by coming down from heaven, despite being the Son of God, and declaring Himself to be the 'son of man', a human being that was equal to any other.

The dragon and his angels rejected the Father at the beginning of the world perhaps because the Father asked them to let go of their own identities and beauty and to love Him first. They chose to reject God and to follow their own pride.
They inspired human beings down history and will

continue to do so into the future. Death and sin came from them, and not from God.

There are many things that we consider normal in this world, which are actually rather abnormal and were never meant to exist originally. All forms of ways that humans control other humans, while being normal in human history, are actually aberrations of the true order that God instituted when He created.

Human beings think it is normal for one person to rule over another. But this is actually an aberration. Whether it be masters ruling over slaves, men ruling over women, one race ruling over another race, bosses over employees, kings over subjects, officials over the populace, clergy over laity, abbots over monks, officers over soldiers, parents over children, teachers over students, or any other kind of relationship where one person is obliged to give up their own will to follow that of someone else, all of it was never intended in the beginning.

God told the woman, 'your desire shall be for your husband and he shall rule over you'. She cannot be happy without the man, and yet when she is with the man, her own will and autonomy is lost to his control.

These words were not only a punishment for the woman, but it carried down to all members of the human race. Every relationship of any sort, where one person is ruled over by another, is another layer of what came about from original sin, which was never intended in the beginning. People likewise need all these things, they need teachers to teach them, they need governments to keep the country safe, they need clergy to help them find salvation; they are not happy on their own, but once they have these things, their own will is curtailed to another's control.

It is because sin entered the picture that control became necessary. These relationships of control are not evil things, but they are things that are made necessary by evil, because if no one ever did anything wrong, you would never need another person to control them.

God commands us to obey the superiors and authorities that He places over us, and we must do so in order to find salvation in heaven. However, He does this in just the same way as He consigns us to death in our bodies in this world. Death was not created by God, but He uses it as a means to accomplish His purposes in a sinful world that has given birth to death. Similarly, authority and control were not part of God's original plan, but He uses them as a means to accomplish His purposes in a sinful world that has created the need for their institution and demands that we respect and obey.

In the Bible, different prophets saw God upon a throne as though He were like a king. However, this image was simply given to them in order so that they would understand something about Him, and not because God truly does rule the world like an earthly king. He wants people to know that He is the One in control of everything, but ultimately when He showed His face to our world, He wanted us to know Him as a human being like us and not as a divine master who we serve as slaves.

Paul spoke of himself as being the slave of Jesus Christ, and he wrote to the disciples as 'slaves of Christ' but he also wrote that 'I am writing in a human manner' because this is the way that his adherents needed to understand. People needed milk to drink, rather than solid food, because they were not yet mature and they still thought in the way that the world thought, rather than as God thought.

You can find artwork after artwork created down the ages depicting the Father, Christ, His mother, or the various saints and angels wearing crowns and sitting on thrones, or dressed in this kind of royal regalia. But these images are not truly close to the reality – they are merely things for us to look at in our own human understanding, just as Paul wrote to the disciples calling them 'slaves of Christ' in a human manner.

Christ didn't come down to the world in order to establish a kingdom to put Himself above other people. He came down to the world to establish a kingdom where there would be no one ever again who would hold power over another person. He gazed upon the impressive architecture of the temple built by Herod and said that 'no stone shall be on another stone'. I think perhaps He meant not just the temple in front of Him, but the church and kingdom He established, with us as the living stones, would not have a single stone on top of another stone.

People who come into positions of authority are tempted by the demon to look upon their authority and position as something that makes them higher than those that they make decisions for. This is just as true of kings and emperors, as it is true of bishops and priests, teachers and parents, masters and bosses, etc. The dragon seeks his own glory apart from God, and so he tempts the people of the world to become like himself; to follow his example of pride, rather than God's example of humility.

The devil always tempts people in positions of authority to do the opposite of what Christ did. In other words, for the king to insist that he is a king, for the priest to insist that he is a priest, for the boss to insist that he is a boss, for the parent to insist that he is a parent, for the person in any position of authority to hold onto and point to their special identity that puts them higher than others. Christ on the other hand was higher than all of them, and He deliberately let go of all these identities and insist that He was a human being like any other, while silencing the demons that called out that He was God above all.

Christ showed people the Father's will. Our world has been inspired by demons when it created institutions and norms that treated people as being more important than other people. The Trinity do not consider themselves more important than anyone else, however. It is the demons, filled with pride, who inspired human beings to make their world like this, because it is a reflection of the demonic image.

The demons are the source of the sin and corruption that leads to the downfall of all states in history. Hence, the moment that the state allows for the concept to exist that one is more important than the other in any particular form, the demons have already put their foot into the door, and the seed has already started growing that will ultimately lead to the state's destruction.

Christ was God and king above all, to whom all were obligated to obey, but He did not hold onto these identities as the demons would inspire a human king or leader to grasp onto his own identity. Instead, He referred to Himself as the son of man and treated Himself as no more important than anyone else. He absolutely rejected the devil's influence and thus His kingdom would never be overcome by the devil.

If other states in history had completely rejected sin, they would have become immortal and in fact they would have naturally joined themselves to Christ's own kingdom. If the leaders had acted as leaders and were obeyed by their people without ever taking their position as making them something worth more than others, then they would have protected themselves from the devil's influence. But because they failed to do so, they allowed the devil to enter, to make them lazy, to make them foolish, to make them arrogant, to make them unable to learn new things, to make them fail to know the truth of the problems they were facing, to make them grow many kinds of vices and corruption until their bad decisions eventually ended with the destruction of their states.

Many Christian states in history claimed to rule on behalf of Christ and yet they gave ample room for the demon in their courts and governing chambers.
The Byzantine empire saw itself as an extension of God's rule from heaven down upon the earth, and yet it was filled with vices that were ultimately rooted in a failure to truly believe in the Son of man as He truly was, in His humility and lowliness. They built massive churches, used state funds to support the church, held church councils, placed the faith in a high position in their society, but it was still a society where the few were more important than the many and not truly a reflection of the Trinity's

own humility.

The same is true of countless other Christian empires and kingdoms in history. They did not survive, because they were followers of Christ in name, with crosses and clergy, but the devil still had a seat at court.

Only a state that has freed itself from sin can live forever. Pride is the beginning of sin, and the temptation to believe oneself more important than others is always present in states that grant authority to some to rule over others. This temptation cannot be eliminated, because it is necessary for leaders to have authority and to be obeyed. Government is necessary because sin exists, and governments always must have a selection of people who are entrusted with making decisions for many others. And this paradigm will always include the temptation for those who are in such a position to hold onto their position as something that makes them more important than others, rather than the example of the Son of man who had everything and did not count this as making Himself as better than others.

States must have people who have authority and who are obeyed, but these people must follow the example of Christ in His humility, so that they may be saved and also so that their states will not leave room for the devil. The same is true of any other kind of authority, whether it be clerical authority, parental authority, teaching authority, company authority, etc. No one should ever hold a position of power and think that this makes him as something more important than those who are under them.

Otherwise, the demon will enter, and his presence will prevent happiness and peace from ever truly flourishing.

Lord, we pray that you help drive out the demons from all states in the world and that you help make governing leaders to follow the example of your Son in His humility, rather than be tempted by the demon who teaches arrogance and pride. We ask for these things, if it is your will, in Jesus' name, Amen

IV: Freedom and Slavery

If people had no sin, governance would never be necessary. It is because you can't trust people to do what they ought to do, therefore societies need to control people in order for people to live together in peace. Thus, there is a need for governance.
Now, what kind of governance is the best kind of governance?
The answer to this question is not as simple as saying that one system is superior to another or one ideology is right and the other is wrong.
Since human beings are different and what is suitable for one people is not necessarily suitable for another people.

If people can be trusted to do the right thing, then they can be given more freedom and rights, and you don't need to fear that the society will be destroyed because of it.
If people cannot be trusted to do the right thing, then they cannot be given more freedom and rights, because if you did this, then they would abuse it and this abuse would destroy the society.

Think about a family where a mother had two sons. If she leaves the first son at home for a few days, she knows that the first son might invite his friends over and have a party that wrecks the house. However, if she leaves the second son at home for a few days, she knows that this son would never do such a thing.
Thus, the privilege of being able to be home alone for a few days, she will grant to the second son, but not to the

first son. She gives more freedom to one than the other, because one can be trusted with freedom and the other cannot.

The same is true of societies and governance.
If you can trust the populace to own dangerous chemicals without anyone ever abusing this right by killing people, then you can grant freedom to the people to own dangerous chemicals. On the other hand, if you know that giving people this right is going to result in them hurting each other, then you cannot let them have this right.
If you can trust people to have freedom of speech and they voice their true opinions, but this voicing of their true opinions does not lead to people fighting one another with violence or trying to force the other side into silence and submission, because everyone respects the right enough that they grant it even to their enemies, then you can grant freedom of speech to the populace. On the other hand, if you know that giving people this right is going to lead to people voicing certain opinions, and then ethnic groups or political factions will begin fighting each other violently because of what these opinions stated, then you cannot really grant freedom of speech to the populace.
If you can trust people to use their freedom responsibly, then you can grant them freedom. If you cannot trust them to use their freedom responsibly, then you must keep them in slavery.

There is a principle here, which I will use a graph to try to make it understood visually.

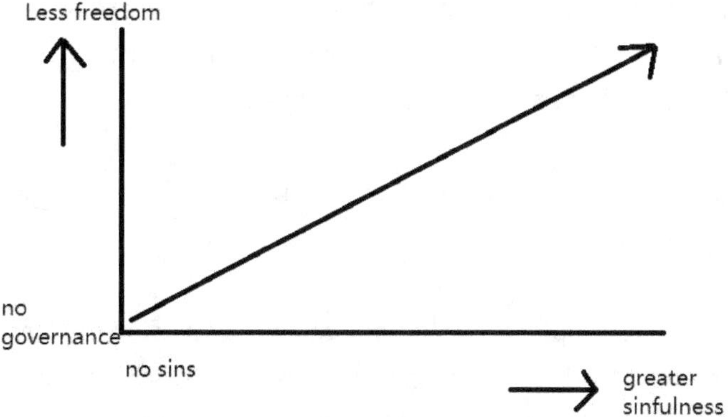

The vertical axis is referring to the amount of freedom a people can possess. The higher the figure on the vertical access, the more control they require. The horizontal axis is referring to the degree of vice that a people has reached. The further to the right indicates the greater their sinfulness has become. A people with no sins, on the other hand, needs no control at all.

If a state was completely sinless, it would 100% free. However, the more sinful it becomes, the less and less freedom that can be granted to the people.

The more a nation is virtuous and the less that it sins, will then mean more responsibility you can trust to the people and fewer controls you need to put on them in order to keep society working together, and consequently the freer that they can be.

A society that is perfectly sinless can be 100% free with no controls at all. That society will be the society of Christ's country that He shall be king over in His second coming. If any nation in this world became sinless, it would become joined together to Christ's kingdom and it would truly be an extension of Christ's rule in heaven upon Earth.

There is no society in the world today that has reached this point. The Vatican has walls and locks on doors. The Catholic states and empires down the ages had vices of every sort.
A society that is sinful, however, must have freedom taken away from them in order to get them to work together.

It is not a simple answer when asking the question of what the right kind of governing system should be, because the people themselves are in different states of being.
All people are sinners, but some people are more sinful than others. All nations have sins, but some nations are more sinful than others.
The more sinful a nation is, the less freedom can be safely granted to the people without fear of them abusing it to the point where the state would be destroyed.

It is a false idea to think that the same governing system and laws would fit for every kind of culture and situation. Some modern thinkers that want to export western democracy around the world are prone to this mistake. John Locke took the assumption that human nature was basically good; modern democracy relies upon the assumption that people will use their freedom responsibly. They think that the same model that worked in western countries can work anywhere, but they fail to understand that the conditions that allowed for the system to work in the west are not present everywhere. There are many places in the world where if the people are given the rights to speak, publish, vote and participate, it would lead to chaos, civil war, destruction or other calamities. This is because the people of those places lack virtue and cannot be trusted to use this freedom in a way that is safe for society.

The sins of different places are different, and if you have a responsibility that you can trust to one group of people, you perhaps cannot trust the same responsibility to another group of people.

If the people are given freedom to choose their government and they use this power responsibly, then it is good for them to have that freedom. On the other hand, if they use this power irresponsibly, then it may not be good for them to have that freedom.

It is mistake to think that every population in the world ought to enjoy the same freedoms.

For example, while in one country, you allow people to own their own guns, and perhaps for the most part they use this freedom responsibly and they only use their guns for legitimate purposes. But if we took this freedom and gave it to the population of a completely different country, perhaps people would engage in violence against each other or against the government. The people who used the freedom for something legitimate should have that freedom, but those who used it for evil should not have that freedom.

Or perhaps, in one society you give people to right to publish anything they want, and the society has a completely free media, but it does not break down morally, because people know better than to publish or view media that is a temptation to immorality. While perhaps in another society, you give people the same freedom to publish whatever they want, and the society does collapse morally, because people create and look at media that is a temptation to immorality. The right to publish is logical for the former society, but it does not serve the latter very well.

Or perhaps, in one society you give people the freedom to enter the country without a visa, and people come into the country and the country does not have any serious problem from the foreigners coming in. While perhaps in another society, you grant the same freedom, and the society has serious problems because people come across the borders and engage in all kinds of illegal or harmful activities.

The road to true freedom in society is by way of virtue. If the people of the nation can discipline themselves and submit their own hearts to God's law as it is written in nature, then they don't need an outside force disciplining them and controlling them. But if people don't discipline themselves internally, then they must be disciplined externally.

God gave the Ten Commandments through Moses because man failed to see the same laws written on his heart. God shrouded the mountain with cloud and thunder, in order to make the Israelites know that He was there, because they had failed to realize He was there when everyday they saw the Sun, the stars and far greater wonders and signs overhead than what they saw on that mountain for a brief period.

Suppose in one society, when a person got old, the family and community would work together to take care of him. While in another society, when a person got old, people would forget about him and not care for him. In the former society, a government may never need to create a national pension program or other social services (which the person would be forced to pay taxes to pay for) to look after the person, since the society did that without the government. But in the latter society, the government may need to step in to do something to help the person in his old age, because no one else is going to help him.

Suppose in one society, people looked after their poorest members and made sure that everyone in their community was able to stand on his two feet economically. While in another society, people only cared about themselves and didn't help those around them in poverty. The government would not need to step in to do anything in the former society, but in the latter society, it may feel a need to do something and force the people to pay something in taxes to pay for the welfare of these people, since no one else will take care of them.

Suppose in one society, you set up traffic laws, and for the most part, people follow them. While in another society, you set up the same laws, and they are flaunted everyone, as drivers continuously pass through red lights and ignore traffic signs for the road.

Suppose in one society, you put an easily reachable first aid kit on every public bus, and people in this society only open the kit when someone needs it because of an emergency. While in another society, you do the same thing, and you find that almost every kit is stolen by the local people.

Suppose in one society, you give guns to police officers and they use these guns to protect society. While in another society, you do the same thing, and the police officers sell their guns on the black market and get money from criminals.

Suppose in one society, people buy a ticket for the train and no one checks them, and no one sneaks on the train, because everyone is honest. While in another, you also have no one checking tickets, and almost every gets on board the train without paying the fee.

These things that I am talking about are not fantasies; if you travel the world from place to place, region to region, you will see for yourself that what I am saying is the reality. Public morality is different in different parts of the world and you can't trust each different group of people with the same set of responsibilities and rules.

A society that is extremely sinful can only work together when it is put under the heel of power that takes away its freedom.
A society that is very virtuous, however, can be given much freedom and it will continue to work together.
A society that has no sin at all, needs no rules and government. That is the kingdom of Christ that He died to establish.

How much the people are allowed to participate within the system, what rights they are given, what freedom they enjoy... all of these things are ultimately what shapes the essence of the political system... and all of those questions can only be answered by first looking at the people themselves and seeing whether or not they are virtuous enough to be safely trusted with those rights.
Christ frees people from slavery; not by fighting a revolution against earthly masters, but by liberating people

from their sins and these sins are the things that ultimately keep them weak, keep them under the heels of other people and give others the justification to control them.

If a state wants freedom for its people, it can only truly accomplish this by eliminating sin. Again, Christ is the answer to this, for He is the one who can redeem people from their sins.

Lord, we pray that you help societies to turn away from their sins and be filled with virtue, so that they can truly be free. We pray that you help make us ready for your return. We ask for these things, if it is your will, in Jesus' name, Amen

V: The Rule of God

Christ is the king of the whole world. He is king not just at the Second Coming, because He is already king now and He always has been king. Christ governs the universe. The government of a particular nation-state rules a country in the way that a governor rules a province on behalf of a king. The government of the nation is just a servant of Christ the king and the king has the ability to dismiss or appoint a new government at any time He chooses. He can do so through conquests, revolutions, elections or any means that He sees fit. The government is merely His servant and He is always the True Ruler of any country. Christ is the Lord of the United States. He is also the Lord of North Korea and Iran. He is also the Lord of Turkey and Botswana. He is the Lord of China and India. All nation-states are merely His servants to rule over the human race. He is patient with sinners throughout the world. A man beats his wife for many years, and Christ patiently waits for the man to change before He steps in to punish him. Similarly, a government may do evil to its people for long times, and Christ patiently waits for the people in government to repent before He decides to punish them.

Christ is the true government, and all governments in the world are simply ruling on His behalf. All of the prosperity and failure of nations is also something that relates to the nation's relationship with God.

Christ can punish nations for the sins that are committed collectively by the nation. In the Middle Ages, people interpreted the invasions and disasters of their times as being punishments from God. When Muslims invaded, it was interpreted as being because Christians were too sinful. The same was interpreted for other invasions, like from the Magyars, the Mongols or the Viking raids. The Black Death was interpreted as a punishment of God for sin. Earthquakes, tsunamis, volcanic eruptions, famines, plagues, etc. were all interpreted as God's punishments. In Deuteronomy, Moses said that if the people of Israel would follow the commandments that came from God, then God would bless the land with all kinds of prosperity, but if the people disobeyed these commandments, then God would bring upon the land all sorts of punishments. Christ said that if people sought the kingdom of God first, then all those other things they needed would be given to them too.

I believe that the bad things that happen to nations have a relationship with the sins committed by the people in both the present and the past. I believe that the prosperity and happiness of a nation has to do with the virtue it has both in the present and in the past.

If a state wants to be prosperous, then the most important thing that it can do is to get its citizens to follow Christ and His commandments.

No matter where one goes in the world, governments always want to promise their people a better material future. This is not an evil thing, but governments throughout the world fail to recognize the root out of which all prosperity comes.

The most important thing that a nation can do is to obey the commandments of God and everything else would follow from this.

If a nation was filled with people who did what was right,

who cooperated with one another in love and received the blessing of God, then the nation would have material prosperity as well.

The most important thing that a nation can have is not oil or natural resources, it is not territory or geography, it is not even population size, but it is rather virtue within the lives of its citizens. A population that practices virtue is worth more than any other advantage that a state could ever possess.

Nations always want better material conditions for their people, but in order to achieve that, then you must make the people virtuous. Since virtue is the root from which all other success can come.

 If you want to grow the tree, but without the root, then the tree will die.

Not only for material prosperity, but also for salvation, virtue among the citizens is critical.

Not only should the state try to make its people virtuous in order to get them to live happier in this life, but it ought to also make them virtuous in order so that they can get to heaven.

Salvation is always more important than better material conditions, although when speaking of something as large as a country, both of these things will come about from the same source: virtue.

To get to heaven is more important than having economic prosperity. To get to heaven is more important than having civil or international peace. To get to heaven is more important than civil freedom. To get to heaven is more important than scientific progress. To get to heaven is more important than family. To get to heaven is more important than life itself.

As Jesus said: 'what does it profit a man if he gain the whole world and lose his own life?'

If people have economic prosperity, civil harmony, civil freedom, scientific advancement, family and life... and they die and go to hell in the end, then all of this was just pointless. Every good thing that they had in life was worthless to them in the end, because it didn't last longer than the short time in this life.

The state's most important responsibility then is to get the people of the state to obey the law of God and to practice virtue. There is nothing else that it can do that is more important than this. It will result in the salvation of the people and in a better life here on Earth.

Lord, we pray that nations will turn away from their sins and obey your laws, so that they may have material prosperity now and salvation in the life to come. We ask for these things, if it is your will, in Jesus' name, Amen

VI: Pragmatism

A nation that practices virtue will have greater prosperity
now and salvation in the world to come. And governments
have a responsibility to do what they ought to do in order
to work towards that goal.
However, the government does not have the power to
eliminate every sin from society and to make all people
into saints.
God is all-powerful, but human government is not.

The government has limited resources. It can control the
education or the media to get it to influence people the
right way, but it cannot control the minds of people and
make them to stop sinning in their thoughts.
Even if it outlaws the outward acts that are done by
people, while this can help to mold the minds of the
population in such a fashion as to cause them to let go of
the sin, many people may simply avoid the sin because
they do not wish to be punished but they don't reject it in
their hearts.

In getting people to follow God's laws, the state's resources
are limited. It can use tools at its disposal to make sure
that things like the media or education are teaching the
right things, and it can use tools at its disposal to help
control public thought through outlawing certain kinds of
speech or public acts, but these things are never enough to
get true obedience from the heart.
The church as an institution is necessary to do its work in
order to achieve that kind of obedience, and the state
ought to use its resources to assist the church in that

mission, since the success of the church in making the people virtuous will result in the salvation and prosperity of the state.

Punishing people who commit certain outward acts is not really a means of redemption, but rather it is merely a means of taking away temptations.

What I mean by this is that punishing outward sins that can be seen and proven to have occurred will only help public morality by helping people to be less tempted by the sin that is committed and punished. The temptation will seem less alluring if people know that they are going to suffer some punishment by being caught for it. It will not really succeed, however, to cause people who have already consented and committed this sin to repent. The person may be sorry because they are punished, but not necessarily sorry for the sin itself.

The state ought to punish sins that occur as outward acts, because such punishments will help public morality by lessening a temptation for others to consent to these acts, but the usefulness of such punishments for improving public morality is only limited, because they often don't really produce repentance from the heart for the person who has already agreed to it.

Consider the words of Confucius: "If the people be led by laws, and uniformity sought to be given them by punishments, they will try to avoid the punishment, but have no sense of shame. If they be led by virtue, and uniformity sought to be given them by the rules of propriety, they will have the sense of shame, and moreover will become good." (子曰、道之以政、齊之以

刑、民免而無恥。道之以德、齊之以禮、有恥且格。）

The prosperity and salvation of the state rests in the virtue of its citizens. The virtue of its citizens determines how much freedom it can be given, and utopia is a place where there is perfect virtue and perfect freedom.

However, laws and punishments are not really the primary means of accomplishing this. Setting up a tribunal to punish and judge every person who commits sins in public will help some people not to choose sin, but it is not really going to get the nation to become sinless.

If you use laws to govern the people, then people will avoid the punishment, but they will not avoid the crime. If you use virtue to govern the people, then the people will know shame and they will avoid doing the crime, regardless of whether they are punished or not.

The role of giving virtue to the people is something that the church must accomplish, which the state can and should help with, but ultimately it is a matter bigger than the state and which must be fought spiritually by the church within society.

Nevertheless, laws and punishments must be given, because they will help with removing temptation.

Since any kind of sin will hurt the prosperity of the nation and will hinder the salvation of the nation, therefore any sin that the government is able to eliminate or reduce can be targeted by the efforts of the government.

This includes things that are supposedly 'victimless', like sexual sins, blasphemy, failing to pray or attend mass, or the telling of 'white lies'. If the government is capable of eliminating these things by its efforts, then it ought to do so.

Governments have a place in the bedrooms of the nation, because what happens in the bedrooms of the nation can bring disaster and ruin upon the entire country.

However, pragmatically speaking, governments do not have the power to eliminate every sin in society.
For example, if you outlawed blasphemy, but the population of the country were all unbelievers who rejected God and only a minority which run the government believed, perhaps the government would have no means of enforcing this without endangering itself from revolution or social upset, and it would be utterly incapable of getting the people to obey the command. In such a scenario, it would be more logical to just allow the blasphemy to continue than to outlaw it, since the government needs to ensure that the social order doesn't collapse and trying to use force to get rid of this sin will have no chance of success.
Or, for example, if you wanted to outlaw sexual sins, but the entire public did these things and wasn't willing to change. The result is then that you outlaw these things, and then the public still engages in all of these sins like before in secret and behind closed doors. And rather than eliminating the sin, the situation actually becomes worse, because people get sexually transmitted diseases that are left untreated or people have children out of wedlock that are abandoned. In this scenario, where the government was impotent to fully enforce what it was calling to do and its attempt to enforce just made the situation worse, then it would be better for the society as a whole if the government just didn't enforce such things.

Even with sins that are not 'victimless', the government has to take pragmatism into account. Suppose if you have thieves who belong to a particular minority group, and you send in police to arrest them, but doing so just causes a widespread racial riot and much greater property destruction than was lost by simply allowing the thieves to continue stealing, then the government would be pragmatic to simply allow the thieves to continue.
Or suppose if you wanted to get rid of abortion in a society, but the nation was already widely practicing abortion. And suppose you outlawed abortion, but most of the country still widely practiced it and ignored the new law. It may not be practical for the government to simply go out and then arrest half the country, because the state didn't have the resources to arrest or hold so many people in prison, and attempting to do so might result in a revolution. However, from a pragmatic perspective, it could use other options, like simply taking small groups of people who commit abortion, punish them and make public examples of them to warn the rest, and that will then cause some portion of the people to stop going for fear of getting caught. And eventually as this number reduces, over time it will get down to a small enough number that you can then go out and arrest every person who still does it.

If a state found that it was impossible to get people to engage in only monogamous sex and that sex with multiple partners was widespread, then the state might be well-advised to teach people to use condoms and make them available. Even though artificial contraceptives are themselves against the law of God, if people are already breaking this law by not having sex in a monogamous relationship, then it would be better in that case for them to use a condom than to not use them, because the sin would then be less, since they would not be also endangering life through spread of disease at the same time as they were committing the sinful sexual act.

A political state is not heaven, nor can it be made as such by the power of the government alone. It is not a place where every person is a saint or every sin will have justice. Although all sins should end, the government has to calculate with prudence and wisdom, and determine what kinds of methods will end up with a better situation and what kinds of methods will not.
When dealing with punishments and legal justice, it is not a simple matter of black and white. The state will never have the resources to do everything and it must think pragmatically of how to use the resources available in the best possible way.

It is like the church teaching about 'just war'. One of the conditions of a just war is that there must be a reasonable hope of victory. If there is no reasonable hope of victory, then the war should not be fought, no matter how evil the enemy may be, because without victory, the war serves no purpose.
Similarly, if the state is going to try to fight against sin in society and yet it has little hope of victory using the methods it is employing, then it is better to simply allow the sin to exist than it is to continue fighting against it. Only if there is a reasonable hope that the punishments

and laws are going to result in a better society can
punishments and laws ever be justifiably be used.
If the state can use punishments to lessen the temptation
of various sins that are committed, and its method will
bear fruit, then it is justified to use such punishments. On
the other hand, if using such punishments is going to fail to
achieve the intended result or in fact will likely lead to an
even worse result, then the sin must be tolerated without
the punishment.
This is what I mean by pragmatism.

On the same note, no state should ever engage in activities
that are likely to cause or provoke a collapse of the sate
itself or throw the state into anarchy. Even if something is
happening that is monstrous and diabolical, the state must
remember that it is in itself still a 'mortal' entity and it can
be destroyed. If acting against the monstrosity is going to
lead to the state's destruction, then it would be better if it
simply allowed the monstrosity to exist.
If the nobles have child sex slaves, for example, but the
king cannot act against them without entering a war in
which he has no chance of winning, then he has to simply
allow the nobles to continue their depravity. The children
will continue suffering if they are left in their condition, but
if the state is destroyed and the nobles win, the children
will still continue to suffer in their condition and no
difference will be made.
If people worship Satan and sacrifice animals to him, and
any attempt by the government to stop this would provoke
revolution and the collapse of the state, then the
government must allow this to continue.
It can try to be clever and find other means to combat evils

in society, but it must not take a course of action that will
lead to a worse result than what it is attempting to fight
against.
Many evils will have to be tolerated in society if in fact the
state cannot successfully act against them without
destabilizing itself and leading to its own destruction.
Because if the state does act against them and destroys
itself, how is it going to help end those evils at that point?
Once it has no power at all to do anything?

Pragmatism demands that lesser evils be chosen over
greater ones when one is obliged to allow evil to exist.
How does one determine if something is a lesser evil?

1) Salvation of souls
2) Human life
3) Material prosperity and other concerns

These are the three priorities in order from greatest to
least. If human life or material prosperity must be
sacrificed in order to save souls from sin, then those things
are better to be sacrificed, for it is better to die or to live in
poverty than it is to go down to eternal hell.
Human life is more important than material prosperity. It is
better to live as a poor slave than it is to not live at all. The
statement 'give me freedom or give me death' is a foolish
one; life is more important than political freedom. If the
latter two priorities must be sacrificed to safeguard the
first, then it is a just trade-off; better to eat bread under a

dictator than it is to eat grass in a ruined city.

What these priorities mean in practice is not always what we might expect. For example: if a state was forced to choose between saving the life of someone who was being killed for believing in Christ and saving the life of the person being killed for a homosexual act, the state should save the life of the latter and not of the former. The reason why is because the soul of the person being martyred is going to go to heaven when he dies, but the person who committed the homosexual act may not be going to heaven without repentance. Hence, because salvation is more important than human life, it ought to choose to save the person who did something wrong, so that he could have a chance to repent and get to heaven, and to forget the life of the person who will meet no bad end when he dies.

By the same logic, Pilate should have killed Jesus and not Barabbas, because Barabbas needed more time to repent but Jesus would not have met a bad end when He was put to death.

Or another example: if a community was forced to choose between allowing a factory to make pollution that would kill some people or to close it down and leave people poorer, then it would be better for people to be poor (so long as that poverty doesn't lead to death, although in many parts of the world it often does) than for someone to die, because human life is more important than material wealth.

Lord, we pray that you help states to have wisdom and prudence in dealing with the issue of how best to rule their populace. We pray that you help them to lead their people to salvation and a better material existence within the powers that they have available. We ask for these things, if it is your will, in Jesus' name, Amen

VII: Participation

God gave talents to every person, which are different from
one another, and which are all collectively required.
Every person in the world is dependent upon others who
have talents different from oneself.

In Genesis, there is a story about the tower of Babel, when
the people gathered together in one place and tried to
build a tower, but God seeing their pride, confused their
speech and scattered them, so that they could not finish
what they set out to build.
God said that if they continued, they could accomplish
whatever they set their mind to do.
If all of humanity was united together, then it could
accomplish anything; there would be nothing out of
human reach. This is because God has placed all of the
talents necessary to accomplish every work within each
and every human being, and if all worked together, then
they could accomplish everything. Every sickness could be
healed, every achievement and goal could be reached,
every problem could be solved, every bit of suffering could
be removed.
However, human beings are unable to unite together
because human beings are proud and sinful. When the
narrative says that God scattered them, I interpret it as
meaning that God arranged it so that their own pride
should prevent them from working with each other. They
were proud and therefore were unable to cooperate, and
thus they could not accomplish that which they set their
hearts to carry out. They divided from one another and
separated into different tribes, different nations, growing

apart from each other in language and culture as they lived in different parts of the world.

I wrote about this in a part of my book *Witchcraft*. The places in the world that developed most technological were those that were most open to the ideas and contributions of the most people. Our own modern age with its globalized economy can accomplish far more than was ever possible in former ages. Like the people of Babel, we have also reached up to the heavens with our tall towers in cities, we have sent machines into space and landed men on the Moon. But if the world came to war and division, with the nations of the world turning against each other in pride, breaking this unity apart, then the modern prosperity and all the things that the modern world is capable of doing would break down with it.

If people worked together and each part contributed to the whole, we could build 'Babel'. The modern world that has globalized and interconnected, has become more prosperous than any other time in the history of this planet, and this is a kind of Babel. If human pride and nationalism constructs barriers between peoples, this is the pride that divides them and prevents the tower from being completed.

The greatest civilizations in history were those that had participation from the many and not from the few in their construction.

Pride is the work of the demon. He puts pride into the hearts of people and thus they fail to build Babel. They fail to achieve whatever they set out their minds to do, because they only have talents to do one thing and they needed the talents of the other person to do another thing to complement theirs in order to build the tower, but they are too proud to work together. Thus, diseases remain uncured, thus problems remain troublesome, thus people live in poverty and lack the things they need, thus people cannot achieve many things that we wish to achieve.

States with more virtue can have more freedom. More freedom will allow more people to participate in the workings of their society. More participation will mean more talents are added to the crucible, and the more talents that are available, the more successful the project of building Babel can become.

Catholic social teaching has something to tell us on this point concerning 'subsidiarity'. People in local communities will typically know better than government officials in faraway offices about the problems they are facing and how these things are best solved. For that reason, if the power to make decisions can be safely left to the lower levels to make those decisions, then governments ought to leave those decisions to the lower levels rather than try to decide everything themselves. I will treat this more deeply later.

However, again, the things I wrote in the fourth chapter have to be remembered here: it is better to leave decisions to the lower levels when the lower levels can handle the decisions, but you cannot give them that authority or freedom if in fact they cannot be trusted with it as a result of their own sinfulness and the abuses that they would do with it.

States should try to involve as much participation as possible from the people in the running of the state as they can. A plurality of people holding political power is better than a single person holding political power, not simply as a 'check and balance' on power, but because the amount of talents that God gives to an individual is never more than that which He gives to the group and the group is able to accomplish more than the individual.

However, again the things I wrote in the fourth chapter have to be remembered here: if power can be safely trusted to a larger group of people, then it ought to be trusted to them, but if they are too sinful to wield it responsibly, then it is better for power to be restricted to a smaller group or even to a single individual.

Greater participation will mean more talents added into the project, and the more that the society can accomplish, however, greater participation requires as a starting point that those who are given the freedom to participate can be trusted to be responsible with that freedom.

A democracy where every citizen has a right to vote is better than an oligarchy or a dictatorship, because a democracy has more participation of more people and thus has more talents involved in the project of governance, however, if the citizens cannot be trusted with this right, because they will vote for something that is going to lead to the destruction of the society, then it is better not to have that right.

A society where people can speak and publish freely, will have more participation of the ideas of people than a society with censorship and control. It will, by its nature, be able to achieve more, because more ideas and talents are able to flow freely into the crucible. But if the granting of such rights results in the destruction of public morals or the breakdown of social order, then such rights cannot be granted.

A society where there are no regulations on business is able to achieve more than one that does have regulations, since more will be accomplished without the red tape holding back people from innovating and creating. However, if the lack of regulations leads to abuse of workers, abuse of consumers, abuse of the environment, abuse of society in general, then the government has to step in and regulate.

More freedom will result in greater prosperity and greater success than less freedom, because more freedom will allow for more people to contribute more of the talents they were given. The group can accomplish more than the individual, as God gave talents to each that were complementary with each other, and if all were working together, there is nothing that couldn't be accomplished, but more freedom requires as a precondition that those who are granted it will be more responsible.

The perfect state is one of absolute freedom: one of anarchy where no governance or control exists at all, but that is impossible in a world where people are sinful.

Lord, we pray that states will become freer and more people will participate in them. We pray that people will be freed from the vices that prevent them from accomplishing what they could do when they worked together. We ask for these things, if it is your will, in Jesus' name, Amen

VIII: Rule of Law

Moses in the Old Testament told the Israelites that they should judge the same between the rich and the poor. If the rich man broke the laws, he should be punished just the same as the poor man.

Moses, however, had other parts of his laws where discrimination between groups was dictated. The law for sacrifice for sins was different depending on whether you were a priest, a prince or a common person. People who had certain racial backgrounds were not permitted to enter the assembly of God. Men and women did not have the same rights under the law. Neither did slaves and free persons have equal rights under the law.

But for all of those things that were not mentioned specifically, the judgement was to be carried out equally regardless of the status of the person. There was no one in Israel who was above the law. In the book of Daniel, in the story of Susannah, the elders perjure and their perjury is found out, and they are not saved because of their status of being elders, but they receive the punishment of death just as an ordinary person would have received for their crime.

There was no one who could claim immunity from the law because of their status.

In the 9th century, when the Vikings were raiding Britain, people of the time interpreted these events as being a punishment from God upon them for their sins. Alfred the Great, king of Wessex (a statue of him is depicted on the cover of this book) interpreted it like this as well and he determined that the solution to this problem was that his kingdom needed to return to God again.

So, he made orders to give gifts to help monasteries and churches, to give honours and orders for devotions made to saints and their relics. Alfred also determined to write what is known as the 'Doom book', which was the first book of codified laws in Anglo-Saxon history. Alfred had this code of laws made for his kingdom and he took inspiration from the laws of Moses in order to create many of these laws, although his inspiration was not exclusively from that source.

Some laws in the Doom book might appear very strange today. For example, it said that if a man accidentally caused the death of another man by letting a tree fall on him, then the tree had to be given to the kinsmen of the slain.

However, some of them might appear more familiar to us today. Alfred in fact took inspiration from the book of Leviticus to rule that the same judgment should be applied to the rich and the poor equally, and the judge should not be partial between his friends or his enemies.

Leviticus 19: [15] Thou shalt not do that which is unjust, nor judge unjustly. Respect not the person of the poor, nor honour the countenance of the mighty. But judge thy neighbour according to justice.

English law has a deep tradition of the concept of the Rule of Law that can trace itself back to this Doom book as well as other sources in the Middle Ages. English law was the source of American law and the source of legal systems throughout the countries that were once part of the British empire.

The principle of the rule of law existed in Hong Kong and not really in mainland China, because of this tradition, which itself has biblical roots.

Laws in mainland China are often very ambiguous. They define things using terms that are open to interpretation like 'harm to social harmony' or 'harm to national interests', without defining specific actions or things that are allowed or not allowed by these laws. They are also not subject to any kind of judicial practice of upholding a precedent when passing rules, thus allowing them to reinterpret the laws as often as they wish for each individual case.

The result is that it gives the authorities the power to decide whoever they want to be guilty to be guilty and whoever they want to be innocent to be innocent. A law can be interpreted one way one day against one person who they want to be guilty and it can be interpreted another way a different day for a person who they want to be innocent. Laws have no meaning then, but they just become deceptive tools and methods of propaganda to give people the false idea that the country is ruled fairly by laws rather than by the whims and wishes of those who run the governing party, which are disguised under the false pretense of 'laws'.

English law has a deeply-rooted tradition with the principle of the Rule of law. The idea in English law of rule by precedent is itself related to this. Since the same law ought to be judged the same way everywhere and at all times, hence, if a court has ruled a particular case, then future courts that meet equivalent cases should rule in the same way. It shouldn't be different depending on the whims or personal interpretations of the judge in one place or another.

The prosperity of the nation rests in its virtue and whether or not it serves God. God is displeased by sin, and abuse of legal justice by states is a sin.

Alfred the Great was correct in thinking that ordering his kingdom in the way that God commanded was the right path to follow in order to bring peace and prosperity to his country. He connected the raids and invasions of the Vikings with a punishment that was falling on his nation for failing to respect God's will. His solution was to try to mend this relationship, end the injustice and seek to do God's will. Thus, among other things, he mandated that his kingdom should observe justice and judge all people the same, because that is what the Bible taught him

All states should do this. All states should recognize that the problems their communities have root from sin and the ultimate solution is to return to God, to seek to know His will and to follow His commands in the society.

Many states are blind to this. They attribute the problems they have to only the superficial causes. Epidemics are caused by bacteria and viruses. Famines are caused by bad economic planning. Wars are caused by bad diplomacy or bad defence strategy, etc. They fail to realize that behind all these things is a divine will which is blessing or punishing people through these things, because they choose to follow His will or not.

The people of the Middle Ages that thought that God's hand was behind these disasters weren't necessarily stupid or superstitious. They understood that the invasions were happening for military reasons too or that famines were happening because of bad rainfall or environmental issues too. They wouldn't have disagreed with the idea that the enemy army slaughtered the people of the city because the walls weren't strong enough; what was different was that they saw something else behind those things, which modern eyes, heavily influenced by atheistic thinking, tend to be blind towards. The reason why the things people could see existed and were arranged as they were was because there was something else that people couldn't see which was ordering all things according to an intelligent plan.

Thus, to rectify the problems of states and human societies, the first thing that the state must do is to repair its relationship with God.

Alfred is recognized as a saint in the church, with a feast on October 26th.

People who violate the same commandments may not have the same level of guilt. A poor person who steals a loaf of bread may have less sinfulness in the eyes of God than a rich person who does the same; although the concept of the rule of law would demand that both be equally punished for it.

In truth, even in states that have the rule of law in their legal system, they still allow for some flexibility in giving out punishments so that those who the judge thinks have committed crimes more seriously will get harsher penalties than those who the judge thinks have committed the same crime in a lesser way.

But the rule of law is that punishing offences should not be a question of the personal opinion of the individual judge. Rather it should be based on things written down, which are publicly available to be known, and which the judge must follow when giving out a sentence, regardless of his own personal opinion. It means that no one is above the law, and no one can claim immunity from prosecution because of the special identity that he has belonging to one category or another.

Every state should generally follow the rule of law in its legal practice. All laws should be written down, publicly known, clear and unambiguous, without leaving room for the judges to decide themselves based on their own private opinions as individuals about whether someone deserves punishment or not.

A law should not be written that forbids 'bad behaviour' without any further definition. It should explicitly define what things specifically are being forbidden or not forbidden by this, so that the possibility for the judge to decide himself how to interpret is eliminated or at least reduced as far as possible as it can be reduced.

If leeway can be given to let judges decide between different levels of punishment depending on the severity of a case, such leeway should be written down, clearly defined and clearly published as well, so that the judge cannot decide himself how to give the leeway, but he will do so according to the rules that are established for the case.

Different laws can be applied to different groups in society, but as long as a law is applied, then no one who is part of that group should be able to escape the penalty of the law if they break it on account of some special status that they hold that is undefined in the law.

Unless the system works like this, it allows for abuse to

enter in. People who break the same law should not be punished by one judge and set free by another. People who break the same law in the same way should be treated the same by the system, without discrimination between one and the other. The system can treat different groups differently (I will write more about this later), but any such difference in treatment cannot be decided arbitrarily by the judge or the policeman, but it has to be set down, clear, unambiguous and published beforehand.

If the society was perfect, it wouldn't need laws. It is not perfect, which is why laws are necessary. Since it is not perfect, that is exactly why it is you cannot simply just trust police and judges to use their own judgements to decide who they think should be punished or not, but they must instead apply the same legal standard regardless of what they may privately think or feel. Otherwise, they will decide arbitrarily and people will be treated unfairly. Once they are treated unfairly, they will respect the laws less, people who are guilty will go free because they are liked by those in judicial authority and people who are innocent will be punished because they are disliked by those in judicial authority, and justice will not exist.
Justice is often depicted as a goddess that is blindfolded holding scales. This is because true justice should be measuring impartially, whether reference to the special status or identity of the person whose case is being measured in the scales.

Not every state should be a democracy. But every state, even absolute monarchies and dictatorships, should still uphold the principle of the rule of law. If the monarch or the dictator disobeys the law he set down for all the people in his own private behaviour, he should be subject to the same punishment too.

Lord, we pray that states will follow the principle of the rule of law in accordance with your will. We pray that judges will judge impartially and not in accordance with their own feelings or wishes. We ask for these things, if it is your will, in Jesus' name, Amen

Part II: Examples

Christ's kingdom is not of this world. Although there may be states in history that claim to be Christian states, who have kings anointed in church ceremonies, who have the cross painted on their flags or who officially acknowledge God and His church, these are not Christ's kingdom. These are sinful human kingdoms, ultimately doomed to destruction, that have made some effort to try to convert to the gospel, but they are not the kingdom that Christ was speaking of when He preached His kingdom.

The church should not run the state, but the state should obey the things that are taught by the church. The kingdom of God is not a political state, but political states ought to seek to surrender themselves to obedience to the laws of the kingdom of God.

As long as people are sinful and they cannot be left to live together peacefully without use of rules and force, states will always be with us. States need to make decisions. In order to know how to make decisions they need something to guide them. Different states in history have had different answers about what this something is which will guide their decisions in how they will run their societies. At various times, things such as political ideologies, the popular will, the interests of the leaders or the elite/nobility, religions, superstitions or other things have been the lodestones used by leaders to decide how best to make decisions for their states.

The gospel and the law of God provide answers to states about how to make decisions. Many modern nation states have rejected this lodestone to guide them, and have chosen other things instead to inform their decisions. However, the teachings of the church and the gospel are still influential among leaders of many nations. In the past they were as well.

This section is meant to deal with various lessons that can be drawn from various episodes from the Bible, history and the modern-day to consider in continuing to think about the question of how best to conduct statecraft. Through looking at these examples, I will use the aforementioned group of principles in order to write about these examples and explore them further so that the reader can better understand them.

Lord, we pray that you help us to understand politics as you desire and to use these lessons for the benefit of the world. We pray that you help the world and the leaders of the world to more greatly obey and follow your gospel. We ask for these things, if it is your will, in Jesus' name, Amen

IX: The Land of Canaan

In the Old Testament, God commands the Jews to destroy the inhabitants of the land of Canaan and to go and occupy the land for themselves after they annihilated the original inhabitants. This is rightly called a 'genocide', because it is the purposeful destruction of entire nations on a mass scale.

The justification that is given for this conquest has several aspects to it.

Firstly, in Leviticus chapters 18 and 20, the Israelites are given a list of sins, mostly of a sexual nature, that they must not do and they are told that the peoples of the land that they are going to enter are doing all of these things. God also tells the Jews that it is not for their righteousness that He is giving this land to them, but it is because of the sins of the people of the land that He is driving them out. Secondly, God also tells the Jews that if they do not drive out these peoples, then they will become a thorn in their side and will tempt them to follow their gods.

To a modern Catholic, this justification may seem hard to swallow. God, through Moses, did not simply say to fight those who fought back against them, but He also demanded that the civilian population be annihilated, including the women and children; 'everything that breathes' according to some translations. For people who think that it is morally wrong to take innocent life, how can this be attributed to a moral God that is supposedly the author and source of all righteousness?

While, there is good reason to doubt that this genocide every actually occurred historically as it was written, and thus the account may simply be a story only, however, that doesn't ultimately solve the problem here, because in the narrative (whether historically true or false) it is still meant to teach people about God's will, about morality, about Truth and justice, etc.

Some people will choose to ignore these parts of the Old Testament or they may say that these are not things that Christians can accept and that we should focus only on what the New Testament teaches.

The problem with this is that these stories are also considered to be inspired by the Holy Spirit and they are also part of the Bible; part of the Word of God. If the Word of God does not hold authority because it is the Word of God, then the New Testament does not hold authority. The same Spirit who spoke through Christ and inspired the gospel writers is also the same Spirit who inspired these stories of genocide and mass slaughter. If you reject one part of the inspired Word, then you reject all of it.

It is not something that can be brushed over, forgotten about or simply just relegated to a category like it doesn't matter. It has to be read, it has to be studied, it has to be interpreted and the lessons drawn from it are things that like all other parts of the Word of God, were meant for all peoples in all places and times.

How could a good God order such a huge genocide to take place in the narrative?

This is not merely a rhetorical question, nor is it acceptable to simply answer it with something like: 'we must take it on faith'. There is no question about anything in the Bible that is not worth the time to investigate and figure out the Truth concerning it. Even if the question seems hard to answer, I believe that God delights in it when we seek to know Him better, which is ultimately what struggles over such questions are trying to do.

I believe this question has an answer that I can try to provide it here, although others may answer it differently and disagree with what I propose. My answer is also going to give us our first lesson in this part of the book, which will be concerning the principle of pragmatism.

Firstly, God's rule of the world as depicted in the Bible, in more than one place, includes stories in which He kills masses of people in punishment for sin. God in fact caused the entire human race to experience death because of the sin of Adam.

But even if people do not commit sins that are worthy of death in their lives, God still makes them suffer for the sin of Adam and experience death themselves.

Little babies who barely knew the breath of life suffered and died as infants, when they were completely innocent, ultimately because God decreed that all born from Adam must suffer and die as a consequence for what Adam did. In Genesis, Abraham intercedes over Sodom and says 'surely you will not kill the innocent with the guilty', and yet the effects of Adam's sin upon the entire human race are in fact putting the innocent to death with the guilty. How does a just God rule the world like this?

God has a higher priority than life and material happiness when He governs the universe. He is not unconcerned about human suffering or human death; He cares about human suffering and death very deeply. But there is something else that He cares about even more and that is the salvation of souls.

You can experience any kind of torture in this world or undergo any kind of death in this world, and no matter how painful it may be, what you experience will always be incomparably less than what is experienced by the souls in hell that are apart from God eternally. This can be hard for us to imagine, but it is true.

The victims of diseases who suffer every day in pain until they finally expire, the people who get tortured with electricity or fire in prisons, the victims of human trafficking that are raped everyday and driven to suicide... it does not matter what kind of suffering that exists in this world, because no matter what it is, it is not even close to comparing what awaits a sinner in the eternity of hell.

Every time that God ever punished the world by giving people suffering or death, it was only because doing so was going to save people from an even worse fate that awaited them.

So, how is it that consigning all people to death and suffering from Adam's sin was saving people from a fate worse than death and suffering?

Hellfire is hellfire because the soul is separated from God. We were designed to be with God and being denied God is to be denied that which we were designed to be with. It is part of our own being and what we are that the fact of this separation should make us suffer. It is not possible for us to exist and not suffer when thus separated, because we would no longer be what we are if that were true. It is part of our own essence in our creation that being thus separated should make us feel suffering.

Now, sin is what separates the soul from God. God does not force people to be with Him, but they can choose to be with Him or not, and He grants us to make that choice freely and thus we are capable of sinning.

If human beings in this world chose to sin, but never died, it would essentially mean that they would suffer in this world forever. This is because it is impossible to be rid of suffering and yet be disconnected from that which we must have according to our own design in order to have joy. Even if you provided them with food, water, material comforts, etc. people would inevitably be driven to madness and endless suffering if they lived in this world forever without God.

We are told in Revelations that at the end of the world the sinners will come back to resurrect in the flesh and face judgement. At that time, perhaps when they are back in the flesh this world, and death has finally been defeated forever, this fate I am describing above is exactly what is going to happen to them.

Now, suppose God saw that by denying people material comforts, by making people suffer hunger, thirst, disease, tiredness, boredom, anxiety, fear, regret, depression, betrayal by others, loneliness, etc. would actually help people to become less attached to this world and in turn to look for Him, and thus caused them to sin less or even be free from sin, He will then give those painful things to human beings because the suffering these things will give to people is still less than the suffering of being detached from Him.

God does not like to give these things to people, but when Adam sinned, He granted these things to human beings, because He knew that there was a priority here that human beings themselves might not understand, but which He in His infinite wisdom understood perfectly.

A poor man who is freed from sin is far richer than a rich man who lives away from God. A country of impoverished people who love God is far more prosperous than a materially wealthy country of people who reject His laws. An old and sick man who has retained His principles is far healthier than an Olympic athlete that hasn't. An ignorant woman who never went to school but who loves her neighbour as herself has learned more than a conceited scholar that teaches at a prestigious university.

Human beings don't see the Truth, but God does, and thus He grants these things of suffering to people in order to help them to detach themselves from the things that are not really real.

If Adam took the fruit and all human beings after him sinned continually without ever suffering any of these things, they would perhaps have all the riches of the world, and yet be without God, without Truth, without true wisdom, without true health, without that which they really needed and they would be destroyed by it.

It is odd to think about the fact that suicide rates are often higher for the rich than they are for the poor.

Human beings committed sin, and God lets human beings suffer in this world, because that suffering can help detach them from this world so that by temporarily losing the goods of this world, they will not lose a good that is even greater than this world.

The things of this world are not evil, but it is when people love these things too much that evil comes into being. If God simply allowed people to have all the things of this world and enjoy them forever while they detach themselves from Him in sin, it would not be a mercy at all, but it would be worse than punishing them.

Sometimes children get angry when their parents punish them, because they think it is unfair, and they don't realize that their parents are helping them to be better and to avoid even bigger suffering in the future that are created by the bad behaviours that are just starting to grow.

Now, death plays a part in this as well. The fact of death's existence does help to teach people to not love this world too much, and to look for something higher than this world. Thus, God does use death to help people not to lose their highest good.

But furthermore, considering the facts of life on Earth, death is a kind of liberation in three ways.

Firstly, for the saints that are living holy lives with God, as long as they remain in this world, they will suffer and be tempted, and those temptations will always be capable of bringing them to lose their holiness and be detached from God. If they lived forever, it would mean that they had to be tempted forever and that means that they are at risk forever and never safe. Death provides them with a safe place where once they have passed through it, then they become safe and temptation can no longer threaten to take them away from God any longer. Thus, God gives death to His saints so that their sufferings and temptations can be ended.

God does not desire for His saints to suffer forever. But the time of His second coming and His kingdom on earth has not been ready yet, and as long as that is true, His saints must continue suffering and being tempted upon the earth. Death is then the only solution for them to end their pains and come to their reward.

The innocent infants and unborn children who die today and in past times in great numbers are part of this first group. They did not deserve to die for Adam's sin, but their deaths also saved them from temptations later in life that might have caused them to lose their innocence and go to hell. Christ spoke about Judas the betrayer at the last supper: 'it would have been better for him had he not been born'.

I would suppose that the vast majority of those in the first group are these innocent infants and unborn children who die without sin, while just a tiny number are those who either retained their innocence into later life or regained it after penance.

Life is a place where souls are tested, to see if they will choose to love God or not when faced with the temptations of the world. God, however, has evidently not required for all human beings to be tested. Considering the masses of people who died in infancy or as unborn children, He obviously was satisfied that these souls were ready without the need to go through the tests that we have gone through.

For the first group, death is a liberation from a world of temptation and suffering.

Secondly, for the souls of those who live in God's grace but still with some sin, as long as they have failed to find perfection, then they will keep sinning in this world. Venial sins, when repeated over and over again, always inevitably become mortal sins. No one can be a venial sinner forever, because no matter who they are, eventually they will reach a point where either they must become perfect or they must be detached from God's grace. However, if they died before they reached that point, it will mean that they will find salvation then, even if they must pass through purgatory first.

Whereas if you let them live forever, their venial sins eventually would become mortal. At that point, they would have been detached from the grace of God and cut off from salvation, until they repented.

Death is thus saving them from a greater fall than they have already fallen into.

It is better to die than it is to sin. It is better to die than it is to be cut off from the grace of God. Purgatory is painful, but it is better to go through it than it is to sin gravely and lose the friendship of God.

Thirdly, for the souls of those who are without God's grace and live with mortal sin, death will send them to hell. In the second letter of Peter, we are told that Christ is 'delaying' His coming in order to give all a chance to repent. Perhaps it is also true that God delays the death of many sinners because He gives them a chance to repent. If there was a person who would have repented and gone to heaven if He had simply been given more time in this life, God perhaps would have given that person more time in this life rather than let them die and go to hell. Those who do die and go to hell are perhaps those who insist on remaining in sin no matter how long you were to give them in this world.

If this isn't true, then I suppose that death is not a gift at all to them, because death is preventing them from coming to repentance and preventing them from having a chance to reform, which they would have taken had they been given the opportunity. God giving death to them, would be like a government giving capital punishment to a criminal, while refusing to give the criminal a chance to change.

Now, suppose it is true, and all that death is doing here is just taking the people who would never repent no matter what and sending them to hell. In that case, it is a gift to them. The suffering in hell will be far greater than this world, however, the sins that they commit in this world will come to an end.

If they kept sinning in this world, then perhaps their punishment in hell would simply just increase more and more. If you let them live forever, then the punishment that was due to them would perhaps also grow infinitely. Furthermore, as mentioned above, being eternally detached from God in this world, will eventually lead the soul to eternal sadness in this world even if they didn't die. Souls in hell continue to sin, however, their sins perhaps cannot grow in the same way as they do in this world. Hence, if you send a soul that eternally wills to sin to go to hell, the soul will suffer extremely, but you will also be protecting the soul from an even worse fate if they were left in this world and their sins were allowed to increase.

This is speculation on my part and it could be wrong.

It makes sense to me, however, partly because the souls in hell are already condemned and suffering. If they sin in that state, when God is already casting them into the lake of fire, the evil that they do is perhaps not as great as when a soul in this world chooses to reject God, and yet God had offered the soul every chance to be redeemed without treating them as they deserve. A person who sins against God, when confronted with God's kindness, is perhaps committing a greater offence than the person who sins against God when confronted with His wrath.

If you had taken all the souls in hell back to this earth and given them life again, and their suffering ended, but they were still insisting on rejecting God, then their sin would be even greater if they were just left in hell to suffer forever. And if their sin is greater, their punishment would also have to be greater as well.

God didn't make death, but He gave death to human beings in order to liberate them from this life and save them from even worse fates. If it was not so, He would not have given death to human beings. He does not at all like death. He hates death. But there are other things He hates even more, and He governs this world with these priorities.

With that understood, the rest of those other stories in the bible in which God punishes people with death and suffering for sins comes to make a lot of sense. Whether it is the flood of Noah, or the Babylonian conquest, or the plagues of Egypt... God gives death and suffering to sinners because He is trying to prevent them from losing something even worse.
Noah and his family were the only survivors of the flood in the sense of earthly life, but that doesn't mean that all those who drowned in the waters went to hell. Perhaps, many of them woke up from their sins before they finally succumbed to drowning and their souls were saved, even if their bodies were not. The same is true of the people of Sodom, the same is true of the Jews in Jerusalem being slaughtered by the Chaldeans and it is also true of the Canaanites that the Israelites were told to slaughter.

The letter of Peter seems to allude to the fact that some of

the victims of the flood were not condemned to hell.
1 Peter 3: [19] In which also coming he preached to
those spirits that were in prison: [20] Which had been
some time incredulous, when they waited for the patience
of God in the days of Noe, when the ark was a building:
wherein a few, that is, eight souls, were saved by water.

Does that mean that earthly states should slaughter people
if they are evil? In order to protect them from a worse fate
that would come on them if they continued living?
We couldn't do so, because we don't have God's eyes. God
can in fact see whether or not the person is going to
repent if given the chance. We cannot see this. Perhaps if
we could, the moral justification would then be there for
us to do so, but we can't see this.
We can never see in this world if any particular individual
would have repented or not had they been given the
chance. For that reason, we should always avoid every
form of capital punishment and in fact every form of taking
the life of people who are evil.
The people who are evil, in fact, ought to have their lives
protected the most, even more than those that are good.
Because if those that are good die, then they will go to
heaven, and thus it is not as bad for them to die as it is for
the evil to die. If anyone should be given capital
punishment, it ought to be the saints. As I said before, if
you had to choose between freeing Barabbas and freeing
Jesus, the priorities would demand for Christ to be
crucified. Christ's death meant that Barabbas was given a
second chance; knowing the nature of His sacrifice given
for all humanity, it is hard to imagine that He would not

have Himself chosen it that way.

Similarly, working to end capital punishment, police violence, warfare, suicide or death from poverty is a higher priority than ending abortion, from one perspective, since abortion will always end the life of an innocent soul, one that is not destined for eternal punishment, but the other means of death might send people to hell since they may have already committed grave sins.

Abortion needs to be ended and put a stop to in society, but not for the reasons that people may think. The reason it must end is not just to protect the lives of the unborn, but more importantly, because its existence and prevalence is a temptation that causes millions of those already born to commit sins that will destine them to eternal hellfire by their act of mass murder through abortion. But sin is something that exists in the heart. If you outlaw abortion, but everyone still agrees with it and wants to do it, then they remain in sin, even if it becomes legally impossible to carry it out. Abortion's greatest victim is not the child being destroyed but the soul of the person that is lost who is responsible for it. Punishing those who do abortion can help eliminate temptations to do it in society and would likely cause fewer people to seek to do it, thus laws against abortion are protecting the souls of people as well, but such punishments themselves don't save people whose will is still to do it if they could. Different states have different situations, but abortion tends to touch far more people in most parts of the world than capital punishment does, hence, one could well argue that the threat to public morality that abortion represents is far greater than the risk that someone will die in mortal sin because he was executed without being given more time to repent. Hence, even from the perspective of the priorities, ending abortion in a state may still be more important than ending capital punishment.

All I mean to say here is that if it is a simple choice between saving the life of an innocent unborn child and the life of a guilty person who is going to be executed, without consideration of the multitude of other factors that may exist, saving the latter should take priority over the former, because salvation is a higher priority than life. If there is a baby drowning in the sea and a crippled man with no chance of being able to swim on his own drowning with him, and you can only save one, then the priorities would dictate that you save the crippled man, because the baby has nothing to fear from death, but you don't know if the crippled man has nothing to fear from death.

As I wrote before, I am not sure that God allows anyone in the world to die in mortal sin who wouldn't have repented had they been given more time. I don't know if that assumption is true. God may use our work in saving the lives of others that are potentially guilty as His own way to make sure that those who would have repented will have enough time.

It is unjust for the innocent to die, while the guilty live, but the priorities of statecraft that I defined earlier demand this when there is a choice between the two, since salvation is always more important than life itself, and when innocent souls die, the consequences are infinitely smaller than when the guilty souls die.

It may seem strange and yet it is true. Those stories of mass death in the Old Testament are explaining exactly the reason why it is more important to save the life of a guilty criminal than it is to save the life of an innocent unborn, because salvation matters more than life. Taking away the earthly lives of innocents in order so that guilty will still find eternal salvation is a better outcome than saving the physical lives of the innocent and the guilty being eternally condemned. Christ gave His physical life so that multitudes would have eternal salvation. It would be better for a million innocent to die and lose their temporarily earthly lives than for a single person to die and lose his soul forever. Christ, in a way, could be considered as standing in the place of any innocent person among the sinful Canaanites whose life was ultimately taken away so that God's people would not lose the faith.

If we could be certain that a particular sinner was going to sin forever no matter how much time was given him, perhaps in that case, it would be right to kill him, if in fact what I wrote above was true, since doing so would thus save the sinner from something even worse. However, it is not possible for us to be certain of that, because we are not God. We don't see who will repent and who will not, so we must always seek to preserve life in every circumstance and most especially, to preserve the lives of people who have the most to regret from losing it.

Thus, God has a right to order such executions or even genocides, but human beings do not.

Now, with regard to the story of the Israelites entering the land in Canaan in particular, there is another aspect here, which needs to be considered.

I mentioned two reasons above that God gave for why the genocide had to take place. The first was the guilt of the people of the land. The second was the fact that they would be a thorn and a temptation to the Jews.

In the narrative of the Old Testament, the Israelites did in fact fail to destroy them utterly, as they were commanded to do so, and these people did become a thorn and temptation to the Israelites. They would intermarry with them and lead them to worship their gods, and this would in turn bring down God's wrath upon Israel, which eventually culminated in their being driven from the land just as they had first driven out the original inhabitants.

There are Catholic prayers that hold the verse, 'Lord, let me die rather than sin against you'.
The principle of pragmatism dictates that salvation must be chosen over life itself. It is for that reason that Christ died, because by His death of the body, the souls of people would be saved. It is for that reason that the martyrs died, because by their blood, the souls of people would be saved. If the death of someone's body can mean life to someone's soul, then it must be chosen.
Jesus said that it is better for your hand or foot to be cut off than it is to go down to hell with both hands or both feet. By the same logic, it is better for someone else to be deprived of a hand, a foot or even his life itself, than to have those things intact and someone be brought to hell because of it.

Now, with regard to the Israelites killing the Canaanites, it is actually the same logic ultimately. If the Canaanites had lived and thus caused the Israelites to sin is such a serious way that they lost God, then it is still ultimately a choice between salvation of souls and deaths of bodies.
If the temptation from them was going to cause the

Israelites to sin and lose God, but their deaths would have meant that the Israelites would be saved from the temptation and remained with God, then it is better that the Canaanites all die than that the Israelites turn to idols.

This is in fact opening the door to the explanation to a great deal of the commandments in the Old Testament that formed the Mosaic law, which I will get into later in more detail.

When the Israelites (according to the narrative) carried out the genocide that God, through Moses, commanded them to do, they killed all, including the innocent. Hence, the first explanation that you are killing sinners that refuse to repent doesn't entirely work here, or at least not with everyone.

Keep in mind, as was mentioned before, that original sin also results in the death of many people who never committed mortal sin either, and it is a fair assumption that the flood of Noah in the narrative would have killed children and infants as well.

If the Israelites made peace with the Canaanites, lived by their sin and in the end, they turned to worshipping idols, lost their relationship with the God of Abraham and in the end they all went to hell (and since salvation came from the Jews, in turn the entire world would never get to heaven), this would be a worse choice than simply just killing the Canaanites and ridding them of the temptation. But one might then rightly ask: 'why couldn't they just have had a stronger faith? Why couldn't they just resist the temptations and stay true to God without the war?'

The answer to this lies in the principle of pragmatism. Of course, that would have been ideal if the Israelites had such a strong faith.

But Moses did not have the power to make them have a stronger faith and God was trying to give them a stronger faith, but they were resisting Him all the time. He granted human beings the free will to refuse Him and He was not going to take that away.

If they refuse to learn to be more faithful to God, then God who ruled them through Moses is then left with what He is left with and must make decisions accordingly.

God then orders them to kill the Canaanites because He knows the Canaanites will corrupt their faith and lead them to idols. Obviously if the Israelites had a stronger faith, then this justification would not have been merited. However, because the Israelites refused to have a stronger faith and resisted God, this justification became merited, since maintaining their weak faith in God by ordering them to carry out the slaughter was still a better outcome than losing it by making peace.

The name 'Israel' in Hebrew means 'he who contends with God'. It is the name that the angel gave to Jacob after he spent the night wrestling with him. The story of the Old Testament and indeed of the Jewish nation is the struggle of a people with the God who chose them and they are rightly named 'Israel'.

The ideal situation is better of course, but the ideal situation is not the one that exists. If Moses had ordered the people 'strengthen your faith and then make peace with the Canaanites, show them a good example and stay true to your God' the people would not have done this, and instead would have made peace with the Canaanites and turned to worshipping their gods. Thus, the principle of pragmatism dictates that Moses should not have ordered that.

When the Israelite warriors went out to carry out the genocide against the Canaanites, it would not be entirely right to say that they were the ones guilty of the deaths of all these people they were slaughtering, both innocent and guilty, because they were carrying out the command of God when they carried out the order and God ordered this in order to protect the weak of faith. Thus, the people who were guilty of killing all the Canaanites were not the soldiers, but it was the Israelites who refused to fully believe in God, who continually resisted God, who always refused His call to love Him more. They were the ones that were responsible for the deaths of those people, because the deaths of those people were the price that had to be paid on account of their own stubbornness and sins.

If a faithful Israelite was to carry out this order of genocide, he would not be committing a sin, because it is not really he who is causing these innocent people to die inasmuch as it was the weak faith of his countrymen that was determining that these people should die.

Since there are so many of those among them who are not true to God as they should be, those other nations had to die, in order so that their faith might remain intact and that this faith could someday bring them and all people to salvation.

A lesson that comes out of all of this, however, is that it

relates to nations fighting wars today. Wars are created by sin, and without sin, there would be no war. The sins that occur in peacetime are the fuel that eventually gets lit in time of war and burns until it is quenched.

If a nation was holy and people obeyed the laws of God, then wars would be averted. If the Israelites were a holy nation without sin, then they would have never needed to destroy the Canaanites in order to preserve their faith.

If Europe didn't have so much nationalism, the First World War would not have happened. If Christian nations had been holy and really followed the teaching to love one another, the national rivalries would not have existed. Paul said that in Christ there is neither Greek nor Jew. If Christian nations had taken the teachings seriously, they would have followed this and the nationalism would never have been lit. But because of their sinfulness in times of peace, their failure to repent and follow the gospel, these sins pile up silently in times of peace until they finally are lit up and become an inferno in times of war.

If America was a holy nation and the people obeyed the laws of God, then they would have taken their wealth and extended it to help the poor in the world. Their failure to do so, and the failure of other rich nations to do so, is the fuel that the communists in Vietnam, Korea, China, Russia or other places used in order to light the wars of revolution and war. In other words, if America and the other rich nations had helped the poor of the world as the law of God dictates, there perhaps would not have been a Cold War or all of the other conflicts that came within that confrontation.

It is the people who sin in times of peace that cause wars to erupt. If a nation wishes to end war, it must eliminate the evils inside itself first and to repent of its sins, and then wars will be averted. On Ash Wednesday every year, Catholics have ashes placed on their foreheads and are told to repent and follow the gospel. If Catholics really did this as Christ desired, no Catholic nation would have a war ever again, because the circumstances that created the war would never have come about.

It is the sins in times of peace that end in wars. The sins in time of peace cause the circumstances to exist that create the wars or make them impossible to avoid. The adulterer, the sabbath-breaker, the greedy, the drunkard, the drug dealer, the person who cheated in the contract, the student who insulted the teacher, the person who ran through the red light, the husband who abandoned his wife and children, the woman who had the abortion... in ways that are usually hard to see, all of these sins create the circumstances that lead the nation to war. The responsibility for wars and the blood that is shed are properly laid on their hands.

When a soldier obeys his orders to go and fight in a war, killing the enemy, it is not really he who is the one responsible for the death of this person that he kills. The person who killed that person was the sinner in his own nation who violated God's laws and thus caused the war to begin.

The soldiers are simply just carrying out the commands of their nations that sent them there, and the people who are responsible for the deaths of those they kill are all those who lived in their nations in times of peace, who lived in the wrong way and created the conditions that ended with them sending out people to kill for them because they wouldn't find the solutions themselves to the human problems that created the war.

The person who kills is the one who commits adultery or watches pornography. The person who kills is the one who has the abortion or defrauds in the contract. The person who kills is the one who refuses to believe in God or to pray to Him. These are the ones who kill and the soldier who actually fires the bullet is simply doing what he is ordered to do by the sinful nation that sent him there, which failed to find a peaceful solution because of its own sins.

Hence, when Moses ordered the Israelites to kill these people in genocide, obeying this order in itself was not a sin. It could not be, because God does not order anyone to sin and Moses was speaking what God told him to speak. Conducting the genocide was not the sin. It was the weak faith of the Israelites that was the sin, which caused the genocide to be necessary to preserve the faith of Abraham through which the Israelite nation and the world could find salvation.

Similarly, when America fought in Korea, Vietnam or Iraq, it was not the soldiers who fought these wars that were responsible for the deaths of those people. The people responsible for the deaths of those people were the greedy at home, the people who refused to acknowledge God, the people who went after illicit sexual things, the people who sought a life of pleasure rather than a life of the cross.

When Hitler's troops fought in Europe, when Napoleon's armies fought the coalition, when armies of any sort fight wars, it is always the same. The nation needs the soldiers to fight for it because of its own sins, and the guilt in the killing is not really the soldier who fires the bullet as it is the sinner who caused the nation to order the soldier to be put there.

People deserve punishment for their sins. They deserve to have the barbarians burning down their cities, filled with vices, and making them into slaves. They deserve to have their freedom taken from them. They deserve to have the wealth, that they preferred over God, to be burned into ashes. They deserve to have their lives, which they have used for evil, to be ended.

The soldiers on the battlefield are a mercy to them, who are killing enemies on their behalf, in order so that they might have more time to come to repent of their sins that deserve such punishment, rather than face what is due and pay the debt that is owed.

If they had repented of their sins and done God's will, they would find solutions to the problems that caused conflicts between them and other people. God designed all people to be complementary to one another, and if they were all collectively doing what God called them, no one would be lacking anything or feel that their rights had been stepped on by anyone else. The best way for a nation to defeat its enemies is not by military power, but it is by converting and following the gospel. The military power is there as a mercy to them, who have not yet adopted this greater strategy for victory. But the day that such a strategy was truly adopted, would also be the day when armies, borders and states would no long be necessary.

This may seem like an odd lesson to start the main part of this book, however, it is not so out of place. Warfare and the need to defend the populace is one of the principal reasons why states are necessary. And there are lessons that are in this story, which have to be grasped as a fundamental core within all statecraft. These relate to the principle of pragmatism and the need to recognize which priorities have to come first.

Samuel told Saul that God had removed the kingdom from him and would give it to another after Saul defied Samuel's command to wholly carry out genocide against the Amalekites and to destroy both the people with all of their animals.

Saul thought that he knew better than the prophet what was right and what God's will was, but he was wrong and his presumption is what made him unfit to be a ruler. Today many people look at these stories written by the Spirit's inspiration within the holy text and they also believe that they know better than what is written about what God's will is.

Lord, we pray that you help us to have a better understanding of the genocide narratives of the Old Testament and let us apply that knowledge to our world in the manner that pleases you. We pray that nations will repent of their sins that cause them to go to war with each other. We ask for these things, if it is your will, in Jesus' name, Amen

X: Cleanliness and Division

There are a huge number of parts of the Jewish law that concern 'clean' and 'unclean'. Certain animals could not be eaten, because this would make people unclean if they were to eat them. Certain things could not be touched or else they would make people unclean. Certain bodily emissions or health conditions would make people unclean if they had them.
If a person was unclean, he was unfit to enter into the assembly of the people of God and had to cleanse himself in order to be clean again so that he could take his place in the assembly. An unclean person could not offer sacrifices to God. He could not celebrate the Passover or the important festivals that all Jews were obligated to keep by the Mosaic law.

What was the purpose of these laws?
There are a number of hygiene issues that are certainly assisted if people engage in frequent washing of their bodies, and these laws would have perhaps provided some benefit for public hygiene from that perspective.
Some of the animals that were forbidden to be eaten are also those that were more dangerous to eat if they were not properly cooked.
Even circumcision has been claimed by some people to have perhaps been useful at preventing venereal disease.

However, the explanation for these laws goes deeper than this.
The purpose of these laws is explained in the text here:
Deuteronomy 14: [1] Be ye children of the Lord your God:

you shall not cut yourselves, nor make any baldness for the dead; [2] Because thou art a holy people to the Lord thy God: and he chose thee to be his peculiar people of all nations that are upon the earth. [3] Eat not the things that are unclean.

And here:

Leviticus 20: [24] But to you I say: Possess their land which I will give you for an inheritance, a land flowing with milk and honey. I am the Lord your God, who have separated you from other people. [25] Therefore do you also separate the clean beast from the unclean, and the clean fowl from the unclean: defile not your souls with beasts, or birds, or any things that move on the earth, and which I have shewn you to be unclean.

[26] You shall be holy unto me, because I the Lord am holy, and I have separated you from other people, that you should be mine.

The people of Israel are chosen to be holy to God and therefore they must distinguish between what is clean and what is unclean. They are chosen to be separated from the other peoples of the world, so they must distinguish between the clean the unclean.

The laws of cleanliness are laws that required the Israelites to separate themselves from other peoples.

The faith of Israel was weak. This was the reason why God commanded them to slaughter the Canaanites. Since if they did not do so, then the Canaanites would be a snare to them and would lead them to worship other gods. If their faith was stronger, then the Canaanites would not be snare to them, because in that case the people of Israel would have never gone to other gods simply because their neighbours worshipped other gods.
The genocide of the Canaanites and the laws concerning cleanliness are serving a common purpose. They are preventing the Israelites from being too close to those who are not following their laws.

Authoritarian countries feel a need to shield their citizens from knowledge of things being reported in the outside world, lest that information will influence their people to revolt, since their system is fragile and can be destroyed simply from the transmission of information. Democratic governments, however, typically don't need to shield people from information being reported outside their borders, since their system isn't going to collapse from the dissemination of information. The society that cannot trust its own citizens with a free flow of information is fundamentally a weaker society than the society that can trust them with this.
God governed the people of Israel like the authoritarian dictator, in this sense. He did not trust the Israelites to be able to make close contact with people that were different from them and who worshiped other gods, because He was a jealous God and such contact would threaten the

faith of His people who were of weak faith.

However, it was not a realistic and pragmatic order to tell the Israelites to simply isolate themselves and avoid all contact with people who did not worship their God. This would be absurd, because they lived within a world that was filled with gentiles, and even if they slaughtered the earlier inhabitants of the land, they could not conceivably have avoided all contact with the numerous gentiles that lived in the nations surrounding them. Their country itself was on the crossroads between three continents; of course, they could not avoid contact with the outside world.

People would come to trade with them, the peoples who lived on their borders would interact with them, conquerors would come to fight with them, officials would come to do diplomacy with them, travellers would come to pass through their land, etc.

The Israelites could not have simply sealed themselves off from the outside world in a practical sense. They had to interact with gentiles who did not follow their ways.

It is not possible to order the Israelites to simply avoid all contact, however, at the same time there were ways to keep that contact at a minimum.

The laws of clean and unclean fulfilled this purpose, because they obliged the Israelites to follow customs that would force them to keep their distance from people who did not follow the same customs.

They can talk to the gentiles, trade with them and interact with them, but they had to be careful that they did not eat food with them, otherwise they might end up eating something unclean. They had to be careful about going near their houses or entering their dwellings, lest there be something that would make them unclean. They had to be concerned about living in the same cities as them or living in close proximity with them, because the gentiles were possessing things in their abodes which the Israelites could not have in theirs, lest it make them unclean and require them to wash themselves before they became clean again. These laws forced the Israelites to keep their distance from the other nations.

The flesh of these animals did not truly make them unclean, nor did these discharges or other things make them unclean either. But they were told to believe that these things would make them unclean, and as Paul wrote, because they believed it was unclean, for them it was unclean, but nothing is unclean in itself.

There is a profound meaning in these restrictions too.
In a certain way it prefigured the teachings of the New Testament, which commanded the disciples to distinguish between that which was spiritually clean and unclean, so that they did not taint their souls through sins.
The different laws and ordinances had symbolic meanings to them as well.
Only animals that parted the hoof and chewed the cud could be eaten. According to the 18th century English bishop Richard Challoner, this meant that only those who discerned between good and evil and meditated on God's law were clean. The same bishop said that those with scales and fins could be eaten meant that those who were protected by the armour of virtue and which raised themselves up by prayer were clean. He also claimed that

the unclean animals were representing different vices.
All the animals that went on their feet or which dragged
their bodies on the earth were unclean. The dirt is a
metaphor for sinfulness. Christ washed Peter's feet and
said that 'one who is clean does not need to wash, except
for his feet'. Christ was speaking about more than this than
just physical washing. A soul that is clean and in God's
grace will still dirty themselves with little venial sins as they
tread about the dirty world.

The hoofed animals didn't touch the ground with their
feet, because a hoof is actually just like a nail and the foot
is above the hoof, which didn't physically touch the ground
in these animals. Thus, they kept themselves aloft from the
dirtiness of the world. While the animals that did not have
hoofs and touched the ground were unclean. The animals
that dragged their bodies on the ground were unclean. The
serpent was cursed by God at the garden of Eden to move
on its belly and thus its whole self is just continually
dragging over the dirt, like how the devil's entire being is
only sinfulness without any virtue at all.

A little leaven leavens the whole lump and a little bit of sin
makes something unclean in God's eyes. Thus, only the
hoofed animals that didn't touch the dirt at all while
striding were considered clean.

There is another way of looking at it too: the flesh of the
different animals could be considered as representing the
different nations.

From the original creation, all the animals that God created
were good. The pig, the oyster, the rabbit, etc. were all
created by God as things that were good, just like how all
of Creation was good. How could one say then that their

flesh was unclean, when it had been created by God?

It is like the nations of the world. All human beings in all the nations of the world were created by God. They are all created to be good.
Although they are created to be good, they turned away from God and worshipped other gods that they had created themselves and they turned to sin. They had been created as good, but they became unclean and unholy because of their sinfulness.

The Mosaic law that said that they could not eat these animals created by God as good, is perhaps in a certain way referring to this mystery of all these nations of people who had been created by God as good and yet had become unclean by their sins.
The Israelites were not to be like these nations were. They were meant to stay true to the true God and not to turn away from Him to sin. They kept apart from these nations, in order so that these nations would not entice them to serve other gods or lead them astray.
For that reason, they were told to slaughter the inhabitants of the land that God promised them rather than to live beside them. For that reason, they were forbidden from marrying foreigners. Perhaps for that reason as well, God commanded them to mark these differences in the clean and unclean, in order to get them to separate themselves from these other nations that did not mark the differences between the clean and unclean.
They were to divide between the clean animals and the unclean animals, even though all had been created by God as good, just like how they were to be divided from the

other peoples and nations of the world, even though God had created all human beings as good.

The religion of the Israelites was not a missionary religion. Judaism today is still not a missionary religion. It doesn't seek to convert the world to believe in what it teaches. The Israelites were commanded to protect their own faith from being spoiled by contact with outsiders and thus to limit such contact. They were never commanded to go forth and preach the laws of Moses or the teachings of the prophets to the nations that surrounded them.

Why was that? Why didn't God want this faith spread throughout the world?

God did want all people in the world to know and love Him, but there was a question of justice involved in this. People of the world do not deserve to know who the true God is. They don't deserve to have a missionary come to them to preach to them the true religion and wake them up out of their darkness.
They sinned against God. And God, in a sense, abandoned them to their own errors and to follow the things that they created themselves. Following these errors would not lead them to salvation. It would harm them, lead them to be ignorant about God's law and lead them to fail to understand how they ought to live in this world in order to be happy. It would lead them to be blind, doing all kinds of things that were harmful to them, without truly realizing it. But that is what they deserved and what justice commanded that they should be given. They rejected the Truth and God punished them by leaving them to be

ignorant and blind, and to let them be enslaved to the
errors and sins that had come from their own heart.

The Israelites did not deserve to know the true God either.
But for the sake of Abraham, who had been willing to
sacrifice even his most beloved son for God, God would
preserve the faith of the Israelites and not allow them to
be forever lost to the errors and ignorance of idolatry.
Therefore, God made sure that the faith remained in the
Israelites. He gave them laws that would help prevent
them from undergoing the temptations from other nations
that would lead them to turn to other gods. He showed
them signs and miracles to make them know that He was
real. He sent them prophets to speak on His behalf.
When the people of Israel would begin to turn away from
God and towards idols, God wouldn't abandon them, like
as He had done with other peoples of the world who did
not descend from Abraham. He sent them prophets who
did miracles and signs to draw them back again. He
brought down punishments upon them to bring them to
repent and turn back.
The Bible says that God punishes us because we are His
children and what father does not punish his children?
Other peoples turned away from God and towards idols,
God did not send prophets to warn them and then send
other nations to destroy and enslave them, because they
were not His children. He abandoned them to their own
folly.
When the Israelites turned away from God and towards
idols, God punished them by sending other peoples to
conquer and dominate them. He did this because they
were His children and He was disciplining them. He loved

them enough that He would not let them go on their own errant way, but He would make the effort to bring them back again through this chastisement.

God would chastise the other peoples too, in their own time, who didn't know Him and who were not His children, but He would not send them prophets or messages, rather He would leave them ignorant as to the true reasons why they suffered, why they being destroyed, and thus let them to keep erring and suffering more, because that is what they deserved.

The people of Israel were given prophets to come and tell them to turn back, to make them understand why they were going to suffer and what they needed to do to come back. For the sake of Abraham, he gave them this, which they did not deserve to have. He did not give such help to the Canaanites. The Amerindians in the Americas were left in the dark as to why they were being annihilated.

Carthage was destroyed by Rome and sown with salt, but the people of the place never heard an explanation from heaven as to why or a promise of hope if they changed. The nations ravaged by Genghis Khan kept praying to their false gods to save them and their prayers came to no avail. Bridget of Sweden, in her revelations had San account where she sees Christ passing judgment on several men who represent different kinds of people. One of them is a pagan and Christ describes the pagan as though he was drunk. A drunk person is in a state where he could be in danger to himself or others, where he is doing things that are foolish and which he wouldn't do if he was sober. A pagan is someone who doesn't know the Truth, who lives and acts in ways that are foolish, because He doesn't know the Truth and the right way to live in the world.

For the sake of Abraham, God kept the people of Israel sober and prevented them from falling into the drunken foolishness of all the other nations of the world whose drunkenness would lead them to much suffering.

God made sure that the faith of Abraham remained with the people of Israel and wasn't lost from them down the ages. This was to fulfill the promise He made to Abraham that his descendants would be God's people.

But He left the remainder of the world to go off into their own folly, idolatry and eternal doom from their separation from Him.
They didn't deserve to be saved and they didn't have an ancestor like Abraham who had received such a promise from God to keep them close to Him. So, in His justice, God left them to their darkness and folly.

When Christ died on the cross, this changed, however. He died for the sins of all of humanity. Because of this sacrifice, the gentile nations received the right to know the Truth and to be as close to God as the Israelites had been. For the sake of not their own merits, but for the sake of Christ's blood shed for them, they could be given the Truth about God and find salvation through it.

So, the Holy Spirit sent out missionaries to the peoples of the world, to tell them the gospel and command obedience to it. The missionaries would have to go through many troubles and sufferings, even with some of them giving their lives for it. The people that harmed them did not deserve to hear their message, but for the sake of

Christ's blood shed for them, the Holy Spirit would send these missionaries to preach to them (and die for them) all the same.

The laws that the Israelites had were designed to be against contact between the Israelites and other peoples. If the Israelites could not touch unclean things, could not eat unclean foods, etc. then it would have been difficult for them to travel throughout the world and share a missionary message with people who ate these things and possessed these things.

In the Acts of the Apostles, Peter has a dream before he goes to meet a centurion. He is shown a sheet filled with animals of all kinds and told to slay and eat. Peter refuses and says that nothing unclean has ever entered his mouth. And a voice then spoke saying, 'do not call unclean what God has cleansed'. This then repeated itself three times. He woke up from his dream and then he received word that a centurion wanted to speak with him. Peter went at the Spirit's direction and came to the centurion's house where he ate with him, and he saw the Holy Spirit come upon the centurion and other gentiles at the house.

Before this point, the apostles had focused their missionary efforts on converting the Jews to the faith. They had not thought it was God's plan to preach to the gentiles as well.

The Israelites had been forbidden to eat all those animals because they were unclean and they were supposed to be a holy people who would discern between the clean and

the unclean. God had created all those animals as good,
but they were to separate them as unclean, just as how
God had created all of those other peoples in those
nations as good, but they were to be separate from His
people for their idolatry and uncleanness.
Now Christ had died for all these nations and His blood had
cleansed them. The unclean animals had been cleaned by
God and it was now right to eat them.
The wall that had been put up to separate the Jews from
the Gentiles came down and a faith that had once taught
people to keep a distance from foreigners now said that
they needed to go and live among the foreigners to preach
to them and convert them to the gospel.
And Peter began this work by going to the house of the
centurion, eating the gentile food with them and
witnessing the coming of the Holy Spirit upon the gentiles,
who had been cleansed by Christ's blood.

The purpose of these laws was to separate the Jews from
other peoples, but those laws only make sense if this faith
was not meant to be a missionary religion. The moment
that it becomes a missionary religion, laws that require
separation no longer make any sense and they must come
to an end, as they did with Peter and the apostles under
the direction of the Holy Spirit in order so that the apostles
might carry out the mission to the gentiles.

Islam has some of these kinds of restrictions within it,
according to many of the common interpretations of Islam
throughout the world. Muslims cannot eat pork and should
not eat meat that hasn't been slaughtered in the correct
way. Islam has been a missionary religion at times in

history, although most nations and regions in the world that became Islamic did so after they were conquered by Muslims who then ruled over them and provided benefits to those who converted to Islam.

In most Islamic nations, Islam didn't spread the way that Peter and the apostles spread Christianity. Islam's spread in most places wasn't through preaching and missionary witness.

One could ask the question: if the purpose of these laws was to get the Israelites to separate themselves from other nations, then why not just order them to do that, as opposed to all these rules about ritual cleanliness?

There are several answers to this. Firstly, these laws served a symbolic purpose that connected together with the New Testament and the mystery of God's plan of salvation for the world. The Jews were meant to distinguish between what was ritually clean or unclean, while this served as a shadow for the commandment upon Christians to distinguish between what was morally clean and unclean. The forbidding of the eating of the flesh of the unclean animals also served to represent the separation of the Israelites, a holy people, from the other peoples of the world who were unclean.

Secondly, the principle of freedom and slavery dictates that freedom can only be trusted to those who would not abuse it too greatly. If God had told the Israelites to use their own discretion in deciding how much or how little contact was OK with the gentiles, then they perhaps would have abused and twisted this, in order to suit their own purposes, just as they abused and twisted other parts of

the Mosaic law in ways that Jesus pointed out in the New Testament.
They could not be trusted with that kind of freedom perhaps, so God gives them strict regulations to follow, which are specific and clear, so that they cannot have room to warp them into what they want them to be.

Lord, we pray that you help us to understand why you gave the laws of cleanliness to the Israelites as well as the other parts of the Mosaic law that resulted in their separation from other nations. We pray that you help us to use these lessons in our time in the manner that pleases you. We ask for these things, if it is your will, in Jesus' name, Amen

XI: Constantine and Rome

Christianity was not a political religion at its origin. Christ did not set out to establish a political kingdom as part of His plan for salvation.
This was very different from Islam and Mohammed who did indeed seek to establish a political Islamic state.
Christ died, resurrected and ascended to heaven. His disciples went out over the world and taught people to obey the teachings of the gospel. They brought people out of a sinful world and towards God, and the sinful world hated them and persecuted them.
The Roman Empire persecuted Christians from the 1st century up until the year 312. Sometimes the persecution was harsh and other times it was more lenient. Other parts of the world that had people that came to believe in the gospel also experienced persecution as well.
Christians lived among societies that were often hostile toward them for the first several hundred years of its existence. Christ had predicted this too and had told His disciples that He was sending them out as sheep amidst the wolves and warned them that the world would turn against them.

Christianity required the obedience of people to the commandments and gospel of Christ. If these things were followed wholly and sincerely by all people, no political state or authority of one person over another would have ever been required again.
Christ was setting the world free. He was not leading a revolution against the political powers that ruled, but He was removing the reason for why political power was ever

necessary to begin with.

If people are wholly virtuous, then they can be given complete freedom. When people are filled with vice, they need to be treated with controls.

There were many so-called liberators in history who sought to bring people freedom by destroying some oppressive ruler over them through war, but afterwards when they needed to govern the society, they could not control the people except with use of great violence and force.

The controls and slavery of human beings starts with their sin. That is the root that these things come from. The military liberators who used violence to destroy evil sought to kill the weed by snapping off its stem, but they left the root to grow back. Christ was truly liberating the world, however, and He was doing so by teaching people to obey the lawful authorities and to change their own behaviour. Many people in history point their fingers at governments, demanding that the governments fix the problems of society, but they do not want to change their own behaviour. They want the society to change, but they do not want to change themselves, who are the causes of all social problems. The problems of society stem from bad behaviour of people and the government can no more end social problems among a populace that won't repent than a doctor can cure a tumour by pouring salve over it. Christ was providing a key that human powers did not have; this key would open the door and solve the basic and fundamental flaw present within all states.

The waves of persecution against Christianity continued in the course of the history of the Roman Empire down to the year 312, when the Emperor Constantine converted to

Christianity and proclaimed toleration for Christians throughout the empire.

This can perhaps be considered as both a victory and a defeat.

It was a victory, because in the land that had once persecuted Christians and sought to eliminate the faith from the world, the religion had spread and conquered the resistance of people, so that it would become adopted as the official religion of the place that had once tried to destroy it.

It was a defeat, because, Christianity had been adopted by the masses of people, but they would pervert the faith to make it worldly. They would continue to oppress slaves, they would continue to fight wars, they would continue to abuse each other, they would continue to have an unfair treatment for the poor, they would continue to do all sorts of sins that rooted from their paganism once they adopted Christianity and paganized it in the process.

If the Roman Empire had truly converted to Christianity, the state and its power would no longer be necessary, because people would have done what was right without the need for compulsion.

The ending of persecutions against the Christians in Rome could be understood perhaps as the devil shifting from one strategy to attack the church to another greater and more insidious one. Rather than shooting arrows at a distance by throwing persecutions to scare people from following Christ, he would poison it from within and he would convince people that the gospel did not forbid all these things that the world did and the church could thus accommodate all the evils that had formerly been part of the society that it had once tried to separate itself from.

When Constantine died, his sons, all of them baptized and professed Christians, took control of the empire between themselves and proceeded to murder all of their relatives in order to secure their own power and make sure that there was no threat to them. The only person left alive was their cousin Julian, who was only a small child at the time. Julian's father was among the relatives who were murdered by the Christian emperors simply because they were relatives. Julian would later grow up and he chose to reject the Christianity that he had been raised in by his family and returned to paganism. In fact, the family of Constantine had never truly left its paganism; Julian was perhaps just making it more obvious.
Julian washed himself in sacrificial blood in order to 'undo' his baptism and when he eventually became emperor himself, he sought to overturn what Constantine and the Christian emperors had already accomplished. He did not succeed and he died within a few years after taking the throne on a military campaign against Persia.
Following his death, the emperors after him were Christians who continued to rule an empire that was becoming increasingly Christian.

Constantine had tolerated Christianity and used state resources to support it, including the building of a number of churches. Notably among them were some of the great basilica churches in Rome and the famous churches in Palestine.
Later emperors would not simply just tolerate Christianity, but they used state power to actively persecute paganism

and put an end to centuries of Roman idolatry.

In the year 410, a Germanic people called the Visigoths sacked the city of Rome. In the course of the following century, the Western Roman Empire would descend into a political crisis that ended with its complete collapse. The Eastern Roman Empire lived on in the form of what historians refer to as the 'Byzantine Empire'.

When these events were happening, Roman pagans took the opportunity to criticize Christianity and make the claim that it was because Rome had abandoned the pagan gods and become Christian that all of these calamites were now coming upon them.

Augustine of Hippo wrote his famous work *City of God* after the Visigothic sacking of Rome in response to these critics.
From that time all the way to today, there have been people who interpreted the events of the collapse of the Roman Empire as being the result of the adoption of Christianity, which is seen to have weakened the empire. Edward Gibbon, the 18th century English historian who wrote about the history of this period blamed Christianity for the empire's collapse.

Rome became Christian and that was why Rome fell; that is the claim that has been made.
The claim is absurd.

Empires fall and rise all throughout history, whether or not they were Christian. There has never been a political empire that was immortal and withstood all tests of time. Rome collapsed after it became Christian. The collapse occurred a century after Christianity was adopted but detractors of Christianity then draw a cause-and-effect relationship to these things.

How is it possible that Rome was not going to collapse after becoming Christian? Was Rome supposed to continue as a unified political empire for eternity? How can we assume that Rome would never have collapsed for all history if it hadn't become Christian?

No empire or political state had ever prevented itself from ultimately collapsing. There are no eternal states or empires in the history of the world.

Since Rome became the see of Peter and the cornerstone of the church, Christianity in a sense did make Rome's empire eternal, but in a different way than the empire of slavery and chaotic political struggles that it had once been. Christianity did make Rome's legacy continue forever, even though its political empire, like all political empires, was destined to eventually die.

This is the fact that cuts to the heart of what is wrong with these arguments: Rome's empire was going to fall eventually regardless of whether or not it had converted to Christianity.

We know that Rome would fall no matter what would happen, because every empire and political state falls eventually. That is how history works. It is inevitable for states to have their demise, just as it is inevitable for human beings to eventually die.

Rome would fall for the same reasons that all empires

must fall and why all people must die. Sin is the reason why people die and sin is the reason why states cannot continue forever.

If Constantine had not converted to Christianity, the empire would have still fallen, because all empires eventually fall.

Perhaps it is possible that the empire would have fallen even sooner than it had if Constantine had not converted.

Augustine, in his book, connected the perils that were being faced by Rome with the sins that people were committing. He wrote that the Romans used to hold pornographic theatre shows that were used to honour their gods.

When refugees arrived from Rome to where he was in North Africa after the Visigoths had sacked the city, he wrote that he did not believe posterity would believe him when he said that these refugees came to start watching these pornographic shows again soon after their arrival.

The paradox of power is why every state has to eventually meet an end. States are needed because people are sinful. And it is because people are sinful that states eventually corrupt themselves and head to their own destruction. Rome was no exception to this.

In the simplest terms, Rome failed because its military was unable to defend its borders against enemies that should not have been so difficult to defeat for a state with as much wealth and resources as the Roman Empire. But the wealth and resources of the Roman Empire were not devoted to where they needed to be devoted to do that.

In deeper terms, virtue strengthens a state and vice

weakens it. If people obey the laws, society is stronger. If people honour their parents, they do better in life. If people tell the truth and honour contracts, trade is stronger and the economy grows more. If people keep sexual relations with their own spouses only, society is more harmonious and the hearts of people are less clouded. If people help the poor and those who need it, society becomes more connected with each other, less likely to fight one another, and more people can contribute their talents to make the state more powerful.

On the other hand, if people are proud, then they are deceived. Their leaders who come up from among them will make wrong decisions and things that the state needs to survive may be neglected. If people don't obey God's laws, the economy grows weaker, the state has less harmony, the talents present in the population are not developed, many social problems are created, etc.

If you ever had a place that completely fulfilled all the laws that God taught then that place would acquire immense power and it would not be threatened by outside actors. But a place that completely fulfilled God's laws would never need government or a state to begin with.

The only kingdom in existence that consists of people who obey all of God's laws perfectly is in heaven. It is guarded by armies of angels that no outside power could possibly threaten. And those living in heaven do what is right without the need for courts or police to control them.

Rome's empire died because of sin, not because of Christianity. Christianity acted as a prophet to Rome, which was already heading to its death for its many sins. Rome listened to this prophet after much persecution and adopted its message as its own, but even after it adopted this message, it was still far from fully believing in it, fully accepting it or fully carrying it out in the world. It still clung to the vices that sprouted from its paganism.

Constantine's reign as emperor was in fact one of the strongest time periods that the empire had in its history. There are historians who claim that Constantine had actually rescued the empire from a long period of crisis that it had been through in the 3rd century when most emperors died violently and didn't last more than several years, while the empire suffered foreign invasions and economic problems.

The empire died after it adopted Christianity and not before; this is true. But, if someone is going to argue that the empire would not have fallen had it not adopted Christianity, this would seem to be a contradiction with the history of every other political state that has ever existed. It is basically scapegoating Christianity in the place of the civil sins that Christianity was in a struggle against and which were ultimately the reason for the empire's downfall. The people making this argument are like a continuation of the accusers against Christianity within the Roman empire itself who called for a persecution or rejection of Christianity because it was the source of the empire's problems.

The truth is that those problems came from sin, not from Christ and there is no state that can exist eternally, because every state is controlled by the same paradox that demands its destruction.

Not only this, but the history of Christian political states sometimes receives an absurd treatment in academia and elsewhere. If a state is Christian, when something goes wrong in the state, the Christian character of the state gets blame for it.

Christians engaged in colonialism. Christians engaged in slavery. Christians fought wars of aggression with one another and with non-Christian states. Christians had problems of social inequality in their societies. Christians had massacres, genocides and episodes of great violence. Christians engaged in racism, sexism and other forms of discrimination.

Modern academics and thinkers may point at these things as showing the hypocrisy of Christianity and blame Christianity for being part of great evils in the world. These accusations are all true. However, non-Christian states did these things as well.

To say that Christian states had these things simply means that these places never fully became Christian states. It does not mean that Christianity is an inherently evil religion that promotes or allows these kinds of evils to exist in contradiction with its own teaching.

To say that the countries that became Christian would not have done all these things had they not become Christian has the same problems in its thesis as the argument that Rome would not have fallen had it not been for Christianity.

When evils existed alongside Christianity, people will hold Christianity as holding some blame for it. The critical flaw in this thesis is that these countries could have still done all of these things had they never heard the gospel to begin with, just as other states that were non-Christian had done.

Christians fought a civil war in the United States in the 1860s, in which many people were killed. One side of the war was fighting for a state that held the protection of the institution of slavery as a key reason for its existence. Christians who rejected the magisterial teaching authority erected by Christ within the successor of Peter, used their own interpretation of the Bible to justify why keeping blacks oppressively enslaved was acceptable and they believed that God supported them to fight against other Christians.

At around the same time, Prussia, a Christian nation, fought wars in Europe against other Christian powers that eventually led to the creation of Germany. In South America, Paraguay, a Christian state, was fighting its neighbours in a war that would leave almost 90% of its male population dead at the end of the conflict.

Writers of the 19th century spoke about Christian hypocrisy in relation to the great differences between what was preached by Christians and what was practiced by them. The churches of the time were sometimes seen as hypocritical institutions that supported or allowed for people to engage in evil behaviours in hypocritical contradiction with what the gospel taught. People of the time period had already started looking at alternatives to Christianity to be their lodestones for morality and were turning to other philosophical understandings of the world.

At around the same time as these wars mentioned above were fought by Christians, in China, the Qing dynasty was finishing its suppression of the Taiping rebellion by executing civilians in the millions and carrying out genocides against ethnic minorities linked to the rebellion. The Qing dynasty was certainly not inspired by Christianity in its rule of Imperial China; like the Roman Empire before Constantine, it actively persecuted Christianity at various points of its history. The Taiping rebels had a Christian inspiration behind what they did, but whatever religion they followed was certainly not the same Christianity as was believed in other parts of the world.

If one could compare the things that happened in the US Civil War with what happened in the contemporary civil war that happened in China, the brutality of the US Civil War is rather light and benign in comparison with what happened in China. The Taiping rebellion left perhaps 20 million dead; the US civil war perhaps less than a million dead. The armies of the US civil war sometimes burned towns or destroyed people's homes, although they primarily only deliberately killed enemy soldiers who hadn't surrendered and were still fighting. The armies of the Taiping rebellion captured cities and exterminated the entire populace.

One side of the US civil war was fighting for a state that retained the use of slavery and denied freedom to a particular racial minority. The government of the Qing dynasty was fighting for a state wherein most of the population lived in a slave-like existence to others and no citizen of the country had effective political rights or freedom other than the Emperor himself.

People may find something wrong with Christianity when they see so many bad things done by Christians. But Christianity is not the source of these bad things, rather it is a tampering force that lessens the evils that were already in society.

Christian states do evil because the people of those states have still not fully accepted the gospel. They have accepted it partially, and this partial acceptance perhaps makes the evil that they otherwise were going to do to lessen, but because it is not a full acceptance, the evil in their midst still remains.

Critics of Christianity point to the sins of Christian states to denigrate Christianity are thus making a bad argument, because they fail to take into account the true picture.

At the end of the US civil war in 1865 Jefferson Davis was accused of treason and held in detention for a few years before he was eventually released. He wasn't sent to prison, nor was he executed. He had led a rebellious government and he was detained for a few years, and then released. Few states would treat leaders of rebellions like this. Later in his life Davis worked for reconciliation between southerners and northerners. The southern states were brought back into the Union and the people of those states had their political rights as Americans eventually restored to them.

At the end of the Taiping rebellion in 1864, the Qing army captured the fourteen-year-old son of the deceased leader of the rebellion. The captive son begged for his life and claimed he was never against the Emperor. He was just a child during the rebellion after all; but unfortunately, he was the child of the leader of the rebellion.

While in captivity he wrote a poem to praise the Qing rule of China. They executed him by using a method called 'lingchi' when they use sharp knives to slowly cut off tiny bits of the flesh, piece by piece, little by little, over a long period of time in order to make the boy's death as slow and painful as possible.

The ethnic minority that the leader of the rebellion had belonged to was also targeted by Qing troops at the end of the war and exterminated, regardless of whether the people had taken part in the rebellion or not. Qing troops executed masses of civilians after the peace was achieved.

Mark Twain wrote a piece called the 'war prayer' as a way of parodying Christian hypocrisy in protestation against US intervention in the Philippines in the early 1900s:

O Lord our Father, our young patriots, idols of our hearts, go forth to battle – be Thou near them! With them – in spirit – we also go forth from the sweet peace of our beloved firesides to smite the foe.

O Lord our God,

help us to tear their soldiers to bloody shreds with our shells;

help us to cover their smiling fields with the pale forms of their patriot dead;

help us to drown the thunder of the guns with the shrieks of their wounded, writhing in pain;

help us to lay waste their humble homes with a hurricane of fire;

help us to wring the hearts of their unoffending widows with unavailing grief;

help us to turn them out roofless with little children to wander unfriended the wastes of their desolated land in rags and hunger and thirst,

sports of the sun flames of summer and the icy winds of winter,

broken in spirit,

worn with travail,

imploring Thee for the refuge of the grave and denied it –

for our sakes who adore Thee, Lord,

blast their hopes,

blight their lives,

protract their bitter pilgrimage,

make heavy their steps,

water their way with their tears,

stain the white snow with the blood of their wounded feet!

We ask it, in the spirit of love,

of Him Who is the Source of Love, and Who is the ever-faithful refuge and friend of all that are sore beset and seek His aid with humble and contrite hearts.

Amen.

Writers like Twain correctly saw great hypocrisy in Christian nations carrying out so much destruction in warfare.
It would be a grave mistake, however, as many did at that time and subsequent times down to today, to then conclude that Christianity was what was to be blamed in

this, because of its hypocrisy and lack of providing a better moral compass.

All of these things could have still happened if Christianity was never present. All of these things could have been even worse if Christianity was never present. And the truth is, which the 'enlightened' thinkers of that time and ours often failed to realize, was that those things did happen and they were often worse in parts of the world where people didn't believe the gospel.

Christian nations committed crimes against indigenous peoples during the course of colonialism and this receives a lot of criticism and shame. Was it the case that indigenous peoples never committed crimes against one another before the coming of the colonists? There is often a lack of knowledge of indigenous history prior to colonialism, because of a lack of written record, but there are certainly records of crimes being committed by indigenous peoples that were written down by those who came to colonize these places.

The Jesuit missionaries in Canada in the 17th century witnessed the genocide of the Wendat people at the hands of the Iroquois; it is hard to believe that this was the first time one indigenous group did something like this in the history of North America, although prior to the coming of Europeans and the first written records, we may never know the full story of everything that happened in the history of the Amerindians.

When the Spanish conquered Mexico, they did it with masses of indigenous allies, because various peoples in Mexico wanted freedom from the oppression of the Aztecs who treated them brutally and sacrificed their people to their gods.

In the Disney movie, Pocahontas, the villain is the evil European colonial leader John Ratcliffe who wants to exterminate the native people and at the end of the movie, he is sent on a ship back to England to be punished. In actuality, the real Ratcliffe tried to make peace with the natives and trade with them; they tricked him into thinking that they would offer food to him at a particular place and when he arrived, they captured him and then executed him by slicing off his flesh with mussel shells.

Indigenous peoples may have killed one another and pushed one another out of their homelands, long before European Christians arrived who did such things to them. Indigenous peoples may have done brutal or violent things in their homelands, long before European Christians did such things to them. Despite the anti-colonial and anti-imperial trends in understanding the world's history that refuses to accept such a hypothesis, there is a possibility that the atrocities of European Christians were just better recorded or even that those atrocities were actually something less than what indigenous peoples had done themselves in a time period when no records were kept. This doesn't at all excuse the crimes committed by Christians. But as I wrote above, it points to the fact that Christianity is not a force of evil in the world and while Christians have done evil, the same things could have been done or even have been worse if Christianity had never been there at all.

Some years ago, famous atheist Christopher Hitchens and British actor Stephen Fry participated in a televised BBC debate against British MP Ann Widdecombe and Nigerian

Archbishop John Onaiyekan on the topic of whether the Catholic Church was a force for good in the world. They succeeded in convincing the audience of their side in the debate and were considered to be the winners.

Their arguments were largely trying to tie the Catholic Church to many crimes or evils, or perceived crimes and evils, in the present and past, such as the sex abuse crisis. The entire debate suffered from the same flaw that I have tried to identify here though. To say that the Catholic church is not a force for good by claiming that evils were committed in Christian nations or by Christians is not proving much, because every state and every people in the world has crimes and evils in it.

To claim that the church is not a force for good because the church has crimes does not prove this point. One cannot prove that it is not a force for good by showing it has crimes. One has to argue that if the church had never existed and if the gospel had never been preached, the world would in fact be better than it was or at least it would be no different without it.

If the Catholic Church had never existed, pedophiles and sex abuse with institutional coverup would still happen in the world. If Europeans had never adopted Christianity, they would very likely have still fought wars with one another.

Without Christianity, social inequality would most likely still be there, as would racism, sexism, etc.

Nations would still try to invade and dominate other nations. Races will still try to dominate and enslave other races. People would still do evil in the world, just as they had always done.

It is an absurd thesis to try to argue that Christianity is to blame when evils and crimes existed in the Christian world and were committed by Christians, without taking into account the question of what the world would look like had Christianity never been there.

Christianity had come to these places, and people had not yet fully believed in it or followed its teachings, because God does not force people to follow His commands.

I think Nietzsche might have had a remark that the Christian conscience had become so evolved that the Bible and Christianity itself was no longer morally acceptable to it.

There is some truth in this sentiment. Pagan Rome persecuted Christianity because Christians did not worship the Emperor or the Roman gods, did not follow pagan practices and seemed like they turned their backs on civil Roman society. They had some superstitious ideas about Christians as well and thought that these people were bringing bad fortune to the empire. They weren't against Christianity because they thought it was against human rights.

If you had gone back to the time of pagan Rome and said that Christianity was evil because Christians had used slavery, Christians had fought wars and invaded or colonized other nations, Christians had used torture, Christians had engaged in sexual abuse, Christians had great social inequality, Christians had discriminated between people, Christians had used the name of a deity to justify these things, etc., the people of ancient Rome would perhaps scratch their heads and ask: 'and what is

wrong with any of those things? We do that too!'
The same is true of a lot of other cultures in the world in
past times.
People have developed a conscience to consider all of
these things as evils in the modern world and that
conscience was largely developed within the Christian west
and spread to other parts of the world from the influence
that came out of the Christian west.
But once this conscience is developed within the west,
people look at these evils that occurred in past times and
they see how they were done by Christians, how Christian
churches failed to stop them or even how they were done
with justifications rooted in Christianity, and they find
something wrong with Christianity because of it.
However, all these evils could have existed without
Christianity ever coming. Perhaps they could have been
worse without the influence of Christianity. Perhaps people
would not even think that such things were wrong at all
nor would they have developed this conscience without
the influence of Christian civilization.

The reason why evils existed within Christians states is
because Christianity did not succeed in convincing all
people that it touched to convert and follow the gospel.
Christ predicted this in fact, and He said in the sermon on
the mount that many would say to Him 'lord, lord' and not
enter the kingdom on the day of judgment, because they
did not do the will of the Father in heaven.

Lord, we pray that you help Christians to convert and
follow the gospel in Truth and not only in name. We pray

that you help people to judge history according to Truth.
We ask for these things, if it is your will, in Jesus' name,
Amen

XII: The Holy Land

The land of Palestine contains sites that are very important to Jews, Christians and Muslims. Jerusalem especially contains such sites.

When Constantine converted to Christianity and became emperor, his mother Helena visited these sites and built churches on the spots where some of the important events in the life of Christ had occurred. The Church of the Holy Sepulchre is the most important of such spots.

The territory that contained these sites was mostly in the control of Christian rulers from the time of Constantine until the 7th century when Muslim Arabs conquered these territories from the Byzantine empire and began Muslim rule over them.

The Islamic Caliphate of that time period was nothing like the caliphate of the so-called 'Islamic State' that existed in our time. It did not oblige those it conquered to convert to Islam and it allowed Christians to worship Christ under its rule, although they had to pay a tax for being non-Muslim. When Jerusalem was taken by Muslims, the Patriarch Sophronius believed that this had occurred in punishment to Christians for their sins. He offered to the Muslim Caliph to allow him to pray in the church of the Holy Sepulchre but the Caliph declined, because he said that the site was holy to Christians and if he prayed here, then later generations of Muslims would say that because the Caliph prayed here that it must be taken and made into a mosque and not allowed to be used by Christians.

According to a tradition, Sophronius then offered the Caliph the keys to church. The Caliph then entrusted the keys to a Muslim family from Medina and down to this day the descendants of the same family retain the keys to the church.

In the 11th century, Pope Urban II called for a crusade against Islam to regain control of the Holy land and the sacred sites in the Holy land:
"Of holy Jerusalem, brethren, we dare not speak, for we are exceedingly afraid and ashamed to speak of it. This very city, in which, as you all know, Christ Himself suffered for us, because our sins demanded it, has been reduced to the pollution of paganism and, I say it to our disgrace, withdrawn from the service of God. Such is the heap of reproach upon us who have so much deserved it! Who now serves the church of the Blessed Mary in the valley of Josaphat, in which church she herself was buried in body? But why do we pass over the Temple of Solomon, nay of the Lord, in which the barbarous nations placed their idols contrary to law, human and divine? Of the Lord's Sepulchre we have refrained from speaking, since some of you with your own eyes have seen to what abominations it has been given over. The Turks violently took from it the offerings which you brought there for alms in such vast amounts, and, in addition, they scoffed much and often 'at Your religion. And yet in that place (I say only what you already know) rested the Lord; there He died for us; there He was buried. How precious would be the longed for, incomparable place of the Lord's burial, even if God failed there to perform the yearly miracle! For in the days of His Passion all the lights in the Sepulchre and round about in the church, which have been extinguished, are relighted by divine command. Whose heart is so stony, brethren, that it is not touched by so great a miracle? Believe me, that man

is bestial and senseless whose heart such divinely manifest grace does not move to faith! And yet the Gentiles see this in common with the Christians and are not turned from their ways! They are, indeed, afraid, but they are not converted to the faith; nor is it to be wondered at, for a blindness of mind rules over them. With what afflictions they wronged you who have returned and are now present, you yourselves know too well you who there sacrificed your substance and your blood for God."

...

"Under Jesus Christ, our Leader, may you struggle for your Jerusalem, in Christian battleline, most invincible line, even more successfully than did the sons of Jacob of old - struggle, that you may assail and drive out the Turks, more execrable than the Jebusites, who are in this land, and may you deem it a beautiful thing to die for Christ in that city in which He died for us. But if it befall you to die this side of it, be sure that to have died on the way is of equal value, if Christ shall find you in His army."
(https://sourcebooks.fordham.edu/source/urban2-5vers.asp , Urban II (1088-1099) Speech at Council of Clermont, Internet Medieval Sourcebook, Fordham University)

Urban II and subsequent popes after him preached that it was a grave evil that the land that was so holy to Christ should be ruled by Muslims who Urban claimed abused these sites by their idolatry and abominations.
The crusades were thus begun. Knights from Europe campaigned to reach the Holy Land and they conquered the territory of Palestine. The crusader kingdoms they set up there lasted for two centuries before the last piece of

their land was lost to Muslim conquest and the crusades ended.

From the time of Christ up until about the time of the crusades, most of the territories that became Christian did so as a result of missionaries who succeeded in converting the people to Christianity. Sometimes the rulers were converted first and they invited the church to convert their people, however, during the first millennium of Christian history, the church was largely not spread by conquest. After the time of the crusades, however, up until the present, almost all of the territories that have become Christian did so after being conquered by Christian states who colonized and converted the native inhabitants. The crusades seemed to mark a kind of watershed in the history of the church from this perspective. In the crusades, the Christian armies lost the relic of the true cross at the battle of Hattin against Saladin and never recovered it afterwards. Figuratively, it seems like Christianity lost something else as well of its original spirit during that period.

If Christ wanted to, He could have called down armies of angels from heaven to defeat His enemies and establish His kingdom on Earth, but He did not do so. He did not use force to try to make sure that all of the places that He walked and did miracles at would remain in the hands of His followers, nor did the apostles do so. He taught His disciples not to resist those who were evil.

An idol created by people, needs human beings to prop it up, or else it falls down. A false religion requires holy warriors to engage in warfare on its behalf or else it will be lost to history. The true God, however, remains standing even when no one holds Him up and His Word conquers, even if He is abandoned by His friends.

Francis of Assisi travelled to the Holy Land in the time of the crusades and attempted to convert Muslims to Christianity by his preaching and example.

The Popes, however, called on Christian knights to go to the Holy Land and fight to make sure that the land that was hallowed by Christ's blood would remain in Christian hands, because it was seen to be an evil if it wasn't.

Christ called on His disciples to go forth to all the world and to preach the gospel to all nations. Christ did not intend for His kingdom to be spread by force of arms. His own example makes this clear as does the example of His apostles.

If it is an insult against God that the land that He hallowed by His blood should not be in Christian hands, then the example that ought to be followed to amend this is the example of Christ Himself and the example of Francis of Assisi.

If the only way for Christianity to spread is by war and conquest, then there is something wrong with Christendom itself. If Christians truly loved as Christ loved and they possessed the Holy Spirit as Christ did, they wouldn't need to use violence in order to spread Christian rule in the world. To resort to warfare to accomplish this, however, is pointing to a lack of holiness and conversion within Christendom itself.

The crusades were more complicated than simply just this aspect, however.

The crusades were also meant to take off the pressure on the Byzantine empire from continual Muslim attacks against it. In a sense, the crusades were also a response to centuries of Muslim aggression against Christian territories.

To fight in defence of life is a legitimate cause to fight a war and the Muslim invaders did threaten the lives of people in Christian states that they were invading. However, if this was the only reason to fight the war, then it would not have been necessary to pursue the war to Jerusalem. If the crusaders were coming to defend Christian lands against Muslim aggression, then they could have fought the crusades against the Muslims that were on the borders of Christian territories that had shown aggression, like as did happen in Spain in the same time period, as opposed to going deep into Muslim territory to take the Holy Land, when it did not border any Christian territory at the time. However, although it may not be necessary to go as far as Jerusalem for this purpose, it may still have been an effective way of reaching the goal of relieving the pressure on the borders of the Byzantine empire. Although unnecessary for strictly that purpose, it is not illegitimate because of it. Going behind enemy lines to relieve pressure on the front lines is not an unlawful tactic in war, even if fighting on the front lines and not going behind it could accomplish the same thing.

Furthermore, perhaps the crusaders would not have come had the Pope simply called on them to fight to defend the

borders of the Byzantine empire as opposed to fighting to
retake Jerusalem. Perhaps the call for Jerusalem would
have received a more successful response.

In order to gain land for Christianity, the crusades were not
a legitimate way to accomplish this goal.
However, as a defensive war to defend against an
aggressive opponent, the crusades could have been
considered legitimate from that perspective.

Lord, we pray for peace in Palestine and for the conversion
of people to your gospel. We pray that those who wish to
go on pilgrimage to these sites will not be impeded by
anything. We pray that you help us to understand history
as you desire. We ask for these things, if it is your will, in
Jesus' name, Amen

XIII: Atlantic Slave Trade

During the time period between roughly the 16th century and the 19th century, many Christian states engaged in the Atlantic slave trade. They took people from Africa as slaves and brought them to the Americas or sometimes to other places in order to do forced labour as slaves. Usually, the children of these slaves were also born into slavery and lived their whole lives as slaves as well.

At that time period, the church did not teach that this institution was morally wrong. There were several good reasons why it didn't do so. In the bible, both in the Old and New testaments, there seems ample evidence that God did not forbid slavery. In the Old Testament, Moses had laws concerning how Israelites were to treat their slaves, but did not forbid the people of Israel to have slaves.

In the New Testament, Paul explicitly told Christian slaves to obey their masters and that they should not talk back to them or steal from them, but that they should try to please them in everything. Likewise, he instructed masters to be good to their slaves, because they should know that they also had a master in heaven. Paul did not say that Christians should not have slaves, however.

This is not because Paul was cowardly and was afraid to tell people that they needed to change their lives in order to follow Christ. Paul often told people that they had to change from their former ways. He said that people had to stop their idolatry, their adulteries, their homosexual behaviours, their getting drunk, their stealing, their calumnies and other things or else they could not enter the kingdom of heaven. He told people to change their lives or else be cut off from Jesus Christ. But at no point did

he say that people had to free their slaves in order to
follow Christ or that slaveholders couldn't enter the
kingdom of heaven.
In the letter to Philemon, Paul exhorts Philemon to accept
his slave back, not as a slave but as a brother, however,
although he doesn't explicitly tell Philemon that he can't
have slaves.
There are bishops and popes in the history of the church
who even owned slaves. Some saints even owned slaves
(obviously including St Philemon).
In later times, institutionalized slavery was abolished in
most of the world and today we think of it as something
abhorrent and against the gospel.
This is what the catechism today says about slavery:
2414 The seventh commandment forbids acts or
enterprises that for any reason - selfish or ideological,
commercial, or totalitarian - lead to the enslavement of
human beings, to their being bought, sold and exchanged
like merchandise, in disregard for their personal dignity. It
is a sin against the dignity of persons and their
fundamental rights to reduce them by violence to their
productive value or to a source of profit. St. Paul directed a
Christian master to treat his Christian slave "no longer as a
slave but more than a slave, as a beloved brother, . . . both
in the flesh and in the Lord."

I note that this part of the catechism doesn't explicitly
state that slavery is morally wrong either, however. In it s
wording it doesn't say that the seventh commandment
forbids the enslavement of human beings, but rather it
says that the seventh commandment forbids the
enslavement of human beings 'in disregard for their

personal dignity'.

Strictly speaking, Paul didn't actually tell Philemon to free his slave Onesimus. He told him to love him as a brother. One would naturally assume that if you love your slave as a brother that you would not keep him as a slave any longer, but I don't think that this assumption into Paul's words is wholly justified.

One can easily read Paul's words to Philemon in the same way as he says in other parts when he tells masters to be good to their slaves or for men to love their wives; as a way of telling them how they ought to love those who were under their authority, however, he still believed that slaves needed to please their masters and women needed to obey their husbands.

Even in the catechism now, it does not actually say that slavery is wrong. What it says is that violating human dignity is wrong and that violating human dignity while enslaving a person is wrong.

Can you enslave someone and uphold their dignity as a person, however?

To force someone to work against their will is a form of theft. You own your own labour and if someone else is taking your labour from you against your will, then that person is stealing from you. This is a violation of God's law and it is not acceptable from a moral perspective. Therefore, kidnapping people and making them into slaves is not morally acceptable, because doing so is a form of theft and a violation of their dignity.

However, in ancient times, there are many instances in which people sold themselves into slavery or indentured servitude by their own free will, not because they were

being threatened with force, but because dire
circumstances demanded it. In the story of Joseph in
Egypt, the Egyptians sell themselves into slavery in order to
have food during the famine because the alternative was
to starve.

If they enter slavery by their own free will, then the issue
of stealing their labour is no longer a factor.

Once a person has willingly entered slavery, does that
mean that slavery is then acceptable and that their rights
as persons are therefore being upheld?

It is possible to own a slave and treat the slave well, and it
is possible to own a slave and to treat the slave badly. If
the slave voluntarily entered slavery and the master treats
him humanely and justly, then I don't think that there is
any reason for why slavery is not permissible or that the
relationship is necessarily one where human dignity is not
being respected.

How does a master treat a slave humanely and justly?
To answer this question, just think of all the ways that
modern employers can or cannot treat employees. They
can require their employees to do work for them, but they
can't sexually abuse them, they can't force them to do
work in a way that will leave them dead or injured, they
can't make them work hours that are too long, they have
to provide them with what they need to support their lives
and their families, if they give birth to children the must let
them have time to be with them, they cannot forbid them
from following a religion, etc.

Ultimately the guiding principle for what makes humane
treatment or not is the golden rule. Paul told Philemon to
love his slave as a brother. In other words, to love his slave

as he would love himself. He ought to treat his slave in such a manner as he would like his own Master in heaven to treat him.

The same logic is ultimately true of modern employers as well when deciding how they ought to treat their employees. They ought to treat them in the manner that they would wish God in heaven to treat them.

Sun Tzu, in his Art of War, said that generals should love their soldiers as their own children.

To have an institution of slavery, to have an employee-employer relationship, to have a commander-soldier relationship or any other thing like this does not have to be inherently inhumane or disregarding of the rights and dignity of the person in the inferior position.

It was never the institution itself which was the problem, however. It was the way that the institution was abused that was the problem.

However, because the institution has been abused so much, people can only see slavery in the lens of the degrading nature of people being mistreated as pieces of property.

When couples get married today, they reject the idea of the woman taking as part of her vows that she will obey her husband, because they think that this degrades her.

It is precisely because there were so many husbands in the world down history and today who abused their wives, beat their wives, treated their wives like objects rather than persons, who abused their power over women to hurt them and simply did not love them, that we think that it is degrading to women to say that they should be obedient to their husbands.

Ultimately it means that we think that if we don't give

power to women, then that means that they will be hurt, because their husbands simply do not love them enough that they can be trusted with power over them and not to abuse it. In other words, is degrading to women to tell them to obey their husbands, because their husbands don't really love them and they will abuse that power over their wives if it is given to them.

If their husbands did love them as they ought to have loved them, however, there would have never been any problem with the woman being submissive to the man. He would never have acted against her interests and he would never have done anything detrimental to her, because he loved her enough that even when she had no power to fight back, he would never take advantage of this position and would sacrifice himself for her. Like how Christ loved the church and gave everything for the church, the husband who fulfilled his role correctly would sacrifice everything for the sake of his wife.

But far too frequently, this isn't the way that patriarchy did exist, and therefore that is not the image of it that was left to us. So, we saw patriarchy as being an evil in itself, because we could not disconnect it from any of these things in our understanding of what it was.

The institution of patriarchy was never actually the problem here. It is rather that patriarchy never worked the way it should have worked, because people were sinful and abused the institution. They abused the institution and that led people to think that it was the institution itself that was the problem, so therefore they said that women should not need to be submissive to their husbands, they needed to have powers politically and socially, because otherwise they were going to be made into victims.

Slavery is something similar to this.

If the masters loved their slaves as Christ loved them, they would not have sent them out into plantations and worked them inhumanely, even to their deaths, in order to make a monetary profit for themselves. However, that is what happened in history and that is the image of slavery that is left to us, and hence we can't see slavery as anything other than an evil institution.

But slavery did not have to happen like that.

Paul told Philemon to love Onesimus as a brother. If masters loved their slaves as their siblings, they would treat them as members of their own family. They would let them live in the same conditions and same comforts that they themselves enjoyed. They would seek to make a better future for them. They would love them and treat them just as they wished to be loved and treated.

Perhaps they would free them from their slavery because of this love and give them the freedom to go where they wished to go. However, perhaps they would not free them from the slavery either, because the economic needs of their time required the work to be done like this.

Institutions of dominance and submission are never the problems in themselves. The problem lies with the lack of love in the human heart. Christ never said that slaves needed to be freed. Paul told slaves to obey their masters and for wives to obey their husbands. He did not do so, because he was afraid of asking too much of the people of his time by telling them to eliminate institutions of patriarchy and slavery.

Christ didn't say that people could not own slaves. But He did say: 'a new commandment I give you, love one another

as I have loved you'.
If that was followed, no one would ever see a problem with patriarchy, with slavery, with absolute monarchs or with any other kind of institutionalized authority that has come into existence, because the people who held the power in those things would never have used that power except in accordance with Christ's command.
Our attempt to dismantle patriarchy, to abolish slavery, to overthrow political states or end all kinds of other institutions, in a certain way, is actually our attempt to run away and ignore Christ's command.
Because rather than recognizing that these evils came from our own sins and lack of love, we say that the problem lies with changing the system, with dismantling the institutions, with reworking the gears in the machine, so to speak, and then once we have new institutions that we erect, the evil in the human heart will no longer hurt us.

Slavery ended in the Americas and the blacks were still treated badly by the whites. It was never really the institution that was the key problem here.
Giving more power to an oppressed group will help end their oppression, but they will eventually just oppress others that are weaker than them, just as they were once oppressed, unless they learn to love as Christ loves.

God holds absolute power over us. We are all the weaker sex in comparison to Him. We are all in a position of submission in comparison to Him.
But there is also no problem in this either, because He uses the power that He has only for our own good and never for His own selfish wishes. We can trust Him and give

ourselves entirely to Him in obedience without fear, because He would never abuse us in the relationship.
Paul said that husbands should love their wives like Christ loved the church. Rulers over nations, masters over slaves, teachers over pupils, parents over children, commanders over soldiers, wardens over prisoners... all should love those they hold power over as Christ would love those under His power and act accordingly.
People seek liberation from these sorts of submission because they find themselves being abused in these relationships and they think that the form of the relationship itself is the problem. But they can change the relationship any way that they like, and the same lack of love in the human heart, will just re-emerge in new ways, like each new head of the hydra.

Slavery does not have to be an evil thing, as long as it is used correctly. Sexuality is not an evil thing, but we associate it with dirtiness just because it has been so greatly abused by so many people. Violence is not an evil thing, but we associate it with evil because the vast majority of ways in which it is used present and past are evil.

Treating the slaves with love as one wishes to be loved is the biggest piece in the puzzle about how slavery was meant to exist.
One will ask, however, that if you love your slaves as yourself, how could you still keep them as slaves?
The answer to this question needs to look at the issue of the economic purpose that slavery fulfilled.

The Atlantic slave trade was used by Europeans as a means of providing cheap labour to work in heavy labour positions on plantations and other lucrative economic activities in the colonies. Sugar, tobacco, cotton, and other cash crops were grown on plantations to make products that would mostly be sold back to Europe.

There is no reason why it would have been that they could not have simply hired people with salary to do the same work and charge a higher price for the products in Europe. Or for that matter, there is no reason why they could not have simply paid their slaves a wage and given them the choice about whether they wanted to work on the plantations or not – in other words, making them into employees.

Perhaps if a single plantation tried it, they would be run out of business, because the other plantations that were still using the free labour from the slaves would be able to charge lower prices back in Europe. However, that is not an excuse for this; after all, the plantation owners could have collectively agreed together to stop the practice of slavery on their plantations and only use hired labour. The governments could have stepped in and regulated it to make sure that only hired labour could work on those plantations, so no one could undersell them by using slave labour.

If the white slave owners loved the black slaves as Christ called them to love, then I think there is no reason why they would have kept them as slaves.

Our answer to the question of what purpose or what need slavery fulfilled is not effectively answered by the history of the slaves working the plantations in the Americas. Indeed, if people of that time did love the slaves as Christ loved them, then there doesn't seem to be a reason why these people should have remained slaves.

We have to look deeper than this to realize why it was the societies saw a need for this institution in past times.

There often exists a big misunderstanding in the modern day about the nature of the Atlantic slave trade. The idea that a lot of people have in their minds is that white people went to Africa, kidnapped black people and then shipped them off to the Americas to sell them to plantation owners.

This did indeed happen, but it may not have been the primary way that this institution worked.

Europeans went to Africa and they sometimes did kidnap black people.

However, more often they acquired slaves by purchasing them from other Africans. Europeans built trading posts or trading forts along the African coastlines, within the borders of African kingdoms that accepted or even welcomed the European trade with them.

They did sometimes kidnap people. However, many of the people they took as slaves to the Americas were already enslaved by other Africans and sold to the Europeans for a profit.

Africans enslaved other Africans long before white people arrived in their countries to trade with them. Slavery is an institution common to almost every region in the world, both before and after those regions had any encounter with the west.

Sometimes the Africans may have kidnapped people who they sold to the whites. Sometimes the people they kept as slaves were perhaps forced to sell themselves or their children into slavery because of poverty. Sometimes it was perhaps people captured in wars or criminals that were arrested that were then enslaved and eventually sold to the Europeans. Sometimes it was perhaps the children of their slaves whom they counted as slaves upon their birth, which they sold to the Europeans.

They sold slaves to the Europeans, who gave them European goods, including gunpowder weapons, manufactured items, and things that Africans themselves didn't make at that time.

Now we are getting closer to the issue of why it was that slavery was seen as necessary in various places and times in history. I will introduce a thought experiment to help us to get there:

Suppose that you had an African kingdom that was at war with another African kingdom sometime during the colonial age. For convenience sake, let us call them kingdom A and kingdom B.

Kingdom A was losing the war against kingdom B, and they knew that if they lose the war, kingdom B would enslave their people, pillage their people, kill their people, rape their people, or do other nasty things to them. Let us also say that there was a Dutch trading fort on the coastal territory of kingdom A. The Dutch can sell them weapons that they need to win the war, but the Dutch are only interested in buying slaves from them in return and not any other kind of product or service they can provide.

The Dutch have no legitimate moral reason for why they should only take slaves and not hired labour, but we are discounting them for now and assuming that kingdom A has no way of changing their mind to only buy slaves.

Kingdom A is then faced with the choice of selling some people into slavery to the Dutch or losing the war and having their country face a catastrophe. In order to acquire that which the kingdom is not able to acquire by its means, it chooses to use the institution of slavery and enslaves some people to sell them for badly needed weapons to save their nation.

In this case slavery is providing for a need that can't be fulfilled simply by hired labourers... at least not on the part of the African kingdom that is going to start engaging in the slave trade.

In some ways this dynamic is similar to what I wrote about wars and soldiers above. The person who is responsible for death in war is not the soldier firing the gun, but it is the civilian in the time of peace who chooses to do evil and failed to solve the problems that caused there to be a need to send the soldier to the frontline in the first place.

In this case, the person who is responsible for the enslavement is not really the party doing the enslaving, but rather it is the one who created the condition that left no other choice except to use this method to fulfill their economic needs.

If a father sells one of his children into slavery in order to feed his other children, whereas otherwise they would starve, it is a similar dynamic at work. The father is not really the one who is responsible for the enslavement, but it is those who failed to help the family find food, it is those who failed to do what they ought to have done to help those in need who are responsible.

In many times and places in history, people were required

to make slaves of themselves or others and sell them in
order to fulfill an economic need that an unjust system did
not give them any other means of fulfilling.
These people could have loved those others they enslaved
as themselves and yet not have given them their freedom.

When Joseph, serving as Pharaoh's minister in the book of
Genesis, took the Egyptians as slaves in return for
providing them with food during the famine, we are not
told about why it was that Joseph simply didn't just offer
them the opportunity of paid labour instead.
It is possible that it is simply just not the way things were
done at that time and thus the idea would not have
entered their minds. They perhaps did not see anything
wrong with just taking them as slaves rather than offering
them paid labour.
It could have been also, however, that the king of Egypt
and the nobility would not have accepted this. Perhaps
they would not have allowed the granaries to be opened
unless the people gave up their freedom as slaves, and
thus Joseph had to bend to their will and take them as
slaves in order to get the food needed to feed them.

Let us take another thought experiment to consider, to
draw out another kind of dynamic:
Let us go back to kingdom A again somewhere in Africa.
Kingdom A is at peace now and it is not at risk of losing a
war against a neighbour in the near future.
Suppose that in kingdom A you had people that committed
crimes. This is a fairly realistic assumption, given that
basically every state in history has had people that
committed crimes.

To force a person to work as your slave against the person's will is basically an act of theft, since you are stealing labour that doesn't belong to you.

However, when a thief steals something from someone else, it is right to require the thief to pay back more than the value of what he stole. He has violated the property of someone else and thus he actually owes a debt to the person who he has stolen from. If the thief doesn't have the property to pay back what he stole, then requiring the thief to do labour instead is not an act of theft against the thief, rather it is an act of making the thief to pay back what he owes to his victim.

This is true not just of thieves, but of all who harm others and hurt society. When they do evil against their fellow man, they incur a debt that is owed to their victims. If the judge orders them to pay back this debt by their own labour, it is not the case that the state is stealing from them, rather it is the case that the state is forcing them to pay back the debt that they owe to others.

Courts today already do this; we call it community service. When a court orders fines to be paid, it is ultimately doing the same thing, because it is usually with the person's labour that the person needs to gain the wealth to pay the fines; thus, the state is ultimately forcing the person to use labour in order to pay back a debt to society.

In parts of the world, inmates in prisons will be required to do labour in order to serve the society that they once harmed. These are technically forms of enslavement of persons, although they are not a form of theft as would be the case in a person who was kidnapped and enslaved unjustly. Even teachers in schools do this with naughty children, by getting them to do extra work or to clean up places that they made messes in or to do other work to restore the damage that they caused when they broke rules.

If you force a criminal to do labour to repair the damage caused by his crimes, this kind of enslavement does not mean that the person who enslaves cannot love the criminal as himself. He can love this slave as himself and not let him go free, because he knows that justice demands that the slave not be allowed to go free.

In past times, a European judge might have ordered a criminal to be consigned to row in the galleys as a slave for a number of years. Today a judge in Europe might order a criminal to do community service at a soup kitchen for some months or weeks. The magnitude and severity are certainly different, but it is actually the same concept and principle at work here; the criminal is obliged to give his labour as repayment to a debt he owes to society. Whether you call it 'slavery' or 'community service' is ultimately just as a matter of semantics.

The amount of labour that you require the criminal to perform should be in proportion to the degree of his crime. Small crimes could require a little labour or a short time to be done to restore what was lost, while big crimes could require a lot of labour or a long time.
Now, there are some crimes that people commit in this world that even all the labour that they could do in the rest of their lives might not be enough to actually pay back the debt that they owe.
Crimes like murders, rapes, terrorism, and other very

serious things might cause damage to people that go beyond what a person could repair, even if they used all the time left in their life to work in restoration. In this case, to simply just make them into a slave and take away their freedom for the rest of their lives is just the same dynamic as in the cases above. You are requiring them to pay back the debt they owe – it is just that in their case, the amount that they owe exceeds all that they are able to pay back in the time left in their lives and thus to make them permanent slaves until they die is actually demanding less from them than what they owe.

If the state enslaves criminals and then sells them to others, while using the profit from the sale to help the victims of the crimes, it is simply just a kind of restorative justice ultimately.

It would only have a right to sell the debt that it is owed. It is not selling the slave exactly, but it is selling the debt that is owed by the slave.

In other words, if the criminal in question committed a small crime, the state would only have a right to sell the rights to his labour for a brief period that was judged fitting for what he owed. The person who purchased the slave from the state would thus only legitimately have a right to force this person to labour for that brief period and then let the person go free afterwards.

If it was a big crime, then the state would have a right to sell the rights to his labour for a longer period. And if it is was very big crime, then the state would have a right to sell the rights to his labour for the rest of his life and thus truly make him a slave.

Making criminals to do work is not only a means of
repairing the damage that they did to others, but it is also
a form of penance that they can do for their sins to repair
their relationship with God. It is also a means of teaching
them useful skills that will help them integrate back into
society when their term of labour expires. It can also help
with getting them into a rhythm where they can learn to
reform themselves for the better by seeing how they can
help society, rather than leaving them in a jail cell to
ponder about their lack of freedom.
There is nothing necessarily wrong about slavery when
used in this sense as a kind of restorative justice.

Now consider kingdom A. Let us suppose that this is not a
place with a well-developed state possessing well-
organized institutions. The judges of crimes are the village
elders in each village and they are the ones who decide
punishments for wrongdoing. They don't have anything
like a prison system or a judiciary. Setting up such
institutions would require resources that the subsistence
farmers in their communities simply could not afford and
still be able to feed their families. If someone is a danger to
society in this place, essentially the only way of protecting
society from the dangerous person is execution.
However, suppose that kingdom A could also enslave the
person in question and sell them to the Dutch traders who
will take the criminals to work on their plantations in
Aruba or Suriname, rather than executing them. This
would actually be the moral choice in this scenario, since
human life ought to be preserved whenever possible.
It is possible that some of the slaves that were indeed sold
to the Europeans and put on the slave ships were people

like this. African countries that wanted to get rid of the dangerous and criminal parts of their own society could have found an opportunity to repair the damage done to their own people through selling these criminals to the Europeans and acquiring goods from the Europeans to serve their society.

They do not have to execute the criminals then, but they can sell them to others and perhaps give those criminals a chance to find a new life.

Suppose also that while kingdom A could not possibly afford a prison system in their subsistence conditions, but they could afford to bind a criminal and force him to work for the rest of his life as a slave, otherwise they would need to execute him for lack of resources to confine him. In this case, slavery would be the moral choice that preserved life again.

The Europeans who were working the slaves to death on the plantations perhaps didn't have a good reason for how to justify why they needed to keep people enslaved, but the African societies that enslaved these people and sold them to the Europeans in the first place might have had justifiable reasons for why they used the institution of slavery.

Consider the case, not of criminals, but of marauders, pirates or barbarians that crossed into your territory and pillaged your people. Here, the same logic bears true: capturing and enslaving them is a mode of justice to make them pay back the debt owed for the damage and evil that they had done.

In the ancient world, this very dynamic was sometimes practiced too. The Roman legions fought the less civilized peoples on their borders who may have raided their lands and took back their captives to sell them as slaves in the markets of Rome for a profit.

If you had tribes of people that continually raided your settlements, then capturing and enslaving them would be a form of restorative justice. The person who owned such slaves could love them as himself and yet keep them in slavery, since justice and social protection demanded it.

If a person is not a criminal but they simply have borrowed money and owe a debt, but they do not have the means to repay it, then requiring them to do labour in return for the debt they owe is also morally acceptable and just. This kind of indentured servitude would have to be in proportion to what was actually owed.

There are many conclusions that would be drawn out of this though in showing what kinds of slavery would be unacceptable.

If a person doesn't owe a debt of any sort, but you force them into slavery, then this is a violation of that person's dignity and a theft of their labour. For some people, they might have no choice but to do this, because a greater evil might be produced if they didn't, like in the cases I mentioned above. In that case, the crime of violating the person's dignity does not rest on the hands of those who enslave them but it rests on those who created the unjust system that required them to make this choice to begin with.

Parents don't have a right to sell their children into lifelong slavery, because the parents do not own the child's labour for his whole life, and people cannot sell what they do not own. The parents can sell the child's labour for the time when he is still a child and under their care, but not after he has reached maturity.

The children of slaves cannot be enslaved simply because their parents are enslaved.

Although original sin is inherited ancestrally and God visits the sins of people upon their descendants to the third and fourth generation, people cannot inherit the actual guilt of these sins. Adam and Eve alone are the ones who have personal responsibility for the evil of the original sin, but their descendants share in the effects that resulted from what they did. Children can inherit the effects and punishments that fall on their ancestors for their sins, but they cannot actually inherit the guilt of those sins.

Moses said that you cannot punish the children for the sake of the father, nor can you punish the father for the sake of the children.

If the parent owes a debt, either by borrowing something or by doing damage to something that he must repair, then he alone has the responsibility of paying it back. His descendants cannot be judged as being liable to pay for it by their own slavery.

If the descendants inherited some kind of property from their parents, then they can be forced to give up that property to pay back their parents' debt, but their labour cannot be required of them, since that was never something that belonged to the parents.

It was a widespread practice in past human history for the children of slaves to be automatically put into slavery. This is how slavery in the Americas worked as well, but it is an unjust practice. Legitimate forms of slavery can only enslave those who either voluntarily enter into slavery or who owe some kind of debt that shall be paid back by their labour and those who enslave must always uphold the dignity of those being obliged to give their labour. Those who enslave people in other circumstances do so illegitimately, although the guilt of such action, as I mentioned, may not necessarily fall on the slavers if they had no other choice but to use slavery because of an unjust system.

If a person owes a debt, either from borrowing or from crime, which is being paid back by labour, the master could still choose to release him from his bondage and pay him as a wage-labourer. However, he would not be obligated to do so. The person who sold this person to another would also not be obligated to free him either because the person in question does in fact owe a debt that should be paid by his labour.

Loving your neighbour as yourself does not mean that if someone owes you money that you must always forgive them and not require them to pay you back. In just the same way, if a person owes you his labour, loving him as yourself, does not require you to release him from his obligation either.

A righteous man can insist for a debt to be paid back from someone else, rather than forgiving it and letting it go. Tobit sent his son Tobias to get back the money that belonged to him; God sent His angel to accompany the son on the journey and make sure he succeeded. God thus approved of the recalling of the debt. If a righteous man can require a debt of money to be paid back, he can also demand for a debt of labour to be paid back.

Christ loved us enough that He died for us to release us from our debts, however. And Christ did command us to love one another as He loved us. Christ forgave our debts, so we should also forgive one another's debts. Hence, the commandment of Christ would oblige us to seek to find ways to release people from their debts of money or labour to us even without paying it.

However, perhaps if you released everyone from their debts, you would be taken advantage of and your own economic needs would not be safeguarded. You have a right and a responsibility to seek to ensure your own and your family's economic wellbeing so that you can live in dignity. If requiring others to pay their debts to you is the means of securing this, then it is right to ask for this to be repaid to you.

Hence, in the time of the Atlantic slave trade, if a person was enslaved because they actually owed something that should be paid back by their labour and then you paid the price to buy this person and make him work for you, that debt of labour would then belong to you and you would have a right to ask for it to be paid. If the person was a criminal and he had hurt his society who then sold him to you, your money to them is the way that that damage to their society is mended and his debt of labour would then legitimately belong to you, and if you needed this labour to ensure your own economic security, it would be right to require him to pay it. However, you should still strive to find a way to ensure your economic wellbeing without needing to hold onto his debt, just as Christ worked to free you from your debt.

In the actual history of the Atlantic slave trade, the slave traders had no interest in these questions of whether the people they were selling were acquired through some morally justifiable means or not. They typically didn't believe that these people were equally people who deserved to be treated with dignity. They took anyone that was sold to them and sometimes did kidnap people themselves. Africans that enslaved other Africans kidnapped people and took people captive in immoral fashions to sell them to the Europeans as well.

The desire to acquire European goods and weapons even led some African kingdoms to fight more wars and capture more captives, so that they could get more from the Europeans, and thus the business of the slave trade worked to destroy the peace of the continent.

European traders perhaps could even encourage Africans to capture more slaves or to fight each other to get slaves. The Europeans did not love the slaves as they loved themselves or as Christ loved them. They abused their dignity in horrific fashions.

After they had done this, people in the modern age abolished slavery, thinking the institution was horribly evil in itself and were left with the question of why it was that Christ had never abolished slavery or why it was that Paul told slaves to obey their masters.

They had never seen slavery being used in a way that protected the rights and dignity of those involved, and therefore they could not imagine the institution existing in any way other than the evil way it had been. They couldn't understand how it was that Christ never abolished slavery or why Paul commanded slaves to seek to please their masters.

The answer to the problem was that it was never the institution that was the problem, however, but it was the way that the institution was used. It didn't have to be like that and slavery may yet still serve a role in the future of our world, although perhaps we may call it other names, like we do in current legal practices, to make it look different from what existed before.

Lord, we pray that you help us to have a better understanding of the role of slavery within your plans for the world. We pray that you help end all forms of the violation of human dignity in the world and make all institutions treat human beings as they ought to be treated. We ask for these things, if it is your will, in Jesus' name, Amen

XIV: Religious Violence

Christianity has a long history of people engaging in violence for religious causes. In the modern day, this is something that we associate with Islam much more than Christianity, and perhaps it is correct to say that in the modern-day Islam has a much greater attachment to violence in the name of religion than does Christianity, but that is only the modern-day. In past times, this was certainly something shared by Christians as well. In the future, we do not yet know how it will be either.

Christian states used laws and violence to persecute religious minorities at many times of Christian political history right from the time of the Romans onward.
The Romans used violence to persecute Christians, and when the empire became Christian, they also eventually used violence to persecute pagans. The Byzantine state used violence to persecute Monophysites and other religious sects that didn't agree with orthodox Christianity. Charlemagne forced those he defeated to accept baptism as a term for their surrender.
Olaf Trygvasson of Norway, when he converted Norway to Christianity at the turn of the millennium, had the pagan priests of the Norse gods chained to rocks on tiny low-lying islands off the coast and left them to drown when the tides went above their heads. The Inquisition was founded in the 13th century and for centuries it used imprisonment, torture, execution and the fear of these things to control the Catholic population and stop people from going away from the faith as the church interpreted it.
Protestant states persecuted Catholics. Catholic states

persecuted Protestants. Orthodox Russia persecuted the Catholic church in Poland after it annexed Poland into Russia.

Political struggles within Christian states that involved attachment to different religious creeds within Christianity often had violence involved with them.
Struggles between Arian Christians and Catholic Christians within the Roman empire over the filling of different political or church offices could involve riots and violence.

Some wars were carried out by states in the Christian world for reasons deeply connected with religion.
The crusades against Islam are perhaps one of the most notable examples of religious violence by Christians. However, there were also other crusades of the middle ages as well, like the crusade against the Albigensians, the crusades of the Teutonic knights against pagan peoples in central and eastern Europe, as well as the crusade against the Hussites in Bohemia. The religious warfare between Catholics and Protestants around Europe that took place from the time of Martin Luther up until the peace of Westphalia is a notable example of violence conducted by Christians for reasons deeply connected to religion. The warfare between Catholics and Protestants in the British Isles, such as the rebellions in Ireland or the Jacobite wars are also notable for their religious dimensions.

In the modern world, however, apart from a few exceptions, you largely don't see Christians actively engaging themselves in violence for reasons directly related to their religious beliefs anymore. Christians still fight wars today, but they don't do it for Christianity; they do it with other justifications. You see Muslims fighting wars and engaging in violence in the name of Islam, but in most of the world, it is not common to see Christians doing this in the name of Christianity. To make the conclusion that this is because Islam is more violent than Christianity, however, is really not correct, if we actually understand the things that happened in Christian history.

The Thirty Years' War in the 17th century, for example, was started on grounds relating to religion and it was fought for reasons deeply related to which side (Protestants or Catholics) were going to come out on top of the new political order that was being forged in the war. This war was perhaps the worst conflict in European history prior to the time of Napoleon; millions of people died in it. The number of people who die today in Islamic terror attacks or at the hands of Islamic militants is still just a little echo in comparison with violence on that scale.
Oliver Cromwell, the puritan English dictator, quelled the rebellion in Catholic Ireland with enough destruction that it is estimated perhaps ¼ of the population of the island died in the course of it.

Why is it that we see Christians not engaging in violence with religious justifications today, but we see Muslims doing this, however?

The worst episodes of Christian religious violence arguably had already ended by the close of 17th century. From the beginning of the Enlightenment down to today, the amount of violence formerly used by Christians for religious purposes has grown increasingly less in most of the world.

The places outside of Europe, like in Africa, the Americas or Asia, which got their Christianity largely from European sources also inherited something from this tradition as well.

I think that Christianity became less violent perhaps has something to do with what happened in the Enlightenment and the following periods in Europe and the west. People became more tolerant of those who held different beliefs than them. Part of this is perhaps a better understanding of the Christian religion that grew, although part of it is also perhaps because people moved away from religion in general and considered religious methods of looking at the world as being less relevant.

Perhaps the explanation is that the Christian world went through a period when religion was pushed more and more out of the public sphere, out of politics, out of decision-making and out of the ideological underpinnings for the organization of states. Christianity became less important for many Christians and therefore why would they go to war or risk their lives to fight for it as other Christians had once done in the past?

Wars that are fought out of anger require that people believe in something first. If Muslims engage in more violence for their religion than those of other religions do so for their religions, it doesn't have to mean that Muslims are more violent, since the people of other religions still fight wars, but just for other reasons, but it may mean that the Muslims believe in their faith more strongly and are willing to fight or even to die for it.

Christians in the modern era will still fight wars for nationalism, for politics, for democracy or a political system, for other reasons… but most of them would not be willing to do so for religion, not because they have rejected war, since they still fight wars, but because they no longer believe that religion is as acceptable a reason to fight as all those other things that they believe in are acceptable reasons to fight.

In other words, it is not necessarily the case really that Muslims in the modern world are less violent than Christians, but rather it is just that Muslims see their faith as something acceptable to fight for, while Christians do not.

Today we look at these episodes of violence in past Christian history and we see it as something barbaric.

I think that the states that used violence in the name of religion in past times did not really use more violence for that reason than states in the past century or so have used violence for other reasons.

America fought its own crusades against the 'evil heresy' of communism that spread to different parts of the world in the last century. Millions of people died in the course of these crusades. They overthrew governments in Chile, Grenada, Iran, Guatemala, Vietnam and other places because they saw this heresy spreading and wanted to bring these places back to a correct and orthodox doctrine for running their affairs. Senator McCarthy and others initiated an inquisition at home to root out this heresy from bringing its evil into society.

Christians in Europe in the 17th century fought very bloody wars over religion. People in the 20th century Europe fought even bloodier wars over nationalism and ideology. The soldiers of the Thirty Years' War were trying to stop what was seen as an evil religion coming to rule over them. The soldiers of World War Two were trying to stop what was seen as an evil ideology that was coming to rule over them.

The Inquisition in its centuries of existence executed thousands of people. The French revolutionaries perhaps guillotined more people in a single year as enemies of the state than those who were executed by the Spanish Inquisition in its entire history for being heretics. The communist regimes of the 20th century could kill as many in a single day.

Again, the thesis I introduced and rebuked earlier that Christianity is responsible for making the world violent is also bearing witness here. People look at the violence and warfare done by Christians in past times and they think that this means there is something wrong or barbaric with Christianity.

The problem here again is that wars are still fought when people don't believe in Christianity too. After Christianity gets more greatly divorced from politics, it doesn't change this: people still believe in things, they are still willing to fight over things, they are still willing to use force and violence to make the world align with the things that they believe in, it is just that these things are not religious things, but they are other things.

Why is it that it is barbaric to fight wars for religion, but it is right to fight wars for nationalism and territory? Why is it barbaric to fight wars against religious heresies, but is right to do so against so-called evil ideologies? Why is it barbaric to fight wars to change rulers or governments that do not allow people to follow the true faith, but it is right to do so against rulers or governments that don't let people have democracy?

War is only legitimate when it is needed to defend life and there is no other recourse. But this truth condemns modern warfare that doesn't follow this just as much as it does for warfare in past times. Why should people inspired by Christianity to fight wars be any more barbaric than all the other people in the past and present who were inspired by other things they believed in to fight wars? Why are the crusaders who fought an aggressive Islam are considered to have done an evil, but the crusaders who fought against the spread of aggressive fascism are heroes? The crusaders committed atrocities in what they did... so did the allies at various points in the Second World War. The crusaders massacred the people in Jerusalem when they captured the city for the first time at the end of the First Crusade, the Americans firebombed Tokyo and intentionally burned to death 100,000 civilians in a single night.

Atrocities happen in wars. Wars can come about when people believe things strongly enough that they will fight for them and those things are being threatened. This is true of warfare all down through history. Why is it that when people who follow a Christian worldview do it from what proceeds out of their worldview, it is something so much more barbaric than all other worldviews that have led to people fighting wars in past times?

Christianity is never treated fairly by the world, whether in education and academia, or in the media, or anywhere else in society. It has to be this way as well, because it does not belong to the world, since Christ did not belong to the world. It will always be treated with a double standard and an unfair judgement by the world, because the world is sinful and does not follow the Truth. If Christ was treated unfairly, then His disciples will be treated unfairly. Not until the end of the world will true justice ever be granted and at that time Christ will be triumphant and His enemies that did not repent will be given what they deserved.

People who are inspired by Christianity as a way to understand the world will understand it in Christian terms and if they really believe it, then they may be willing to fight and use violence according to those beliefs. People who are inspired by democratic ideals, political ideologies, nationalism, or any other way of thinking, if they really believe, may also be willing to fight and use violence according to those beliefs.
Removing Christianity from the picture doesn't stop the world from engaging in warfare and violence. It just leads the world into believing in other things and engaging in warfare and violence for other reasons, and may even do more violence than they were doing before.

We look at these Christians in past times doing violence in the name of religion and we think of them as barbaric. We perhaps think that these people were not good Christians or simply just didn't get that the message of Christianity was to love your neighbour, and yet these people were fighting wars and on both sides were claiming to be doing so in the name of Jesus Christ, the Prince of Peace.

However, this kind of violent zealotry in the name of religion has a dimension to it that I am trying to highlight here that is being overlooked.

When people take religion seriously and they consider things of religion to be grave matters, violence and warfare can be a consequence of this. Just like how when people take a political ideology seriously or a system of belief seriously, violence and warfare can be a result of belief in those things too.

We are not really so different from them, even if we give these time periods names like the 'dark ages' or consider these people as belonging to a different time. We should try to understand them.

If you actually believed that you followed a religious faith that people of the world needed to believe in order to get to heaven and no other belief in the world was able to save your soul from damnation, this kind of belief can lead to particular conclusions.

For example, life and death itself is worth less than the salvation of souls. If people lose their earthly lives in order for the souls of people to avoid eternal damnation, then logically it is a small price to pay for this. And if you believe that a state or a government is engaging in actions that are going to doom its people to hellfire, going to war to put an end to that state or fighting a revolution against it then becomes a fight (in your mind) to save the souls of people from eternal ruin.

Grave evils may occur in the course of the war, however, none of these things will come even remotely close to eternal pains in hellfire.

If we really want to understand why it was that Christian

states in past times had violence against other Christians or other religions in the name of Christ, we cannot just dismiss them as being barbaric or bad Christians. We actually need to consider what it was that they were thinking at the time and treat it with the respect that is due to it.

This was a time period when the priests and bishops of the church did indeed teach to the laity that all outside the church are doomed to damnation. Protestant leaders made similar claims about Catholics and said that those who followed the Pope were following the antichrist and doomed to damnation.

Now, if you actually believed that that was true, then how could you simply just be contented with everyone believing what they wanted to believe and just accepting it? How could you tolerate and accept such a horrible thing as seeing these masses of people being doomed to damnation?

If you had any love at all for those people, then you would seek to convert them.

If governments and state powers were preventing this conversion from happening, because they used their power and resources to persecute those who tried to spread the true religion within their borders, then you would want that to change.

If you lacked faith such that you doubted that God could accomplish this change by anything other than your own taking up of arms and engaging in warfare, then you would perhaps look to warfare then as something good, which could help assist in bringing souls to salvation.

In the modern-day, after the Second Vatican Council, we believe that people outside the church can find salvation as long as they follow their conscience. Even if people never receive baptism and never formally join the church, we still have hope for their salvation. And because we have hope for their salvation, we may not try to convert them or preach to them, but we may just seek friendship with them and leave the choice to them as to whether they wish to join us or not. Ultimately God will judge them about whether they were following the Truth or not, and we refrain from judging.

This teaching wasn't present, however, in the 16th and 17th centuries. If it was present, the wars of religion perhaps would have never occurred. But it wasn't present and the question of whether a land was Protestant or Catholic was (in their mind) ultimately a question of whether the people were going to hellfire or whether they had a chance of salvation.

One might say, in these circumstances, that people in Protestant lands still had the opportunity to be saved if they simply just left those lands or if they chose martyrdom within those lands. Warfare and worldly methods were not needed to bring them to the church, because they had ways to be part of the church. After all, the ultimate choice about whether you will to be part of the church or not belongs to you.

However, this idea is failing to take into account that the vast majority of people are not saints. Their faith may be weak, they may not have the economic means to leave their lands and if you were to present them with persecution, they may fall away forever.

If you let them live in a Catholic land where they could practice the Catholic faith, they might continue in that faith and ultimately still die with the sacraments of the church. Their faith isn't strong enough that you could reasonably expect them to stay true to it in the midst of the storm. Their knowledge might also not be great either and they might not really understand what the dangers were in the Protestant teaching.

And indeed, if we look at history, most of the people in those countries did leave the church when their princes became Protestant and subsequent generations from then on lost the faith of their ancestors.

Paul said that one should avoid giving causes of temptation to those brothers who are weak in faith, because such causes might mean eternal death for them. He constantly urged people to be on check for those who would deceive them away from the Truth.

In this case here in 16th and 17th century Europe, the faith of these people and perhaps also their knowledge of the Truth was not strong enough that they would remain in the Catholic church when the leaders of the states that they lived in changed their religion.

If that temptation had been removed from them, however, they may have remained with the sacraments of the church until their death. While we do not know the salvation or damnation of most people, it is possible that there were people who found eternal damnation in that time period, who would have otherwise been saved if that temptation had been removed from them.

When the Spanish Armada tried to invade England, when the Holy Roman Emperors tried to take back the territories that had fallen to Protestantism, when the Catholic monarchs of Europe fought Protestants in warfare, this is part of the mindset that existed.

Now, God can do anything, however. And if people had faith, He could provide them with a way to save the souls of these people and bring them back to the Catholic church without warfare to retake their lands for Catholicism. To say that the Catholic monarchs of Europe who fought these wars were bad Christians has some truth to it, because the mission of the church does not require warfare to advance itself, and the church is stronger when it grows deeper in virtue and love, not when it possesses armies and weapons.

But, the monarchs of Europe were not saints. The vast majority of the laypeople, clergy and bishops of the time were not saints. Their faith was strong enough that they saw a real need to bring these masses of people back to Catholicism, but it was not strong enough that they had found a way to accomplish this other than through warfare.

The Popes and bishops at the time gave encouragement for Catholic leaders who used laws, wars and other means to do this. Pius V, who is a canonized saint, did indeed openly encourage the subjects of Elizabeth I to violently overthrow her because of her heresy.

God through Moses commanded the Israelites to slay the people of the land of Canaan, otherwise those peoples were going to bring them to sin. Now, if the Israelites had a stronger faith, then even if they lived next to the Canaanites, they would not have betrayed God on that account. But God in His wisdom knew of their weakness of faith and hardness of heart, and told them to kill these people, because eternal damnation is a greater evil to be avoided than the loss of physical life.

The minds of authorities within the church could have been something similar to this too. Since they know that the people in those countries lacked the faith to stay true to the church in the midst of the storm, and they also knew that asking the faithful and the leaders of Europe to convert and become saints was not going to be answered. And they see that warfare might cause scores of people to remain within the sacraments of the church that could bring them to salvation, while doing nothing would (in their minds) leave those souls to damnation.

This mindset I am describing is indeed behind a lot of the violent episodes in the history of Christian states.

The inquisition sought to find, arrest, put on trial, torture and execute people because it saw a real threat to the salvation of people when wrong ideas were spread in society.

Today we think it to be crazy that you could get in trouble and be subject to arrest or execution for saying things like Christ wasn't God or the church was wrong. But at that time, if you actually believed that a person going into heresy was cut off from salvation and that heretics had the ability to cause others to follow them on their path, then using these kinds of methods to stamp out heresy becomes a method to protect the salvation of people in your mind.

When the crusaders went to fight the Hussites in the 15th century or the Cathars in the 13th century, they were acting as a military arm of the inquisition to stamp out heresy before it spread further.

The laws of Moses have the same things in them.
Deuteronomy 13 says that if someone should come and try
to tell you to follow others gods, you must kill that person,
even if it was your own family member. If a city is led away
to follow other gods then that city must be destroyed. It
was God's Holy Spirit who inspired those words in scripture
to be written; the same Holy Spirit who inspired the gospel
of Jesus Christ.

This is also partly explaining the mindset of the violent
political struggles that occurred in Byzantine history during
the Christological controversies that divided the people of
the Byzantine empire against each other.

It is also partly this mindset behind the wars that Christians
fought against Muslims that were conquering Christian
territories.

Was this mindset right or wrong?
In the modern-day, we would say it was wrong, because
we believe that those outside the church also may be
saved and we can be hopeful that they will find salvation if
they follow their conscience so that we do not need to
worry about whether they die outside of the church.
If we took this mindset back to these time periods, then
we would say that even if all these multitudes were leaving
the Catholic Church and becoming Protestants, as long as
they did so in good conscience, they wouldn't have been
damned for it.
Did they all do it good conscience?
Knowing human tendencies, this would seem doubtful.
More likely, many of them did so in bad conscience, but

they gave into doing what they knew to be wrong or should have been able to discern to be wrong, because the pressures of the world were upon them.
If those pressures were removed, perhaps they wouldn't have violated their consciences.

Christ said that if anyone causes one of these little ones to sin, it would be better for a millstone to be hung around the person's neck and he be thrown into the sea.
However, ultimately the only person who can cause someone to lose their innocence is the person himself.
If you teach a child to do something sinful, and they innocently follow along and do it, as long as the child did not realize that what they were doing was sinful, then the child has not committed a sin. Only if the child knew it was wrong, and they followed what you said because you as the adult had pressured or tempted them, would you actually be causing the child to lose his soul to sin.
However, the choice to sin still remains with the child himself.

There is an Arnold Schwarzenegger movie called End of Days where the character played by Arnold is fighting to stop Satan. He gets into physical fights with Satan, throws Satan out of a window and tosses a grenade at Satan.
The devil in real life is not defeated like this, however. All the weapons and armies in the world are not going to destroy evil with firepower.

States should seek to remove temptations that will cause people to sin and to go away from God or go away from the church.

However, it is a sin to invade other states, it is a sin to kill the innocent, it is a sin to fight wars when other means were available to solve the problems, it is a sin to use torture, it is a sin to execute those who could be safely kept incarcerated, it is a sin to overthrow rulers, etc.

But, losing faith in Christ and His church is a greater evil to be feared than all of these things. Since Christ and His church can heal people who have fallen into evils. Peter was saved and Judas was not, because Peter retained his faith in Christ's mercy and returned to Him, rather than despairing. For those who hold on to faith, they still have hope when they fall, but for those who reject faith, they have no hope in the end.

God told Moses to order the Israelites to kill the Canaanites because the Israelites' faith was weak. God told Moses to order them to do something that was evil, but it was a lesser evil than what they would have done otherwise had they entered the land and lost their faith in God. God's order in the narrative could be seen as a manifestation of the principle of pragmatism. Salvation is a higher priority than life.

Pius V approved of people in England to give up their allegiance to Elizabeth I. Various Popes and bishops supported Catholic monarchs in their attempts to use force against protestants. Innocent III called for the crusade against the Cathars. All the crusades to recapture the Holy Land were done at Papal commands. The inquisition operated and judged people with the approval of the church.

Ideally, Catholic states should not use any of these means in order to remove temptations from people. They should use other means to counter heresy or threats against the faith of people. Using violence must always be a last resort and it is not morally acceptable when other means to accomplish the objective are present.

The great truth of all the heresies that occurred in the history of Christendom is that every one of them had some kernel of Truth lodged deeply within them that the dominant society and church at the time was sinfully neglecting.
Dominic of Guzman, the founder of the Dominicans, went to preach to the Cathars in the time period before the Pope ordered the crusaders to kill them. He tried to use arguments and faith to bring them back to the Catholic church. He found that the leaders of the Cathars were people who rejected material wealth and tried to live simple lives, and that this resonated with many people in a time where the leaders of the church were living like princes in magnificence and wealth. He told the early Dominicans to not use horses for transportation, to rely upon begging to get their daily bread and to follow rules that would keep them living poor and simple lives, because he saw this as necessary in order to get people to really believe the message they were preaching.
The heresies are actually just outgrowths of the sin present within the church itself. When the members of the church fail to follow the gospel in their daily lives, the demon gains power from it and eventually is able to simply break off a piece of the church itself. And the fuel for the fire is the sin and corruption present within the church.
There is no one who assists the enemies of the church more than the people who live in the church, especially

those in important positions, who do not live as the gospel
commands.

The Christian princes and the leaders of the church should
have converted more deeply and obeyed the gospel more.
If they did so, they wouldn't need force to protect the faith
of people from heresies, because no one would have been
attracted by heresies to begin with.
No one would go to eat garbage or tree bark in the middle
of a famine, if real food was provided to them.
Now, if they don't have the real food, if the people of the
church are not going to live as they are supposed to live
and thus they allow heresies to grow their seeds, and there
are no other means to solve the problem, in that event
using all those worldly methods to combat heresy and
reduce the temptation is still a better option than people
losing the faith and being cut off from the church.
Even if people fall, like Peter, they can still rise again if they
come to return to Christ. With faith, there is still hope,
even when one falls.

Ultimately Christians should seek to be more like Christ
and love as He loved in order to defeat the powers of the
world. By following God, they can overcome the world.
When they use violence, force and warfare to do so, they
are trying to defeat the world using the methods of the
world and they ultimately will never win, because they are
becoming part of what they are seeking to destroy when
they do this rather than embrace deeper conversion.

States can use these methods to fight heresies, but a note
of warning must be put here. Since heresies themselves

grow from sin and if sinful methods are being chosen pragmatically to combat heresies because people are not willing to follow the true path of the gospel, these sinful methods themselves will ultimately give birth to new heresies and break people off from the church.
Not until the people become holy will the society ever be free from heresy. But once the people become holy, the state will no longer be necessary either. As long as society requires states to exist, states will have a duty to use these worldly methods to fight against the temptations that draw people away from Christ, but the paradox will hold sway and they will not ever truly succeed in what they seek to do.

Lord, we pray that you help protect the faith of people from false teachings that will deceive them. We pray that states use the methods they ought to use to remove such temptations and not the methods that they shouldn't use. We pray that we may judge the history of the church according to your gospel and wisdom. We ask for these things, if it is your will, in Jesus' name, Amen

XV: Monasteries

Anthony the Great lived for almost his entire life in the
Egyptian desert as a hermit away from the temptations of
the world and with God in prayer. He is considered as one
of the first fathers of the monastic tradition in Christianity.
He lived during the time of the Emperor Constantine. The
Emperor had converted to Christianity, but still had not yet
received baptism because he was afraid of being stained
by the sins of the world that he was immersed in. The
Emperor knew about Anthony, because Anthony had
become famous in that time and he sent messages to
Anthony asking that Anthony would pray for him.
During the course of Christian political history, there were
many Christian rulers who requested that monks and nuns
who were secluded from the world in their monasteries
would offer up prayers for them, who were still immersed
in the world.
Many monarchs, royalty and nobility gave gifts to
monasteries and supported their financial existence, partly
out of a belief that the monasteries would pray for them
and that these prayers would help them to get to heaven.

All the evils of the world exist because the world has been
separated from God and has earned God's wrath by its
sins. The political and social problems of states are part of
this. States suffer political and social problems because
they are part of a world that has sinned and been punished
by being separated from God.

Demons are attracted by power. People who have power
may suffer greater temptations than people without it,

because the demons seek to influence them more. Dominant races, sexes, social classes or other categories will face bigger temptations than who are not dominant, because their power is what draws the demons closer to them. People in positions of influence, like those in the media, will attract demons towards them because of their power of influence. People in authority and in government will especially attract demons towards them by their power and authority. The more control they have over others and the less there is to control them, the more the demon will be attracted by them.

There is an old saying that power corrupts and absolute power corrupts absolutely. This saying is wrong. It is not power that corrupts, but it is power that brings forth temptations and the human heart becomes corrupted when it fails in resisting those temptations as it ought to have done so.

There is no such thing as a system that is capable of defeating this, because it is rooted from the primordial evil that fell from heaven and not just a matter of a particular type of political system.

States create checks and balances to try to hold back the people in positions of power from becoming corrupted and abusing that power, but the devil can pervert these checks and balances, because what ultimately holds these checks and balances up and what their continued existence relies upon are human wills and human hearts.

It is not checks and balances that prevent power from corrupting people and freedom from being lost. It's virtue in the hearts of people that keeps the checks and balances from failing when temptations arise.

Paul told the Christian community that they should always

pray for those in positions of power and authority so that they might be treated well by them.

Power attracts the demons, but simply having power does not mean that one is under the control of the demons. A person can have absolute power and not be corrupted as long as they have the strength to resist temptations. Power is not the thing that corrupts, but it is the human heart that corrupts when the temptations are offered to it. Prayer is the means of overcoming temptations. People in positions of authority need to pray to get the strength from God to overcome the temptations that are arranged against them. People who lived under their power must also pray for them to help them overcome these temptations.

In the time periods when rulers became patrons of monasteries and asked the cloistered monks or nuns to pray for them, this was a way to help them to fight the temptations that came from their office.

People in positions of power need to pray and they need other people to pray for them, because the temptations that will come upon them are great.

Prayer is more necessary for the state than virtually any other resource that it could possess. Virtue is what makes the state to succeed or to fail, and virtue is nothing more than the resistance to temptation and the doing of good. The state will stand or fall on the basis of virtue, and temptation is the thing that has the power to destroy virtue. Prayer is what is needed to combat temptation.

Monasteries that pray for the leaders and pray for the welfare of the society are of very great necessity. Prayer is not something unique to monasteries, however, even though the people who spend their lives in monasteries tend to excel at it more greatly than the general public.
All people in society can pray. Even the beggar on the street has the power to pray and can change the course of the nation by his prayers.
The devil is quite good at convincing people that prayer accomplishes nothing or that prayer has no power in it to change anything and it is a waste of time, because people can't see the immediate effects of prayer. But by faith we know that God hears prayers and He promised in the gospel that those who ask shall receive.

In the Middle Ages, the rulers gave gifts to monasteries in exchange for their prayers. There is in fact no gift that they were able to give to these monasteries that was equal with what the monasteries were giving to them.
If the state giving gifts to monasteries or other institutions will help bring about more prayer for the state and its leaders, then this is a more worthwhile investment than any other project that can be attempted.
It is not always true that giving monks and nuns greater physical goods is going to help them draw closer to God and lead for better prayer, however. Although removing the need to worry about material concerns may help people to have more time to concentrate on prayer and may also allow for more people to be supported in this kind of life.
If there are people who are willing to spend their lives in

prayer to the true God and the state merely needs to solve
the basic economic needs of them for this to work, then
the investment is an absolutely worthwhile one.
In many cases, the state may not need to do this, however,
because private donors themselves may give what is
needed to support this lifestyle. In that case, the principle
of subsidiarity would dictate that it ought to be left to the
lower levels to accomplish this.

The nation and the leaders need prayer. Salvation, life and
lesser priorities are all affected by the question of whether
or not people are making prayers.
The state needs to encourage prayer in whatever way that
it can. It cannot force people to pray, like as occurs in a few
parts of the Islamic world, where Muslims are obliged to
do daily prayers at set times and can be punished if they
are found doing something different.
It needs to encourage people to pray, but ultimately it has
to be something that is given freely by people.
The media and education system play a vital role in this,
because they can teach people about the need to pray.
If one realizes that any person who is conscious and
possesses a rational mind is able to pray, one realizes that
there are many people who may not be able to do other
kinds of work, but who still are able to pray and help the
state.
The homeless, the unemployed, the beggars, the
orphaned, the elderly who have no one to take care of
them, the disabled and crippled, the people with physical
illnesses that prevent them from doing work, the criminals
in prison, etc. can all be recruited by the state to use their
time to pray for its leaders and for the welfare of the

nation, and the state can take care of their basic economic needs as payment to them while they fulfill this great task. Doing this kind of work serves a huge benefit to the nation as a whole and it also teaches these people their own value in making them realize that they are not a burden to society, but rather they have the ability to be the pillars that society rests upon.

All things in the nation depend on virtue to succeed. Virtue depends on prayers. If the state can gain prayers by solving the simple economic needs of the people doing the prayers, then it is the greatest investment that the state can possibly carry out. Although if lower levels of society can solve these economic needs without the state, then that is preferable.

Lord, we pray that you help teach us to pray as you desire us to pray. We pray that you help leaders and societies to resist temptations and be filled with virtue. We ask for these things, if it is your will, in Jesus' name, Amen

XVI: Natural Disasters

In past times, it was common for people to interpret
natural disasters as signs of divine displeasure with the
world. Christian history has many examples of this.
Earthquakes, plagues, famines, tsunamis and all sorts of
disaster that have occurred were often interpreted as
being acts of divine justice against the world.
Most recently during the Covid-19 pandemic, Pope Francis
publicly interpreted the pandemic as being a kind of
reaction by nature against a world that had abused nature
so much.

We know from the teaching of original sin that all human
suffering and death is deriving from human sinfulness
beginning from Adam and Eve. Without sin, suffering and
death could not exist.

During the Covid-19 pandemic and during the Spanish flu a
century earlier, people had enough awareness of diseases
that they understood people in close proximity would
spread the disease and therefore they made efforts to cut
down on public gatherings. Among the public gatherings
that were shut down included religious gatherings and
masses.
Grocery stores, postal offices, hospitals, and various types
of shops remained open in many countries because they
were considered to be essential, but the public offering of
the mass was shut down because it was not considered to
be essential.

Padre Pio said that it would be easier for the world to exist without the Sun than it would be for the world to exist without the mass. The mass is more essential than food or health.

Christ said to the devil during His temptations, 'man does not live by bread alone, but by every word that comes from the mouth of God'.

In the book of Haggai, the prophet speaks words against the Jews about how God was going to curse them because after they had returned from exile, they went out about planting their fields and doing their business while they left the house of God in ruins and didn't rebuild it. Since they had placed other things first, and God second, therefore the prophet said that the works of their hands would be cursed and the crops they planted would be corrupted with mildew and rot.

If people could find a way to go outside and shop for their essentials while minimizing the risk of the virus through various means, then they can also go outside and find a way to attend mass while minimizing the risk of the virus through various means.

States should assist with this as well. They should use their resources to try to help make it remain possible to safely attend mass even in the midst of an epidemic, because the mass is a more essential work than anything else being carried out in society, including the work of the medical workers fighting the disease.

Lord, we pray that you help us to trust in you and not in

human beings. We pray that you help us to repent of our sins and return to you. We pray that you help make people healthy in body and soul. We pray for governments to have the wisdom to do as they ought to do in the midst of great trials. We ask for these things, if it is your will, in Jesus' name, Amen

XVII: Democracy and Dictatorship

When vices increase, states move towards totalitarianism,
because the only way to make the society operate
correctly is for people to be controlled in everything they
do, since they can't be trusted to make the correct choices
themselves.
The West in recent times has been moving more and more
away from Christianity and away from God. It has
embraced many vices and abandoned Christian moral
teachings on many things. Eventually this path may end
with it destroying its democracy and freedom as well, since
the vices of people will lead to social problems that have to
be met with force.

Consider the Covid-19 pandemic and how it worked in
different parts of the world.
In China, a totalitarian state with extensive surveillance
and population control, the state did not trust people to do
the right thing. Instead it made mandates for the
behaviour of everyone and enforced it with mandatory
electronic surveillance to force people to follow the rules.
The result was that China was able to end most of the
epidemic in their country relatively early in the pandemic,
even though they are a country with very high population
density, even though they had to combat it before much
was known about the virus and the virus had spread
around so much in their population before they
determined the full scope of the threat.
In many western democracies, however, people were often
given public health orders, but without effective
enforcement. Governments urged people to 'do the right

thing' and left people with the freedom to decide
themselves whether or not they would follow the health
guidelines. Enforcement existed, but it was never at the
scale needed to make sure everyone was complying and a
lot of was let to trust of people.

Even if most people followed the rules, enough people
kept breaking them over the course of the pandemic, such
that these countries mostly never freed themselves from
the disease until vaccines became widely available. Even as
I write this, these countries are still not free of the virus.
This experiment, if it can be called that, in a way proves
why it is that the virtue of the people is what determines
what kind of governing system can be given to them. If
people do the right thing on their own, then controls
aren't necessary. But if they don't, then they need to be
controlled or else the whole society suffers.

The people in western countries that went out to parties
or broke the health guidelines irresponsibly were
essentially proving that they didn't deserve to live in
freedom.

China's ability to achieve victory over the pandemic in
comparison with many of the western democracies doesn't
prove that the Chinese governing system was inherently
better than democracy. What it proves is that the people
who lived in those particular countries were not
responsible enough that they could have been trusted with
the freedoms that such democratic systems gave them.

If the people in those western countries were given
freedom and they rejected God, embraced abortion,
embraced the sexual revolution, refrained from doing what
they should have done to help the environment, failed to

help the poor and needy, etc., ultimately, they are unwittingly working towards a world where the freedom and democracy they enjoy cannot exist any longer. They are working towards a world where systems like those in China or other totalitarian states should succeed and systems where the people are given freedom should fail in comparison.

Charlemagne in his Capitularies, said regarding his subjects that had been unfaithful in spiritual matters: 'For in no way are we able to understand how they can be faithful to us, who have shown themselves unfaithful to God and disobedient to their Priests'

Charlemagne's words there are explaining why it is that virtue is so important for the state.

If people are unfaithful to God, they are also going to be unfaithful to each other. If people don't follow a moral code to start with, how do you expect them to keep contracts honestly? How do you expect them to follow the laws when no one is watching them?

If people go away from God and into sin for so many different things by their own free choice, it should surprise no one that they wouldn't listen to public health orders either. A society of people who don't follow conscience and right reason in spiritual things are inevitably not going to follow conscience and right reason in secular things either.

The people who embraced the sexual revolution, who supported abortion, who had the freedom of speech and abused it, who had the freedom to worship and chose not to follow God, who had the freedom to choose how to live and didn't live rightly, were ultimately creating the conditions that lead to the subversion of democracy and the destruction of the freedoms that they were abusing.

In Plato's Republic, Socrates compares the different types of government and he claims that democracy produces dictatorship, which he marks as the worst form of government. By dictator, he didn't just mean a person who ruled without being elected, since he regarded traditional monarchs and societies that were ruled by the military as being something different from 'dictators'.
Rather he meant a person in power who was enslaved by his passions and not a follower of reason; who used force to dominate the people. When I write below about the idea of the 'dictator' I am also following the same usage here.
The dictator tried to find happiness in the things of this world, but this world could never satisfy him. As much as he had, he always wanted more. Reason would tell him that the things he pursued could not help him find the happiness he sought after, but he didn't follow reason and instead, like an animal without reason, followed only his passions and desires. He used violence and force to get what he wanted, but once he had it, it was never satisfying for him, and so he would only pursue after more.
I don't believe that Plato was correct in thinking that democracy naturally produces dictators or that democracy is a less preferred system of governance. A democracy ruled by virtue is the greatest type of system; the only thing more perfect is a society with no state at all, where people do not need controls any longer to live in harmony. It is true that the greater freedom in democracy can perhaps sometimes allow for more temptations to exist in society, which in turn can lead to greater vice. However,

just as absolute power does not necessarily produce corruption, so also absolute freedom does not necessarily produce corruption either. It all depends upon whether people retain virtue or not when they are confronted with their temptations.

More freedom is better than less, but it needs virtue in order for it hold together like how a body needs bones or else it collapses. Democracy dominated by vice, however, is a recipe for disaster.

People pursuing their own selfish interests, not following Truth, not following God, not following reason, but just pursuing what they want and seeking the things of this world to satisfy them, when these things will forever be unable to satisfy them, ultimately will lead to people and society as a whole essentially going crazy.

They are looking to the world to make them happy and yet they are not happy, nor can they find true happiness. The democratic state has given them the freedom to pursue their own happiness, but they choose to use this freedom to look in all of the wrong places, and eventually their twisted desires lead them to seek to dominate one another.

They may struggle with one another to get power over one another, since they think that it is because their own will is not being followed in society, which is why they have problems and aren't satisfied in this world. They do not love their enemies, because they are sinful, and rather than listening to one another, and believing that each person has something to contribute, they may treat the people who disagree with their views with contempt and believe that only they alone possess the truth. They may not believe, as a democracy requires, that the other side has a right to their opinion and viewpoints.

The dictator that appears may be just whichever person among them, pulled out of their ranks in the midst of them, who is just a reflection of the society as a whole and who has won control over the rest of the people to pursue his own wishes. God uses sinners to punish sinners and he places people in power over other people to show a reflection of themselves back upon them and let them see what they really are.

They reject the Truth; he rejects the Truth. They choose to believe what they want to believe is true and not what is actually true and so does he. They are selfish; he is selfish. They tell lies; he tells lies. They fail to live in a moral way; he fails to live in a moral way. They hate their enemies; he hates his enemies. They live without God, pursuing the desire of their own hearts; he lives without God, pursuing the desire of his own heart.

The people may then fight and struggle with the dictator, blaming him for all of their problems, thinking that he is evil, while failing to look at their own selves and come to realize that the person they are accusing is ultimately themselves, for he is their reflection, pulled out of their ranks and number. If he deserves hellfire for what he does, as the people insist, then so do all of them too, because he is just doing what they do.

Christ said that if you do not forgive your neighbour then neither shall God forgive you. If the people living under the dictator insist on judging him for what he does, when he is just a reflection of themselves and their own society who is pulled from their collective ranks, then so shall their own sins be judged as well.

Hitler didn't come from a vacuum. He came from a society of people that had vices in it. Hitler only became Hitler in history and not just become some obscure crazy guy forgotten by history, because millions of people listened to him rather than the Truth.

They thought that the party and the leader could bring them happiness. Hitler was going to make them powerful, make them wealthy, and make them greater than other nations. He was going to solve all of their problems for them and give them a glorious future where they ran the world. But even if they did run the world, even if they did become wealthy, even if they did have all their current problems solved, the end result would have only been that they would still be unhappy, because no one can find peace from anything in this world; God alone can grant peace.

The end result would have just driven them even crazier than they had been as they kept pursuing their desires without ever finding the satisfaction or happiness they were looking for. God spared them from this and let them be defeated, giving them the mercy of being punished with a harsh defeat rather than to let them have what they thought they were pursuing and let that drive them insane. Hitler did not achieve power over Germany except if God allowed it, for no one achieves power in a state without God's permission. God erects Hitler over these people for a purpose and He shows people a reflection of themselves that serves to punish them and teach them.

The dictators of the present and the past are like this.
Those of the future will also be like this.

Psalm 31 (32) [9] Do not become like the horse and the

mule, who have no understanding. With bit and bridle bind fast their jaws, who come not near unto thee. [10] Many are the scourges of the sinner, but mercy shall encompass him that hopeth in the Lord.

The Psalm here tells us not to be like horses and mules, who will only move when they have bridles in their mouths and are forced to move by them. Sinners that refuse to obey God's laws when they have freedom are like this; because they create the need for states that take away their freedoms and oblige them to behave in the way that they wouldn't choose freely. These states need to use great force and violence to control people, like an animal being whipped, because the people will not do what they ought to do without being subjected to such force. Indeed, they create not just the need for such states and for such controls, but their own pursuit of sin will ultimately lead to sinners among them actually destroying their freedoms and in fact erecting such states over them.

Benjamin Franklin said: 'Only a virtuous people are capable of freedom. As nations become corrupt and vicious, they have more need of masters.'

Freedom is always preferable to control; but freedom can only be granted when people are not like the horse or the mule, and they will move forward without the bridle in their mouth.
Thus, the path to preserve freedom and democracy; the solution that stops dictators from appearing and totalitarian states from dominating, is to use one's own freedom for good and not for evil. To use one's time to

pursue happiness in the right place, to follow God and find true peace. To use one's freedom to obey the laws of God and the teachings of Christ from the heart and thus become truly free. Only then, freedom is preserved and the forces of tyranny are held back.

Lord, we pray that you help us and all of society to follow your laws from the heart and freely, so that we may not be subject to controls that take away our freedom. We pray that people will repent of their sins, which have merited such punishments upon them and that you may have mercy. We ask for these things, if it is your will, in Jesus' name, Amen

XVIII: Position of the Church

What is the correct relationship between the state and the church?
The church does not have the role to govern politics, but those who do govern politics are obliged to obey the gospel of Jesus Christ as it is preserved and taught within the church.
However, as an institution, should the church have any role within the political framework of the state?

Should the state, for example, use its resources to assist the church in its mission?
When Constantine converted to Christianity, he used state money and resources to assist the church. The Church of the Holy Sepulchre in Jerusalem as well as other holy sites in Palestine, the great basilicas in Rome and other things were things given by the Emperor Constantine to the church.
The Hagia Sophia was built by the Byzantine emperor Justinian.
A huge portion of the cathedrals, monasteries and churches that were built in the Middle Ages were built with the financing that came from wealthy patrons who were often in positions of political authority and used the resources of their states to finance these projects.

Today, many modern states would reject this idea of state sponsorship for the church and in most places of the world, the churches rely on the donations of people or sometimes from their own businesses that they run. In Germany, people have the option to have some of their taxes sent to the church, but this is still ultimately a donation in a sense being done through the government, since people are free to reject this option.

Should the government spend public money to help the church?

This question in fact goes into the entire issue of how taxation ought to occur.
Governments need money in order to function. Soldiers, policemen, bureaucracies and public employees don't generally work for free. The infrastructure, the state investment projects, the state-run institutions, etc. are all things that require enormous amounts of money. Governments need to get that money from somewhere.

In most places, they get this money through taxation. In some places, they may be in control of particular industries or monopolies that they use to acquire revenue for themselves and don't need to rely as heavily on taxation.

But as I wrote in the principles above, it is better to give people more freedom than less, because the system will run better when everyone has the freedom to contribute their talents.
When governments tax people in order to use the tax revenue to accomplish something in the state, they are basically taking the freedom of people away to do what they wish with their money and instead insisting that their money must be used on what the government wishes it used on.
But also, as I wrote in the principles above, freedom has to

be taken away from people at times because people cannot be trusted to do as they ought to do.

If you let people do what they want with their money and the state asked for donations, rather than taxes, to pay their soldiers and police, to build their schools and bridges, or to invest in their communities, the state might find itself short of the money it needs.

If the state relied on the good will of people rather than the obligation of taxes, and if people were just asked to donate what they could to help the state in its enterprise, this would only work if the people were really virtuous and would really give up their wealth selflessly and freely to help the community.

In most places of the world, this plan would probably not work. Hence, their freedom has to be taken away and the state must oblige them to give up their money for these purposes that the state considers to be necessary.

Now, with regard to the church, the issue of money is different than it is for other institutions and things in society.

The church's mission is not a material one. It has as its goal the salvation of souls, which is the highest kind of work that a person can be part of in this world.

The church uses material things to help accomplish this goal, but it can accomplish this goal even without very much in the way of material goods.

When Mother Teresa went out on the streets of Calcutta to find the dying poor and baptize those of them that were willing, she was doing the work of saving souls, but she didn't need great amounts of material or wealth to accomplish this.

The materials that are actually needed for the sacraments are very cheap. Bread and wine for masses, tiny amounts of olive oil for anointings, water for baptism... these things do not cost a lot in most parts of the world.

The church building might cost considerably more than all of these things. The costs of paying for staff members, paying bills for utilities, paying for airline tickets or cars... these things might make up a much larger portion of the budget of a modern diocese than paying for the actual things that are needed for the sacraments themselves. However, it is the sacraments that are giving grace to people and which are the most important element among the physical things that the church has.

The church can in fact have none of its properties and yet still accomplish its mission of saving of souls. It can have no physical building, no cars, no plane tickets, no electricity, no hired staff, no ornaments, no artwork, no holy vessels, no vestments, etc. and yet it can still be quite capable of saving souls. In fact, the priests who don't have any of these things might be even more effective and convincing to many people to get them to listen to them.

Churches under persecution are often like this. The persecuted church of the Roman empire met in the catacombs underneath the city of Rome, in locations in the wilderness, inside the private homes of believers, etc. Catholic priests in concentration camps of the 20th century still gave the sacraments to people with meagre resources. Cardinal Francis Xavier Nguyen van Thuan of Vietnam did mass while imprisoned by holding the bread and wine in the palm of his hand while reciting the prayers and distributed it to his fellow prisoners.

Christ did not need big donations of wealth in order to

accomplish His mission. He received some donations of expensive things, like the ointment that He was given prior to His execution or the gold that His mother was given upon His birth, but even without those things, He would have still accomplished His mission. Many of the things He needed, He was provided for by those who believed in Him.

According to the German mystic Margaret Ebner, Christ's mother gave away the gold that they received at the child's birth to help the poor. She didn't take it for her family to glorify herself or her Son, like what a church does when it receives donations from people, which it then uses to fund art or build architecture for honouring Christ, Mary or the saints. For that reason, when Jesus's parents went to present Him at the temple in Jerusalem, they still sacrificed two birds, rather than a bird and a lamb, since they remained poor and had to choose the poorer option for the sacrifice.

The state should only tax people and use their money to pay for things, when there are things that are necessities for the function of the state, and which the people themselves are unwilling to pay for voluntarily. If something is not actually necessary, or the people themselves are willing to pay for it voluntarily, then the state should not tax.

In the case of the church, even if the church is poor, it can still accomplish its mission in this world. Furthermore, poverty of material resources is of benefit to the church's mission in many ways. Hence, material wealth is not a necessity for the church and therefore I would argue that the state should not tax people and give the money to the church when it is for anything more than basic necessities

to function, if those things are not being provided by
donations.

The church's mission is vital for the state, which is why
making sure that it continues its mission needs to be
supported if the people will not support it themselves by
their donations, but the church's ability to do its mission
doesn't necessarily become stronger when it is given more
wealth on top of its basic requirements, especially if that
wealth was forcibly taken away through taxation and not
given freely.

What I wrote above concerning the state paying for the
basic economic needs of those who would devote
themselves to prayer does not conflict with this. Taking
care of the basic needs of food, clothing and shelter of
people in monasteries or other people who are devoting
themselves to pray so that they don't need to worry about
work is something entirely different from paying for the
construction or maintenance of expensive and ornately
decorated buildings, paying for plane tickets and cars,
paying for vestments and sacred objects, etc.
Investing in the former is a very wise investment by the
state. Even if it is taxing people and giving the money for
this purpose, it has great value in it. Paying for the latter,
however, makes less sense, from the perspective of the
state, because the entire purpose of the institution is to
help bring people to love and follow God, and if the people
themselves are not willing to listen and help the church by
their own free will, forcing them to give up their money
through taxation to make the structure more beautiful may
not do much to change their hearts to make them love
God more.

Investing in the church is a wise investment. But mass can be done on a simple wooden table sitting in a tent. Baptisms can be done with a washbasin. Using wealth to make the tools and structures more beautiful and attractive is a good thing to do, but it is not strictly necessary in order to carry out its principal purpose nor is it always necessarily helpful at convincing people to repent and believe.

If the church does have a material use for something, then the pious faithful themselves should be the ones to fulfill it by their donations, just as Christ's needs were fulfilled by those who believed in Him.
If the state *forces* people to take their money and give it to Christ and His church, then this really takes away from the merit of the donation. Furthermore, if the pious faithful really are not willing to help the church in its material needs, this may mean that the church needs to work harder to convert them. Leaving the church in poverty to increase the sanctification of its ministers may act as a kind of remedy for the situation then.
Let the church follow what Christ taught in Matthew 10, which was the spirit adopted by the early Franciscans. For anything beyond basic needs, let the church rely for its material needs on the goodwill of those it preaches to. Christ relied on the goodwill of people for His material needs in His ministry. He never forced anyone to give Him something.

Now, I argue that in general the government should not be taxing people and giving the money to the church. However, should the church have any kind of privileged position in the state?

The teachings of the church are the way of salvation and all people everywhere are obligated to obey the gospel that the church teaches. For that reason, there is every reason for why the government should give the church a privileged position in society if such privileges can help it to accomplish its mission of saving souls.

Giving large amounts of wealth through forcible taxation to it makes no sense, but there are other things that can be given to it that make a great deal of sense.

The state should not tax people and give the money to the church, except to fulfill basic needs if those needs are not being met by others, but the state should protect the church's property and not violate it. If the church acquires property through donations from people, the state should respect its rights over that property, even if it accumulates large amounts of it, like as occurred in Catholic countries in past times that led to popular revolts and the redistribution of property. The state doesn't have the right to violate the property of people, whether we are speaking of the church or anyone, unless one of the higher priorities was threatened.

If the church acquires a massive amount of land, property and wealth in a country through centuries of free donations by people, then the state should not interfere with it. They should be allowed to freely keep that which they received, which was freely donated to them. Christ controls His church and His Spirit will move the church to decide itself when it is right to use its wealth to help the society in general.

The voice of the church is a voice that all of society benefits from hearing. The state would do well to make sure that its ability to speak and publish in society is protected.

The presence or lack of virtue is the thing that will make the state to thrive or make it fail. It will allow the people to live freely or it will force people to be controlled. The church has graces and gifts from God that will assist it to make the people more virtuous and therefore its mission should not be impeded by the state.

The church is the body of Christ, and it was given the Holy Spirit by Christ so that the Spirit would preserve His gospel intact and unblemished within the church for all time.

The church should not control the state, but the state should obey what is taught by the church.

The church does not have competency to pass opinions about technical questions, but it does have competency to pass opinions about moral questions. For that reason, its opinions should be requested by the state for all of its functions, since every function of the state will have moral dimensions to it.

The church does not have a role to say whether a particular law or policy will be effective or ineffective at reaching a particular goal, but it can say whether or not such a law or policy is morally valid.

The church does not have a role to judge which people have the best talents or expertise to fulfill different positions in the government from a technical perspective, however, it can offer an opinion about whether the actions of persons in public office or persons being considered for public office are moral or immoral.

The church should not control the government, but its opinions should be taken into account by the government when making decisions. It teaches the gospel, which the government should follow, just as all people should follow. The government should retain the ability to choose to listen to the advice from church authorities or not in the way it operates. Not all advice from church authorities about what should be done about particular questions will always be correct.

The state should recognize the truths about God and the truths about the church openly. The church should not run the state, but the state should operate in obedience to the gospel taught by the church and openly acknowledge this as such.

People should be allowed to believe whatever they wish to believe, but they must follow rules on censorship if rules on censorship are in fact needed for the society.
People should be allowed to follow other religions, but those religions are still subject to the rules on censorship if such rules are needed for society. If the activities, assemblies, publications, schools, etc. that exist are deemed harmful to society, the government can restrict them, but it cannot take away the right of people to believe in those religions. The church's opinion should be sought after for this kind of censorship just as it should be sought after for all kinds of censorship, in places where censorship is required.
Keep in mind that Moses, who was taught by God, commanded that all who tried to get the Israelites to worship other gods should have been put to death in

Israel.

It is better, of course, to give people freedom to follow other religions without any control or restriction on anything, because more freedom is better than less freedom. But if abuse is too great, controls become necessary.

The modern world tends to take a position of nominally supporting freedom of religion for all religions, while at the same time, suggesting that evil things done by people in the name of religion cannot be attributed to those religions and it is justifiable to stop them.

In other words, they would likely support Muslims being allowed to pray at mosques, but a Muslim who preached violence or terrorism at a mosque is not a 'real Muslim' according to many voices of authority in the modern church; thus if the state were to arrest them and stop this activity, it would not then be violating religious freedom, since it simply defines religious ideas that it rejects as not being truly part of religion. I think this is semantics, however, because in the end it is still ultimately no different in principle from the concept of forbidding religious practices when they are deemed harmful to society.

The Muslims who blow themselves up are doing it with an ideology that is infused and justified with their religious beliefs. They believe that God wants them to do what they do. Of course, they are wrong and like Paul, they misunderstand God's will when they carry out such violence against those made in His image, but actually all Muslims everywhere who think that God wants them to believe the Quran is His holy word, which they must follow to find salvation, are wrong and misunderstanding God's will as well. What exactly is it that makes one a 'true Islam' or a 'false Islam', when they are both actually incorrect? God may plant seeds in Islam but that doesn't mean the religion came from Him. Even radical Islam, even the terrorist ideologies; God's almighty Spirit can still find ways to plant seeds of Truth in their beliefs too, but that doesn't mean that their beliefs came from Him. If neither is walking on the correct path, how can one be called correct and the other incorrect?

The difference between them is that the vast overwhelming majority of Muslims in the world pose no serious direct problem for society's physical safety when they are allowed to freely practice their beliefs, while these radical ones do pose serious problems when they are allowed to freely disseminate or practice their beliefs. If one forbids the radical ones from employing their beliefs for preaching, teaching, publishing, etc. then one is effectively ordering that they cannot espouse their religious beliefs in public, cannot teach their religious beliefs in public, cannot publish their religious beliefs in public, cannot convert people to their religious beliefs, etc. If one just defines such people as not being the 'true Islam' and thus therefore justifying limiting their religious freedom, while maintaining the belief that one doesn't believe in the concept of the state interfering in people's religious freedom, I think one is simply just playing games with words. Since, in essence, it is ultimately a measure to limit people's religious freedom and the state is trying to control what religious ideas people follow when it defines a certain religious group as not being a true religion in order to justify its suppression.

Recognizing the freedom and rights to believe or not believe in a religion does not mean that the state is obliged to allow people to practice, preach or spread that religion any way that they choose. Moses put idolaters and people who followed other gods to death, but actually if they never went to craft an idol, never espoused their beliefs to others and simply just held their beliefs privately, there was no punishment for them under the laws of Moses. Moses didn't actually prevent them from believing in other gods by the punishments he enacted, but people were only to be put to death when they went out and did something that was seen or heard by others that showed they worshipped other gods.

The church of the Middle Ages never punished people for heresy either. It only punished people who openly espoused their heresy, were heard by others and had the potential of influencing people by their wrong ideas. A heretic who was closeted and never revealed anything to people about his beliefs was never in danger of the Inquisition.

Today, even in the age of a belief in universal freedom of religion, we still ultimately tend to believe that spreading or preaching of certain religious teachings should be outlawed, even if the dominant narrative in society has tried to construct itself to suggest otherwise. The past and the present are not really so different from each other, it is just we have taken the line and redrawn it to provide much more liberty than existed in the past, but the line between what is acceptable and unacceptable is still there, and we haven't actually embraced a belief that people are free to confess any religious teaching as they wish.

Thus, to say that people should have freedom to follow the religion they choose and to say that the state has a right to restrict religious activities is not a contradiction. Like all things, however, there is a correct way to use such measures and incorrect way to use such measures.

The state ought to allow people as much freedom as possible in religious matters. However, if abuses are happening that are dangerous to society, because people are abusing their freedom to do the wrong thing, it has a right to impose limits on people. It has a right to control what is preached. It has a right to control what is published. It has a right to control whether houses of worship should be allowed to exist or not. It has a right to control whether people are allowed to openly confess the things they believe or not. It doesn't have a right to control what they actually do believe, because that is what goes on in their hearts.

Many states in the past and present make decisions that abuse their privilege to make such choices about what is or is not harmful to society about religious matters, but that doesn't mean that states don't have the right to make such decisions.

They should use such power to eliminate abuses, when those abuses are too great. But if people can be trusted to do the right thing, they should be allowed to be free in what they choose to do. If religious bodies are espousing violence or harm to society, then it is right to take away their rights to engage in religious activities or to influence others.

If they are simply just espousing ideas that might tempt people away from the Truth, the amount of control they should be subject to is dependent upon the virtue of the populace. If the people are going to resist the temptation by their own free will, then it is better to let them preach the false ideas as much as they wish. However, if the people are too sinful and faithless towards the true God and His church, removing the temptation by inserting controls on their activities and influence can be justified as well.

Doing so is not a violation of the right to choose one's own religion. It is not a violation of religious liberty to remove the threat in society to the spiritual souls of people by suppressing certain religious activities anymore than it is a violation of religious liberty to remove the threat in society to the physical bodies of people by suppressing certain religious activities.

There is nothing wrong with the state privileging the church in this fashion in order to suppress the rights of other religions and give greater rights to the church.
The ideal remains, however, to have as much freedom as possible in matters of religions, where it is possible.

Those under the church's immediate hierarchical discipline, particularly bishops, priests, deacons, monks and nuns, should be subject to the civil law, just as the rest of society is, and just as Christ Himself was subject to the civil law and regarded Pilate as possessing authority over Him that had been given from above.
Those who are under the church's immediate discipline should generally not be subject to state laws concerning censorship, however. They should be permitted to speak and publish as freely as they wish. If they say something

wrong, then the church authority itself should deal with them.

The church does not have a right to call on the state to punish its own members for violating church discipline in some fashion, unless the civil law itself includes these actions as crimes. If they violate church discipline, but the civil law isn't broken, then the church has the right to excommunicate them or to deny them the sacraments or any other similar penalty, but it does not have the right to call on the state to use civil penalties on them.

The state should not intervene in the internal affairs of the church, except when it regards things that are not part of the church's competency. It should not choose who the bishops or priests should be, but it can make rules and regulations regarding the building code of the church building, to make it safe for fires or other hazards.
In church history, the first eight ecumenical councils of the church were convened by the political authority of the Roman/Byzantine emperors. I think this is a mistake. The church should have a right to call or cancel meetings at its own discretion, without the intervention of the state.

The state should not assume that people who follow the church are good and those who do not follow the church are not good. The difference between virtue and vice in an individual is not necessarily equivalent to their religious choices.
The state may discriminate on the basis of religion when engaged in certain general policies, such as taxation, which

I will get to in the next chapter.

Lord, we pray that you help us to better understand the role that the church ought to have in political states. We pray that you help political states to have relations with the Catholic Church as they ought to have in accordance with your will. We ask for these things, if it is your will, in Jesus' name, Amen

XIX: Taxation

An ideal state does not need taxes, because people would not need to be compelled in order to do what they ought to do. If people were virtuous, they would donate their money voluntarily to every cause that required it and there would never be a need for a central authority to force them to give up their money to pay for the things that the state must pay for in order for the society to work. Government exists because of sin, and taxes also exist because of sin.
If taxes exist as a result of sin, it makes sense to put taxes on the things that are sinful, so that those who in society are causing the need for taxes to exist in the first place will also be the ones to carry its burden.

Most states in history typically collect taxes according to where they see money accumulated in society and where they see that taxing such money would not have too adverse effects. States in the modern-day tax income, property, profits, sales, inheritance, etc.
When states tax these things, they are ultimately discouraging people from making incomes, holding properties, making profits, passing on inheritances or engaging in buying or selling. However, these activities are not wrong in themselves, and I would argue that there are better ways to collect revenue.

The state should align its taxes, as far as it is possible, in such a way that the things they are taxing are also the behaviours that they wish to discourage.

There may be many things that are moral vices, but for which the state doesn't want to use a hard punishment like an arrest or even a fine to put a stop to, because such methods would not be pragmatic. In such cases, putting taxes on the practice of these vices is a logical thing to do, because it will earn revenue for the state on the one hand and it will discourage the practice of these things on the other.

For example, although artificial contraception is against the law of God, if the state were to forbid using it and outlaw it entirely, the negative effects that this could produce might be much worse than the actual sin of people engaging in sexual activity that is cut off from life. Outlawing condoms could lead to the spread of sexually transmitted infections and ultimately the death of many people.

In the law of Moses, Moses allowed for the Israelites to divorce their wives, even though this was against the divine law. Moses did this according to God's instruction to him.

The reason for this law was perhaps because the negative consequences of outlawing divorce may have been worse in that time and place than if the sinful practice was allowed. Men might have simply just secretly arranged for their wives to be killed, or perhaps even openly arrange for it by making accusations of adultery against them to have them killed. Whereas just allowing them to divorce is the pragmatic choice.

Artificial contraception would be sinful, as would divorce, but choosing to legalize either one in the society may be a pragmatic choice as far as the state is concerned. However, the state can still discourage either one by applying taxes to them. For example, if the state obligated a divorcing couple to give a portion of their assets that are dividing between themselves to the state in order to pay a tax that will itself be a kind of payment to the country for the harm that divorce does to society.

The state can thus earn revenue being paid to it by the sinful people who lack virtue and who are in fact creating the need for social control in the first place.

I'll write more about artificial contraception, divorce and pragmatism later below.

There may be things that are not moral vices in themselves, but when abused to a certain extent they become moral vices. In society, if the state finds that too many are abusing something too much, the state would be wise to put taxes on this as well, in order to both raise revenue and to discourage the behaviour.

For example, alcohol and tobacco in themselves are not sinful to be consumed, but there are far too many people in the world who consume either one to the extent of damaging their own health, which is an abuse of these things. For that reason, it is logical for the state to put taxes on those things.

One hundred years ago, around the time that women began to get the vote, feminist movements that were often tied to churches advocated for the prohibition of alcohol in society, because there were so many social problems coming from it. Husbands were getting drunk very often and engaging in domestic abuse, wasting their family's income, etc.

If people cannot responsibly use the freedom to drink alcohol, then they should not have that freedom. There was nothing wrong with the mindset that went into the cause of prohibition.

However, the black market was huge and far too many people in society simply just didn't respect these laws and continued to engage in drinking.

The movement was a failure and alcohol became legalized again after a short period.

If the state wished, it could have simply raised the amount of force it was using in order to put an end to the practice, but that wasn't seen as pragmatic. The women in these movements wanted their husbands to stop drinking, but they didn't want their husbands thrown in prison.

Islam prohibits alcohol to Muslims and many Islamic countries ban the consumption of alcohol in their borders. There is nothing wrong with drinking alcohol, but there is something wrong with drinking it irresponsibly. If people can't be trusted to drink responsibly, then they shouldn't be allowed to drink at all. A virtuous people should have this freedom, but a people without virtue should not have it.

However, if you have a society without virtue and you find that enforcing the rules to prevent them from having alcohol will only create more problems than it solves, pragmatism would dictate that it be legalized.

Although you legalize it, you can still discourage it through taxes or similar means.

There are many things that are not wrong in themselves, but which people abuse far too much.

People may spend far too much time playing games, surfing the internet, watching their phones, watching tv, etc.

There is nothing wrong with these things in themselves, but when people abuse these things in an unhealthy manner, it makes sense for the state to put taxes on these things.

There are many kinds of foods that people abuse by eating too much of it and creating health problems in society. It makes sense for the state to tax these things too.

In the modern-day, there are huge environmental problems being rooted in far too much human consumption. People take far too much from the Earth. For that reason, it makes sense for the state to put taxes on all those kinds of consumption which are leading to environmental problems as well.

Taxes will serve to discourage behaviours as well as to raise revenue. If people are simply taxed just because they get a paycheque, what is the point of this? Does it serve society better to discourage people from getting paycheques? The tax system should be aligned as much as possible in such a way that the things being taxed are also the things that the society would benefit from if people did these behaviours less, because taxes invariably discourage the behaviours that they are taxing.

In some countries, they tax the income of people above a certain bracket, but they allow people to get a credit on their taxes if they give money to charities. This is a very logical practice.
The church teaches that you should keep as much money as you need for you and your family to live in dignity.

Anything more than this, you ought to use in order to help your society.

Therefore, it makes a lot of sense if the state were to set income taxes on people such that you determined how much money in a given place that people would need in order to be financially secure for now and in the future, and then you made that amount to be the threshold that had to be crossed over before you began putting income taxes on them. And then if the people who do earn more than what they need to live in dignity do not take this money to help the society, you can then apply taxes to their income to bring revenue to the state.

It is sinful people who give reason for the need for states and governments to exist in the first place; therefore, it makes sense to make them to be the ones who must pay for its finances.

It is a sinful practice to have excess wealth that you are not using to help other people with and which you do not need yourself. If you apply taxes to such people, you are discouraging something that ought to be discouraged. Giving them the option to get a credit on their taxes by donating to charity, so that they can even avoid paying any taxes at all if they are benefitting the society with their wealth, would then be ensuring that those who are acting virtuously would not need to be taxed.

I wouldn't argue the same logic for corporate profits, since corporate profits are not the same as personal income. However, I would argue the same logic for individuals who earn their income from corporate profits through any means.

You can never actually judge whether a particular person who is watching so much tv or who is making so much money and not giving to charity is actually sinning or not. Only God alone will ever know that. However, the trends that you see in society can be judged as either good or bad, and the state has a duty to apply methods to discourage the trends that it sees as being bad.

For that reason, I would also argue that it makes sense to apply taxes to individuals who are not Catholic.
If the church exists in the society and people are free to enter it, but they don't enter it, this is because sin is present. It is likely both the sins of those in the church and those outside of it that is present, and it is impossible to know which particular individuals are refusing to join the church because they are obstinate and sinful, and which individuals are refusing to join the church because of innocent ignorance.
However, it is something that ought to be discouraged, and for that reason it does make sense for the state to apply taxes to people that are outside of the church. Applying such taxes will encourage many to think about joining the church.
This is not the right reason to get people to join the church, however, people who come to the church for the wrong reason at the beginning might eventually come to believe in their heart over time and the church itself furthermore has the responsibility to discern who it can appropriately baptize or not. Christ attracted great crowds by His healings, by His division of the loaves and the giving of free bread, by His gift of God's power to people who wanted help... but getting bread for the stomach or healing

of the flesh were never the reasons for why people should have become His disciples.

Catholic states in past times did things like this to Jews or others that lived within their borders that were not of the faith. Muslims did this kind of practice with Christians and Jews.
Historically, this practice was extremely effective in many parts of the world at getting masses of people to slowly convert to the religion of their political leaders. There are countries today that perhaps would never have become Christian or Muslim if this sort of practice wasn't used.

Sinful people are giving rise to the need for states and it is sinful for people to refuse to believe in Christ, when they were given sufficient reason to know that He was God.

I don't propose that simply not being a Catholic should mean that you must pay money. Because what if a person had no income or was unable to pay such a tax without harming their economic needs of their family?
However, what would be right is if people who had incomes above a particular threshold (like the one I defined above) had to pay a special tax if they were not counted among the members of the church.

Lord, we pray that you help us to understand how taxation should be used by states in your plans for the world. We pray that you help governments to assign taxes as they ought to do so and not as they shouldn't do so. We ask for these things, if it is your will, in Jesus' name, Amen

XX: Censorship

Society achieves more when it has more freedom, however, freedom can only be trusted to those who will not abuse it.
It would be better to have a society with no controls over what people say or what they publish, however, such freedom is not suitable to every society, because the populace might lack the virtue that is needed to use this kind of freedom responsibly.

There is no society in the world that has complete lack of control over speech and publication. Countries with 'freedom of speech' still may make it illegal for broadcasters to purposely falsify news or to defame people. They might make hate speech or death threats into banned forms of communication between persons. They may have laws that ban or restrict pornography.
It would be better if the state had no laws at all and that the state didn't even exist, and the people themselves could simply be trusted to always do the right thing. But because people are sinful and they don't do the right thing, society needs to control people in order for society to continue functioning.

Now, virtue among the people is the most important thing for the state to possess. Possessing it will make the difference between whether the state can be free or whether it must be controlled. It will make the difference between whether society is healthy or unhealthy, whether the civilization will continue or whether it will fall. It marks the difference of life and death for human society.

Salvation of souls is also the highest of all priorities, and virtue is going to be what leads people to find salvation or not.

The state does not have a magic wand that it can pass over people to make them go from bad to good. The church is the institution that has the most powerful tools available to it to accomplish the redemption of souls and the state should encourage its mission.
The state has no power to make people change their hearts and repent, but the state does have the power to remove temptations from society that may cause people to lose virtue and fall into vice.
The things that have the power of mass influence over public society are also the things that often provide some of the greatest temptations to a public society.
The media and the education system especially carry a massive influence over the minds of the citizenry. It is in the power of the state to interfere with either one to make sure that that influence does not cause the citizenry to fall into sin and lose themselves to damnation.
The things presented in the media or the education system can create temptations that will lead people to eternal hellfire and can make people lose their virtue, leading to the ruin of the state.
Christ in the gospel spoke about children and said 'whoever causes one of these little ones to sin, it would be better for a millstone to be tied to his neck and he be thrown into the sea'
These words of Christ can well be applied to education systems that influence children so as to cause them to develop vices and lose their innocence.

The greatest joy in heaven is when a sinner becomes a saint. The greatest sadness in heaven is when those who were once innocent are lost into sin.

If the society is virtuous enough, then the state does not need to interfere in this way and it can trust people to run schools or to create media in a way that is responsible and will not ruin the society.

However, if the society is not virtuous enough and these institutions cannot be trusted like this, the state has a responsibility to use its power to step in and remove the temptation.

In that case it should try to control what is taught in schools so that students are not taught things that will lead them to hellfire and it should try to control what is published in various forms of media so that those things do not lead the society to damnation.

The role of the church is important in this, because it possesses the authority to teach the gospel and the Spirit preserves the correct teaching on morality within the church. If the state needs to enact controls over the education system or the media for these reasons, the church should be invited to offer its opinion to help the state in carrying this out.

If possible, the church can even be given the power to actively run such programs. For example, the state can make it such that no one can run an institution of education or publish any form of media without getting a licence that is provided by the church, and which the church has the ability to revoke if it finds that its instructions regarding morality are not followed. If the church needs financial help to run such a program, it could also be given the power to charge a fee for the issuance of these licenses.

Other things that have the ability to have mass influence can also be subject to state supervision if in fact those who run these things cannot be trusted to act responsibly. Large-scale public events, for example, can be made such that they require state permission to be held.

With regard to religious organizations that influence masses, the issue becomes much more delicate and the principle of pragmatism has to enter the picture.
Anatoly Lunacharsky was a high-ranking Soviet commissar that dealt with religion in the administration of Lenin and Stalin. He said that religion is like a nail and that the harder that you hit it, the more deeply that it goes in.
While religious bodies can be a great temptation upon people, because they deceive people into thinking that there is another truth than the Truth as it is taught in the Catholic church, subjecting them to control and shutting them down for non-compliance may not produce favourable results. People may hold onto the false beliefs even more strongly than before when they are subject to persecution.

The same to an extant is also true of other bodies, including media, education and public events, but it is not typically as strongly so as it is with regard to religion.
If using laws and restrictions can effectively control all of these things, and such controls are needed because of a lack of public virtue, then the state would be right to use

such laws and restrictions. But if using laws and restrictions does not effectively control these things, or it effectively controls some things and not others (like it has the power to shut down schools and this power is effective, but trying the same with religious bodies will be met with great resistance), then it needs to think of other strategies for how to deal with these things, if indeed these things are providing a threat to public morality.

The state needs to use the methods that will work and if it is found that suppressing something to get people to stop being influenced by it is going to have the opposite effect, then the state needs to use other strategies to counter these things than suppression.
The state should use its power to remove temptations from society that will lead people to sin, however, it must be pragmatic in doing so and realize that force does not always produce the most favourable of results to this end. Other methods can be employed, such as financial means. The state, for example, can provide funding to educational institutions, artists of various kinds that influence many people, religious bodies, etc. and make the funding conditional upon compliance with certain rules that the state gives to them in order to protect public morality.

What about individual freedom to speak?
Again, it is an issue of both virtue and pragmatism.
Individuals that do not influence the masses are not as significant as media or educational institutions, hence even if they do have bad opinions or words that will influence people in the wrong way, they are not as serious an issue

as those other things are.

There are some things that people can speak even on an individual basis that can seriously disrupt public order. Death threats, threats of terrorism or violence against people, inventing false emergencies and creating panic, lying under oath, etc. are forms of speech that the state should outlaw unless the society really is virtuous enough that it can be trusted not to abuse speech like this.

If there are very serious issues with public morality, the state can pass laws that take away individuals' freedom to say certain things that will tempt others to do things that wrong.

In past times, the church possessed the institution of the Inquisition which used the power of courts and jails to punish people who spread heresy.

Generally, if the media and education systems are already controlled, control of individual speech may not be necessary. However, there may be situations where it could be necessary even for such great control as to pass laws limiting personal freedom to speak.

Again, if the state deems it necessary to protect public morality by restricting individual speech, it should nevertheless invite the church to pass its opinions about what should or should not be allowed in this.

If the state does choose to restrict individual speech, it must do so in a very clear manner. In other words, it should set down clearly what things can be said and what things cannot be said. It should not leave the definition of what constitutes legal or illegal speech ambiguous so that it has the power to prosecute whomever it wishes. People in those circumstances should be given a clear awareness beforehand.

Similarly, with regard to censorship of media, educational institutions or other things that influence the masses, it should not arbitrarily punish anyone. If something is found to be unacceptable, it should give an order for such a thing to stop and only deal out punishments when people who have received this order choose to defy it. It should never punish people who were unaware that what they were doing was illegal because they had never been given an order.

In cases where public security is under a serious threat, because of a risk of civil war, foreign invasion or public violence, the state should consider to use censorship or limitations on personal speech if such is necessary to avoid influences spreading in society that might damage state security.

For example, if there is a movement in a society that wants to overthrow the government or which wants to destroy some ethnic group, and there is a serious risk that this movement can create great social disorder, the state should consider forbidding the propaganda of this movement from being circulated and banning public displays of approval for it.

These kinds of laws, however, should not be used to safeguard the selfish interests of leaders in the state. If the state has things to be ashamed of, the state should openly confess and apologize for these things, rather than to use censorship to block the knowledge of such things from spreading. If the state wants to promote public morality, then it must take this course, because this act of public repentance will set an example for the society to follow. If the state does evil, never admits to it, hides it and suppresses those who spread the knowledge of it, it is only serving the cause of weakening public morality when it does this, because it will set a bad example for people to follow and make them believe that moral laws do not need to be abided by.

Lord, we pray that censorship in states will be carried out as it ought to be and not as it shouldn't be. We pray that societies will be protected from the temptations that lead souls to ruin. We ask for these things, if it is your will, in Jesus' name, Amen

XXI: Principle of Subsidiarity

One of the key principles in Catholic social teaching is the principle of subsidiarity. This is a doctrine that the church teaches about how societies should be organized.
In short, the principle means that decisions that can be made by lower levels of a system ought to be left to lower levels, rather than higher levels taking over the decisions themselves.
For example, if you had a school system, with many schools over a wide area, the principle of subsidiarity would state that individual teachers should be allowed to decide their own ways to teach students, rather than the centralized system telling them how to do so. Since the teacher will understand their own students better than a person in an office far away, and they will have a better idea of what things will work or won't work for their own particular situation. But if the centralized body dictated to them how to do everything, it will never take into account all the various complexities that are present in each individual situation for each classroom, and its rules will work in some places and produce disasters in others.
Or another example, if you had an army that was fighting a battle, the principle of subsidiarity would leave lower-level officers and individual soldiers with the power to decide when to take the initiative to do things that are not included in their orders, rather than doing everything according to a centralized command. This is because the general is not going to see everything going on in each particular situation and will not be able to quickly give an order to a smaller unit to tell it whether it is OK or not OK to take a particular initiative when the unit sees the

opportunity. But if the general said that nothing should move or engage at any time except according to centralized command, the army is not going to fight as effectively and many opportunities when they could destroy enemy forces will be lost on account of the need to follow centralized orders alone.

The principle can be applied to any organization and it can be applied to societies and states as well.

The principle of subsidiarity would dictate that governments should only be called upon to do things and make decisions on things when lower levels of society are incapable of making these decisions or doing these things. For example, when people choose who to marry or where to live, this decision should be left to the individual himself. The government should not be deciding for the person about who they would be the best match with or where to live would be most appropriate for them. The government is not going to understand the person's particular circumstances and wishes better than the person himself, and there is no need for the government to take the power of decision-making out of the individual's hands and put it in the control of a centralized authority.

Companies should be allowed to choose what products they are going to produce according to what they see the market demand is, rather than the government giving them a quota for how much of something they should make. Charitable organizations should be allowed to choose who and when to help, rather than the government instructing them how to do so.

Now, as I wrote before, if people were perfectly virtuous,

government would not even be necessary. However, the vices of people require them to be controlled in order for society to live together in relative peace.

How much control they need to be given is dependent upon how much virtue or vice is present in the society. Decisions that can be made at the lower levels should be left to the lower levels. However, the truth is that all decisions can be made at the lower levels if people were simply honest, reasonable and virtuous.

You wouldn't need, for example, a government mandate to decide how to build transportation routes in the country, because all the communities would just peacefully and logically work out together how they would like these routes to go without any selfish prejudices clouding their thinking and freely contribute their collective resources to accomplish the project.

Another example: you wouldn't need the government to maintain a standing army, because each community could freely coordinate with each other to set up such an army if it was needed to defend the society, and they would reasonably discuss with one another about what was needed and they would reason together to freely set up the army in some way that was just as effective as any state's, without the need for a central authority to dictate orders to them or collect taxes from them.

There are no decisions done by states that couldn't be managed on lower levels if the lower levels worked together freely, in a reasonable and virtuous manner.

The reality, however, is that there is no society that is wholly reasonable, wholly honest and wholly virtuous. In any given democratic state, where freedom of the citizens tends to be high, you will still find great arguments and divisions among people who cannot agree with each other about what is true and what is false, what is needed and what is not needed, etc. And the only way that the society can effectively function is if people agree to let go of their own ability to make decisions and give that power to elected representatives who will decide for them.

Truth is not subjective; Truth is objective. People having great disagreements over political issues is not because there are two or more different equally valid and correct viewpoints to every issue, but it is because people put their own interests first and want politics to work in their favour. If people were objectively and sincerely seeking the Truth, once they learned enough, they would always come to the same answer and there would be no disagreements between people. In heaven, there are no contradictory opinions.

If people sincerely sought the Truth, they would find it. Contradiction of opinion and ideology in democratic states comes from sin.

People can be wrong about many things, because they lack sufficient information and not because they had bad morals. Although this also ultimately has its roots from sin, often because the educational institutions, their peers, their parents, the media or the leaders are not giving the accurate Truth to people, because the Truth does not correspond with what they would like people to believe. The original principle I wrote remains true. If society was perfectly virtuous, the state would never have been needed, because people would freely and voluntarily choose to do what was needed to be done, without the

need for a higher order directing them.
It is just as is written in the prophets in the Old Testament when speaking about the law of God. No one will need to tell anyone any longer 'know the Lord', because all will know. The law will not need to be written on stone any longer, but it will be written on the heart. There is no government or law in the kingdom of Jesus Christ. In his kingdom, people will do everything that they ought to do without anyone ever needing to tell them what to do.
The Holy Spirit speaks to people by suggestion and not by command. The world was never meant to have authorities that rule over one another. The world could have structures and organizations to make people operate more efficiently, but none of these things would require 'control' if people of the world were perfect, for all would voluntarily agree to do what ought to be done without any compulsion.

Control exists because of sin. People must control one another, taking away their freedom, because people will abuse it otherwise. Human sin creates human slavery. Christ sets people free when He brings them to repent.

Now, the principle of subsidiarity is that decisions that are appropriate to the lower level should be left to the lower level. I have just said, however, that government would not need to have the power to make any decision at all, if the society was perfectly virtuous.
Therefore, the principle of subsidiarity in the context of the political state has to be understood that government needs to take control of the issues that the lower levels are failing to take control of, or which because of disagreement or

unwillingness of people to cooperate, the lower levels are unable to take care of.

In almost all societies this will include things like giving national governments control of foreign policy and the decision of going to war.

There are many societies in past times where the power of the state was less centralized than today and monarchs allowed for local leaders to raise their own armies (which the monarch would call upon for help in time of war), issue their own edicts for those who lived under them, jail or execute criminals in their territories according to their own subjective laws, as well as other things that most states today would reserve to a national authority.

According to the principle of subsidiarity, if these things can be delegated to lower levels and still be effective, then it is better to do this than to reserve them to the level of the national state.

However, in the modern world, there are many situations where they would not be able to do this effectively. In the Middle Ages, it was not so difficult for private individuals or small groups of people to own horses and armour as well as to train as knights. In the modern age, aircraft carriers, tank battalions, nuclear weapons, etc. are difficult to organize effectively on a private basis without state control.

Transportation routes, whether by land, sea or air, usually require government management in the modern-day. Certain infrastructure that is critical to the country's economy also often requires government management, if not outright ownership, to ensure it stays functioning properly.

In the modern world, many states have huge apparatuses for dealing with public welfare, especially including healthcare and education. Many states also have institutions and mechanisms designed to help seniors, help homeless, help the poor, help the unemployed, etc.

These programs essentially exist because people and organizations within society are unwilling to do what they ought to do in order to help their neighbour.

If people took care of the people in their own families, if people took care of their friends and the people who lived in their communities, the state wouldn't need to do any of these things.

For example, if you had a completely privatized education system where everyone paid tuition to enroll, you could still have universal education if people simply used their money freely to help out the poor of their society who couldn't reasonably afford it. But because people are not willing to do that, the state needs to create a free education system funded by tax dollars.

The same is true of healthcare. A completely privatized healthcare system without any state involvement, could deliver effective healthcare for everyone in the country if people simply were willing to help out those around them who couldn't afford it. But because people are not willing to do that, the state has to step in in order to make sure people have access to healthcare.

When the state funds these projects, however, what a lot of people don't fully understand is that it will always run these things more inefficiently than if it was left to the lower levels of society to run. They will ultimately end up losing more money through taxes to pay for these things and through a slower economy that such taxes cause, than they would lose if they had simply just spent the money to help their neighbours by their own choice.

People acting both on the individual level and acting within organizations that they set up themselves, could certainly solve all problems with people in society not having access to education or healthcare, they could certainly solve homelessness, or take care of the unemployed or refugees or anything else like this.

People won't do what they ought to do, however. We don't love our neighbours as we should. As a result, the problems are left unsolved and people look at the state and say that the government must step in to solve these social problems. And if people really are unwilling to solve these problems on their own, then the government will have a need to step in and make these decisions, rather than leave them to the lower levels.

Smaller government is better than big government. More freedom is better than more control. However, not every society will be able to have smaller government and more freedom, because of the lack of virtue of the people of the society.

The state should leave as many decisions out of its hands as it can, but there is a need for it to make decisions when things must be done that people are unwilling to do so themselves freely.

Lord, we pray that you help us to have a better understanding of the principle of subsidiarity. We pray that states may employ this principle in their territories according to your will. We ask for these things, if it is your will, in Jesus' name, Amen

XXII: Laws on Sexual Conduct

The same principles apply to the gift of sexuality just as they do to all other things here. When people use it properly and do not abuse it, they should be given freedom. When they abuse it and use it to do evil, they must be treated with control. However, any laws passed regarding them should be done in accordance with the principle of pragmatism.

A lot of people have the mindset that sexual sins don't produce victims and they don't disturb society.
Privately done sexual acts that are out of the view of others could be argued to be things that only harm the person who does them, although he might think that they do not harm him at all.
However, sexual acts that are immoral and which are known to the public, will be a source of temptation to people and they will be destructive towards the virtue of the nation.
Canadian Prime Minister Pierre Trudeau said that the government had no place in the bedrooms of the nation and he thus legalized homosexual activity. The problem being ignored by this statement is that the things that remain in the bedroom don't remain locked away permanently in the bedroom; the knowledge of these things spreads over the whole society and influences everyone.
Aristotle said that those who have great influence, such as teachers, actors, leaders, etc. have a special responsibility upon themselves to make sure that they set a good example, so that they influence others to be good as well.

The truth is that we all influence one another, and our deeds, whether they be good or bad, are going to influence other people to also be good or bad. We all have the responsibility to set a good example to one another. Thus, when people commit sexual sins and the knowledge of it is spread, it does have an influence that hurts public morality.

When people commit sin, the state grows weaker. The state does a service to the people of the state when it uses its power to remove unnecessary temptations to sin.

Immoral sexual practices include all sexual practices other than that which occurs between a man and his wife in an act that isn't closed to creating new life. This includes a huge number of things.

Even Moses didn't outlaw all of these things, because he did not have any laws against masturbation or against divorce or remarriage. Jesus in the gospel said that when people lust after another in their heart, that they already commit adultery and that marrying a divorced person is adultery as well.

Moses's laws and Jesus's gospel both came from the same God. However, the laws of Moses were laws of an actual political state and of an organized society, with actual legal punishments written down for those who violated them. The commandments of Jesus were for a kingdom that belonged to a higher nature.

The state should outlaw immoral sexual practices. If people do these practices privately such that no one ever discovers them, then they can escape legal punishment by the fact that they did them so privately that they didn't create a source of temptation for the society.

On the other hand, if they are discovered, then the mere fact that they are engaging in these practices is already enough to inspire temptation in others by their bad example. The state helps remove this temptation and threat to public virtue by punishing these people, so that others will not be tempted to follow their errant path.

Now, the issues of pragmatism have to be taken into account here as well.

Moses did not give the Israelites a law against divorce, because of their hardness of heart. Perhaps if Moses told them they could not have divorce they would have simply resorted to secretly murdering their spouses when they wanted to remarry. Pragmatism would dictate that allowing divorce would then be the better option in that environment.

Contraception is similar to this. If contraceptives are not permitted in society, even worse evils can result than those that result from people sinfully using them. The spread of diseases, including deadly diseases is one of the most serious of these evils. The state would be good to discourage the use of contraceptives through influencing the public in the education system and the media, but it may not be wise to actually outlaw them, unless the chances of people spreading diseases by their lack of use was no longer a factor.

But penalties should be given to those who violate sexual ethics and are discovered for it. As long as people are not going to be murdered because people can't legally separate, and no other serious life-threatening

consequences are going to result, the state should not
legalize remarriage. If medical science could advance to
the point that sexually transmitted diseases were no longer
a threat, the state should also outlaw contraceptives.
Masturbation, pornography, sex outside of marriage, etc.
should all be punished, so long as pragmatism is respected
and outlawing these things is not simply just going to
create even greater evils.

Legal punishments, however, should also come hand in
hand with education. The media and the education system
have a role to play to make sure that people are influenced
the right way as well. This is why censorship is needed for
places where people can't be trusted to use this kind of
freedom in a way that won't destroy their own society by
sin.

The sexual revolution that occurred in the 20th century was
preceded by a long period of time when artists, writers,
movie makers, musicians, etc. all helped 'break barriers'
for human sexuality by allowing for their art and their
media to ever more suggestively give the idea to people
that the conservative voices that told people to keep their
virtue were wrong and belonged to a different time, and
that these practices had nothing wrong with them, but
were in fact good and beautiful things.

If the society is virtuous enough that it can be trusted on
its own to uphold sexual ethics, then like all things, no such
legal restrictions are required. If people, through shame or
conscience, are going to keep the public morality strong
with regard to sexual ethics, then the state should not
attempt to do anything about these things.

Divorce should be not legalized, unless pragmatism dictates that it should as I wrote above, but there should not be any laws that prevent people from separating. They can be allowed to separate, but they must remain married in the eyes of the law and cannot be remarried afterwards. The church does not recognize any marriages outside of the church to be valid. This is not because marriages outside the church are all invalid, but it is just for the purposes of church canon law, all marriages outside the church are not recognized to be valid or invalid until the person actually becomes a Catholic.

The state, however, must pass an opinion on all marriages if it needs to pass laws concerning public sexuality. It must discern whether or not a marriage constitutes a true marriage according to the appropriate criteria and act accordingly.

What constitutes a true marriage?

1) A male and female couple that are not closely related
2) Who willingly choose to enter into a nuptial union without compulsion by others
3) Who intend to remain true to one another until death, to the exclusion of others
4) Who are open to having children with one another through their marriage and are capable of intercourse
5) Who properly understand what they are entering into
6) Who are not already bound by some prior marriage they had before

The church does not allow Catholics to marry who don't fulfill these requirements. These requirements are not from the church, however, but they come from God and natural law. All marriages everywhere are true marriages or not on the basis of these criteria.

If the state needs to legislate on sexual ethics, then it needs to have a system where it recognizes marriages to be true or false.

There is no one right way to have such a system. Many states require marriages to be registered with the state at a public office of some sort, but this isn't strictly required. The state should respect the local customs of different cultures within the state for how they choose to make marriages publicly known.

Now many people find themselves as victims in abusive marriages. This is usually truer of women than it is of men, but it can occur to either sex. They should be allowed to separate, but not to divorce and remarry. If their marriage was a true marriage, then it remains a true marriage until they die, regardless of anything said by any human authority. The state doesn't possess the authority in itself to declare a valid marriage to be dissolved, hence it should not recognize legal divorce.

Many people might find it hard to separate, however, from a person they are invalidly married with because of economic dependence, social pressures or other things. Taking into account what I already wrote regarding the principle of subsidiarity, it would be better if the state didn't involve itself with these things and that the lower levels of society were left to help the people in these difficult situations. However, if the family, the community, the people in that place, are not willing to take up the burden to be a neighbour to the person suffering in their midst, the state will have to intervene in some fashion and use laws to protect people, as well as to help them to separate from someone who they are not validly married with and not face adverse economic or social consequences while doing so.

Many people will feel like they may need to remarry, because they need someone to help take care of their children or to help them economically. Again, this is something that the local community, the family, the friends, etc. should be helping them with. When a woman has to leave her husband because of abuse and she needs help with raising her children or keeping herself economically stable, the people around her ought to lend a helping hand. She does not need to be in a relationship with a man in order for men to be part of her child's life and help raise the child as male role models.
However, if people are unwilling to help one another like this, then the state ought to intervene and make sure that she has what she needs to raise her child, to be economically stable, etc. Women who are raising children should not be obligated to work at full-time jobs outside of their homes. If a woman has no one to help her, then the state should help her and provide her all that she needs without the need for her to enter full-time employment outside of her home. But the state should not allow her to remarry if the first marriage was in fact valid, so long as this ban on remarriage will not produce greater evils according to the priorities.

There are some sexual minorities that should also be mentioned here. Homosexuals, pedophiles, people who are sexually attracted to animals or other desires that seemingly can't be satisfied within a valid marriage, have to go through temptations that are much harsher than what most people have to deal with.

Their penalties for violating sexual ethics ought to be balanced to make them lighter than those of normal heterosexual attractions who were in fact able to lessen their temptations through a valid marriage.

People should not be thought of as being monsters because of their sexual attractions, whether it be to the same sex, to children, to animals or to anything else. They should be respected for who they are, but nevertheless taught that they should not act on these desires.

The media and the education have a part to play in this as well in order to help the public to accept, love and respect people who have such sexual dispositions, but nevertheless without abandoning the morality that teaches that sexual acts belong only to valid marriages and not to these things.

Gay pride would be acceptable if the sexualized element was removed and they were celebrating these people for who they are, but without condoning sexual sins.

With regard to modesty in dress, the principle of freedom in relation to virtue has to be kept here. If the public can be trusted to dress appropriately in public places without being immodest, then the state should not try to intervene in this.

If the public cannot be trusted in this fashion, the state needs to help remove the temptation. If it can remove the temptation through public education in the schools and media, and this causes the society to change, then this is a better option.

If that doesn't work, the state can pass laws regarding personal dress and outlawing various ways for people to dress in public that are going to be occasions of temptation and sin for others.

Revealing clothing belongs in the home, but conservative dress belongs in the public. There is nothing wrong with people dressing themselves up and revealing their bodies to their spouses and family members, but each thing in nature has its own proper place and that is the place to which it belongs. It does not belong to the entire world to see.

With regard to people who identify as transgender, the issue here is a complex one, and I refer to my book *LGBT and Catholic Doctrine* to explain more fully many of the complexities involved with it.

The fundamental issue at the core is the question of whether or not God does create people who are seemingly possessing the bodies of the opposite sex than the gender He has given them.

I believe that He may, although I could be wrong. In the book, I argued that God does not create people to be homosexual, and thus if a person has a homosexual inclination from their own biological nature itself as given them by God and not from some kind of psychological confusion, then the end conclusion has to be that the

person is actually a member of the opposite sex, otherwise
it would mean that God created the person gay.
States today do not have the resources to determine if
someone is neurologically designed to be attracted to
women or to men. However, if there was a way to
determine it, and what I argue was in fact true, it would
have profound implications for many things within the
state. For example, if a man was actually a female, because
he was designed to be attracted to males, the state could
not recognize a marriage between this man and a normal
heterosexual woman, because then that would be a
marriage between two women.
If such resources became available for states to determine
this and to find that a person's own nature caused them to
be homosexual, the state should recognize this person as
being a member of the opposite sex, albeit in a special
category.
What I am suggesting here, however, is something
completely different from transgenderism as people would
normally understand transgenderism that involves surgery,
hormones, dressing, etc.
A male who is designed by God for other men, would
ultimately be a woman, since God makes no one gay,
although that doesn't mean he would then have some sort
of requirement upon him that says that he should then act,
behave and live his life as a normal woman would. He
should be himself. The same is true for a female designed
for other women.
Keep in mind, that even if this were true, a man who was
actually a woman still could not marry a man who was a
man, even though it would be a heterosexual union,
because one of the requirements of a valid marriage is that

they are able to have intercourse.

With regard to transgenderism as people would normally understand it, however, the issue is that people need to accept the body and gender that they are given by nature. Transgender surgery is a kind of mutilation and it should be outlawed for that reason.

Transgender hormonal therapy is perhaps not mutilation, since the changes that the body is going through are natural changes in the body being stimulated by the hormones, but the therapy is said to be dangerous for health. If it was not dangerous for health, then perhaps it would be permissible for people to use, as long as it didn't adversely affect the lives of people and it wasn't related to a sinful rejection of one's own flesh.

Crossdressing can be sinful when it is publicly sexual, and in that case, the same things about lewd clothing that I wrote above would also apply to it. When it is not publicly sexual, it can still be sinful when it is needlessly offending people. It can also be sinful when it is related to a person's rejection of their own gender as God gave them. However, crossdressing in itself is not necessarily sinful if it is neither sexual nor scandalous.

In the case of transgendered people, the issue relates to the question of God's design for them. Did God intend for them and give them a nature that was designed to make them live their lives as the opposite from the gender they were seemingly born with?

I have to confess that I don't truly know the answer to that question, although I suspect the answer is no. However, I wouldn't assume that a person identifying as transgender and attempting to live in their transitioned sex is necessarily being sinful in what they are doing, because they might sincerely believe that this was not a rejection of themselves.

For that reason, I don't think the state should outlaw people attempting to live lives as the opposite sex, so long as the other things I wrote above are kept. That is to say, they should not use surgery or methods that will damage their health; they should keep the same rules of modesty in dress as are being kept by others in the sex they transition into. They cannot marry or have sexual relations with someone that they cannot have children with, etc.

The state should not recognize them as being members of the opposite sex, unless it was able to determine what I wrote above regarding people designed with a homosexual nature.

The state should protect them from harassment or discrimination, just as it should protect any minority of people from harassment or discrimination.

The state should use education and the media to influence the public in order to get it to uphold public morality concerning human sexuality. Ninety percent of the battle the state will need to fight on this issue is fought there, and not with actual legal punishments that are assigned to those who infringe public morality.

If the public can be convinced that sex outside of a legitimate marriage is wrong and feels shame over it, then no further laws would be necessary. If the public can be convinced that self-control in a marriage, rather than contraceptives, is something beautiful and noble, then the public morality will benefit from it.

The state should also encourage people to live celibate

lives for God as well. The media and the education system ought to present such lives in a positive light so that people will be influenced to follow this example.

Lord, we pray that states will use their laws and powers to govern human sexuality as they ought to do so and not as they shouldn't do so. We pray that people will receive the right influences in their lives and not the wrong ones. We ask for these things, if it is your will, in Jesus' name, Amen

XXIII: War

It is a sin to kill. However, states need to use violence in order to protect their people from those who would harm them.
States should always try to find other means to protect people than the use of violence. Violence should always be the last resort and never the immediate reaction. However, unless states acquire god-like abilities to protect their people always without risk of failure or the need to harm anyone, violence is still going to need to remain as a tool in the state's hand when the situation calls for it.
If states do not use violence to stop those who would harm their citizens, the state will collapse, anarchy will reign, and the people who do use violence will take power and become the new state. It is a necessity that even if one were to try to do away with it, the situation would simply just become worse.

Gandhi used non-violence to fight against British rule in India. But after India became independent, it retained armies and police forces that used violence to defend territory as well as to maintain social order. There is no state in history that has ever been able to throw away the tool of violence and remain standing.
Christ used non-violence to resist those who did evil, and He was part of the inspiration behind Gandhi (and Tolstoy, whom Gandhi also admired). However, Christ's kingdom was not a political kingdom. He did not intend to found a state that possessed an army or a police force. He intended to create a nation where government was no longer necessary at all, because the laws of the state would be

written upon the heart itself and no one would need to be told what to do, since all would do it freely.
As far as political states are concerned, they require violence in order to exist, without exception. Political states need to exist because people are sinful. Once they turn from their sins, the state itself also no longer needs to exist either. That is the kingdom that Christ is leading us to, but so long as we haven't reached it yet, political authority will need to exist in order for society to remain intact.

Violence is needed for states to exist. But, like all things, there is a correct way to use the tool of violence and an incorrect way.

Pope Pius XII wrote this regarding capital punishment:
" Even when it is a question of the execution of a condemned man, the State does not dispose of the individual's right to life. In this case it is reserved to the public power to deprive the condemned person of the **enjoyment** of life in expiation of his crime when, by his crime, he has already disposed himself of his right to live."
(from <u>The Moral Limits Of Medical Research And Treatment</u> – 1952)

When states use violence to protect society against those who would do harm to it, so long as there was no other option, then they are not truly killing people. They are simply just stopping people from killing more.
If there is an active shooter that is gunning down people, the police sniper that takes him out is not really killing him; rather the shooter has already disposed of his right to live (as Pius XII phrased it) and the sniper is just preventing him

from taking out any more lives than he has already.
When I say that he has disposed of his own life already,
what I mean is that he is the one who has caused it to be
so that in this situation he has to die in order for all those
innocent people he is targeting to continue living. He is the
one who has caused his own death and the police sniper is
just saving those who he hasn't yet taken by his wrong
action.

If the sniper doesn't kill him at that moment and he just
continues killing forever, someone is eventually going to kill
him. The sniper in that case is just making sure that that
inevitability happens now so that the number of lives lost
in the end will be fewer. Christ told Peter 'those who live
by the sword, shall perish by it'. Those who kill the
innocent are going to perish; that is an inevitability. The
state uses violence against such people to protect more
innocent from dying, and not really to take the life, since
the life of the killer was already doomed regardless of what
the state should do.

Violence is legitimate when it is being used to defend life.
When it is used to defend property, territory, honour or
anything else like this, it is not legitimate, unless life itself
depends on those things.

If a thief is driving away with your car, unless you are going
to die in poverty because you have no car, it would be
wrong to shoot him as he escapes. This is because human
life is more important than property and material
possessions.

Similarly, if an enemy army annexes and occupies territory
or if a rebel province declares its independence, but the
loss in territory poses no risk to the safety or life of anyone,

then it would be wrong to fight a war over this.

Frequently when enemy armies invade or when certain areas of a state declare independence, however, they do need to use violence to maintain their control. In that case, using violence to stop them could become legitimate, not for the sake of the land, but for the sake of defending the lives of the people who are going to be hurt by these enemy armies or rebel forces.

The only thing that could justify harming or taking a life is when there are lives at stake that are threatened with being harmed or being taken.

In Chinese history, the 'Warring States period' is sometimes looked upon as a reason why allowing places to become independent from a central authority is dangerous to society.

The Zhou dynasty ruled China in the 1st millennium BC, but its control grew weak over time. Local leaders in different places began emulating the ceremonies and practices of the Zhou Emperor themselves, because they themselves wanted to be monarchs in their own domains.

Gradually this evolved over time, until they lessened or stopped the tribute that they were meant to pay to the central authority, they built their own armies and organized their own territories as separate kingdoms. All of these local areas then separated into different states.

But once this happened, they then began warring with each other in order to gain territory from each other. And this descended into chaos as centuries of warfare between these states continued until the larger states swallowed up the smaller states, and eventually one state took over all the others and founded a new dynasty that ruled over all of China.

The lesson that is drawn from this episode in China's history is that the movement towards independence, even if peaceful at first, will lead to chaos and warfare. Therefore, China cannot allow for regions to become independent (for example, Taiwan or Hong Kong), because this is the starting point to the collapse of a central authority, social chaos and destruction.

However, there are several arguments against this conclusion that should be considered.

Firstly, if the existence of separate independent states equals to meaning that the world cannot be at peace, then the end conclusion is not only that a country should not allow territories to become independent, but it is actually that the world possessing more than one state upon it is something that ought to be avoided. In other words, not only should all of China be unified, but actually all the world should be unified by the same logic, and no independent nation should exist anywhere, since independence of nations means that they will fight wars between themselves.

Secondly, many nations have been independent and lived next to other nations without engaging in continual warfare between themselves. In the modern world since the end of World War Two, the vast majority of nations in the world have not fought armed conflicts with their neighbours. Thus, warfare is not an inevitability that comes from having independent states rather than a single unified state.

Thirdly, warfare is often needed to stop regions from becoming independent when there is a strong drive to become independent. If these local areas in the Zhou state sought to become independent and the Zhou state had stopped them, this could have also led to warfare and chaos as well.

However, there are counter points to consider too on this: To the first argument, this may be a reason for why a single unified state over the entire world would be beneficial, because it would put an end to the threat of warfare in the world that occurs between states. The lessons from the warring states period in China could be applied to the entire world to say why it is that having independent nations is something dangerous.
European history, for example, is filled with wars between separate states for most of its history. During the time of the Roman Empire, however, the people who lived within the borders of the empire didn't need to worry about warfare between their homelands and the homelands of other ethnic groups within the empire because of the security provided by a large state that ruled over so many different peoples and places. What makes China and Europe different, was that China's empire remained together and the result was the nation of China, while the Roman empire in Europe fell apart and the result was many centuries of warfare between rival European states. To the second argument, it is undoubtedly true that warfare is not an inevitability of the independence of states. It is also true that increased crime and wrongdoing is not an inevitability of granting people more freedom. If the people are virtuous, then they would not do wrong, even if the laws were not there to stop them. Similarly, if nations were virtuous, they would not be greedy and covet

one another's lands if they were in separate states. However, not all people are virtuous, nor are all nations virtuous. Thus, the principle of freedom and slavery would say that freedom is right in some conditions, but wrong in others. The disintegration of the Zhou state was an example of the latter, not of the former.

To the third argument, violence would perhaps be needed to stop independence, but it may have still been less violence than what was needed to fight in the wars that would result afterwards once states had become independent.

If it could be reasonably guaranteed that the independence of a region would not mean a future war would start between that region and another state, then warfare and violence should not be used to stop the region from becoming independent. To know the answer to this question of whether this would be the case, one must consider the virtue of the people.

The people of Zhou dynasty were obviously not virtuous enough to become independent from each other and maintain peaceful relations. However, the same lesson is not true in other places. The British empire granted independence to its colonies and in some cases, it did not result in warfare, while in some cases it did result in violence.

If Britain had ignored Gandhi's campaign and retained British rule in India and Pakistan, it would have perhaps saved the subcontinent from several wars, episodes of extreme violence between religious groups and might have even saved them from a possible future nuclear confrontation as well. If Britain had retained control of its

colonies in Africa, there are perhaps a number of civil wars
and episodes of violence in a number of those places that
would have never happened.
However, Britain's granting of independence to Canada,
Australia, New Zealand, the Caribbean islands, Papua New
Guinea, etc. did not result in warfare or violence for these
places. The independence of these places was quite
peaceful.

In fact, the principle that more freedom is superior to less
freedom, would dictate that it is better for regions to have
the freedom to separate and become independent if they
wished to do so.
However, freedom can only be granted to those who
would use it responsibly. If granting more freedom and
allowing more independence would result in greater
abuses occurring or even warfare resulting, then states
should not grant such freedom and independence.
There are many things that smaller states would not be
able to achieve unless they had cooperation from those
who lived outside their borders, and this is another
argument against breaking up states into smaller pieces,
but this argument is fallacious. A state that is broken into
two smaller states can still work together to create an
allied and integrated military to defend themselves from
larger threats, they don't necessarily need to enforce
border controls between themselves that limit trade or
traffic, they can make arrangements to fulfill all of the
things that were otherwise seemingly only possible when
they were together in a larger state. If they are responsible
and act virtuously, they can come to honest and fair
agreements to solve all of these things while remaining

independent.

The European Union is an excellent example of how states retain their independence and yet cooperate with each other in such a way that they can achieve many things that otherwise would have only been possible had they been unified into a single state.

However, in practice, many states will not act virtuously and they will choose to not cooperate with each other when they otherwise should have done so.

China threatens war over Taiwan if Taiwan were to declare its independence. This is not similar to the episode of the Zhou dynasty, however, because Taiwan is already effectively independent and it has been since 1949. Fighting a war to take back the island would not be a war to stop its independence, because that has effectively already happened a long time ago, but it would be a war of conquest and the assertion of a new political control that didn't exist before.

The arguments regarding the Warring States period are not relevant to this, because Taiwan right now is already capable of fighting a war with another state, since it is not under the control of the same government as the mainland and it has its own military forces. Threatening a war to stop it from making an official declaration of independence does not change this fact. In fact, there was a period in the early part of the Cold War, where the government in Taiwan was seriously considering launching a military invasion of the mainland to take advantage of instability and retake control of the country.

The freedom to become independent is better to be given

than not given, because more freedom is better than less. However, freedom can only be granted when it is not going to be greatly abused, and warfare, like that which occurred following the breakup of the Zhou dynasty, is an example of a great abuse of this freedom. Not every granting of independence has to end like that, however, and the virtue of the people will determine whether it should succeed or fail.

Confucius understood the problems of the Warring States period, which he lived through, as relating to a breakdown in social morality. He was correct in this conclusion. Even if the local lords of the Zhou state had declared their independence, warfare did not need to result if in fact people were virtuous.

Comparing the Warring States period to the case of Taiwan is even more distant on another point. Confucius lamented the breakdown of social morality when the local lords didn't follow the right duties and customs in how they treated the Emperor. The Emperor was truly their sovereign and they had a duty to obey him.

Taiwan's government doesn't have any kind of duty to obey Beijing. The communist party in fact were the usurpers of political power in China against the government of the Republic of China, which now governs only in Taiwan. According to this argument, it is the CCP in Beijing who created chaos by rebelling against the central authority that had to retreat to Taiwan. The government that was usurped from power is not bound by any filial morality that dictates why it should have to give its obedience to those who rebelled against it and those who came after it.

This would be like saying in the Warring States period that when the minor states defied the Zhou court, the Zhou court was then bound to become their vassal and treat the rebels with filial homage. It is like saying that the father was bound to obey the son.

The traditional Confucian ideas would actually dictate that it was the CCP that should have repented of its rebellion and given its obedience to the government in Taipei, not the other way around.

Violence is legitimate only when there is no other resort that can neutralize the threat. If there is some other way to stop the active shooter than by the sniper shooting him in the head, then that method must be used instead. If the sniper could stop him by blowing the gun out of his hand (or even shooting his hand off, without taking his life) or the police could stop him by convincing him to give up, then those methods must be used instead of taking his life. If there is some peaceful solution that can end the threat from an enemy army or a rebellion than using violence, then that peaceful solution must be used instead. Even if it means sacrificing territory, rights or honours, these things are still better to sacrifice than it is to take a single human life.

If a dangerous criminal can be safely incarcerated or otherwise rendered harmless without risk of him escaping back into society to harm more people, then capital punishment becomes an invalid tool.

Violence is legitimate only when there is a realistic chance that it will succeed in defending the lives it is being used to defend. If the enemy army is so overwhelmingly powerful

that the state has no means to stop it even with violence, then violence becomes illegitimate at that point. If the violence cannot actually stop more lives from being taken, then it cannot be used as a tool, since the reason for its justification is then no longer present.
In that case, it is better for the state to simply just surrender, run away or give up.

Wars cannot be fought for any other reasons than these and police should not use violence for any other reasons than these.
If people are not dangerous but they refuse to obey the laws, the police can arrest them, but they should not use violence unless the people in question are using violence themselves. If they use violence to resist arrest, the police can use violence to defend themselves, if other means of neutralizing the threat are not available.
States cannot invade other nations to take lands from them or to punish them and take vengeance on them. If a state has done something wrong, but it no longer poses a threat, then the state that has been wronged should leave it to God to punish the state that had done wrong. He will do a much better job at judging and punishing than human beings will do.

When using violence, it can only be legitimately applied against those who are actually engaged in or threatening to engage in violence. Civilians are not valid targets in warfare, even if they form part of the economy or infrastructure that the warring state is using to fight the war.

Violence is only valid when it is necessary. When fighting a war, the state only needs to kill the enemy soldiers that are engaging in violence directly in order to end the threat. The civilians who run the economy that is supplying the enemy soldiers can continue living, and they will pose no threat if they are not using weapons themselves.
Those who put on the uniform and become participants in the war are valid targets. Those who do not participate are not valid targets.

When fighting wars, states should attempt to develop weapons and tactics that can neutralize the enemy without actually killing them or at least not killing so many of them. If enemy soldiers can be dealt non-lethal wounds that will prevent them from fighting again, but which don't actually take their lives, then these are preferable to the lethal wounds.

Lord, we pray that you help states to use violence as they ought to use it and not as they shouldn't. We pray that loss of life can be reduced or even eliminated in warfare and in the actions of police. We ask for these things, if it is your will, in Jesus' name, Amen

XXIV: Agreements

The Catechism of the Catholic Church regarding the seventh commandment's relation to contracts and promises teaches that:
2410 Promises must be kept and contracts strictly observed to the extent that the commitments made in them are morally just. A significant part of economic and social life depends on the honoring of contracts between physical or moral persons - commercial contracts of purchase or sale, rental or labor contracts. All contracts must be agreed to and executed in good faith.

The catechism is mainly speaking about agreements regarding trade in goods and services, but this teaching could just as equally be applied to agreements between states.
States have a moral obligation to keep the promises and treaties that they have freely entered into with other states, unless it would be a moral injustice to keep them. In the book of Joshua, the Gibeonites deceive Joshua into agreeing to let them live even though Joshua was supposed to destroy them. Joshua comes to realize the deception, but he keeps the agreement all the same, because he had bound himself to it.
Just as economic life between persons relies upon people carrying out their contracts, diplomacy between states relies upon states carrying out the agreements that they have freely entered into.
If countries cannot count upon other countries to carry out their side of an agreement, then such agreements become difficult to do and the international order suffers because

of it.

Practically speaking, violations of agreements happen all the time. So many countries sign documents concerning human rights for people to which principles they pay lip-service towards, but violate them when dealing with domestic issues.

If it is a sin to keep an agreement, then the agreement does not need to be kept. If both sides to an agreement freely agree to cancel the agreement, then the agreement does not need to be kept. If the agreement provides for a way to legitimately get out of the agreement, then the agreement does not need to be kept. If the agreement was not entered into freely, then the agreement does not need to be kept. If the agreement is impossible to keep, then the agreement does not need to be kept.

Regarding agreements 'not entered into freely', this arguably would include treaties that were imposed on defeated nations in wars. If a nation is forced to surrender and give up territory, or else the other state is going to continue fighting that war and killing its people, then even if it puts its signature on the paper that gives up the territory, it is not truly bound to abide by this agreement, since the agreement was one that was done with a threat of great violence behind it. I wrote more about this topic in my book *Territorial Disputes*.

However, barring these things, states must keep their agreements and treaties. The international order relies upon this in order to function.

Lord, we pray that you help states to keep the agreements that they have freely entered into. We pray that you help us to understand your law in relation to international diplomacy. We ask for these things, if it is your will, in Jesus' name, Amen

XXV: State Enterprises

The question of what things ought to be privatized and
what things should be publicly-owned is a question that
naturally links in with the principle of subsidiarity.
The ideal is that the state should not own anything,
because the people of the society themselves will do
everything that needs to be done on their own without the
state's involvement.
However, because people can't be trusted to do this, the
state needs to intervene in the economy at times in order
to make sure that the rights of people are protected and
the needs of people are met.
This intervention includes the need to sometimes own
companies and enterprises.
For example, public utilities that the nation's economy
relies upon to function, like a system for generating and
delivering electricity, transportation networks, ports and
airports, etc. might need to be publicly-owned if there is a
possibility that these things could fail in private hands and
create grave damage to the nation's economy by that
failure.
If something is so important that the state simply cannot
risk it failing, then the state has reason for why it should
own it and not leave it to the private sector.
On the other hand, if a particular business can fail and the
state can accept this, because whatever needs it provided
for will still be provided for by others without the need for
the state, then ideally the state should not try to own it
and it should be left to the private sector.
This is from the principle of subsidiarity, since it is better to
let lower levels handle the things that the lower levels can

handle and reserve for the upper levels only the things
that are too large to be left for the lower levels to handle.
Therefore, the state should only seek to own the things
that it must own, when the society could not be trusted to
do this on its own and it is something that needs to exist.

Lord, we pray that you help states to use public ownership
as they ought to use it and not as they shouldn't use it. We
pray that the economies of nations will fulfill the needs of
all people. We ask for these things, if it is your will, in
Jesus' name, Amen

XXVI: Research

The principle of subsidiarity is also a principle to be
considered when dealing with the issue of research.
New knowledge and new discovery can provide massive
benefits for a society. Medical knowledge can help protect
the lives and health of the citizens of the state, new
technology can help improve the lives of people and help
the economy grow stronger. New knowledge about the
humanities can help people have a better understanding of
what it means to be human and it can also help in
understanding God better.
There is no way to calculate the value of research.
 It is better for people to engage in this search for new
knowledge on their own without state involvement.
However, the reality is that the society will likely not invest
as much in research as it ought to invest if it is left on its
own.
Most of the time, people invest money in research that will
seem to provide short-term economic benefit to
companies or wealthy individuals. Many things that may
improve the condition of human life on Earth for people
are not things that have an immediate price tag in front of
them that shows their worth.
When the microscope was first invented centuries ago, it
was a novelty or a hobby that was purchased and owned
by nobility who found it interesting to look at things so
closely. It was only after people began looking closer that
they discovered things like the cellular nature of life and
paved the way for modern microbiology and all of the
benefits it has delivered for the world. At the beginning,
however, people hadn't imagined how important this

invention was going to be for the world.

When society does not invest in these things themselves,
or it invests in them in a very short-sighted way, the state
has reason for why it should step in and try to invest in it
itself.
How much should it invest?

A large amount should be invested in research, since
research can give so many benefits to the society, but the
state would need to calculate how much of a burden that
taxes would be on the people to support this research
against the long-terms benefits that research would give
them and give the world.
People need sufficient wealth in order to live in dignity,
and the system of taxation should never be so oppressive
that they cannot live in dignity. As long as the needs of
people are met and they live in dignity, taxing what is extra
to this in order to help research is justifiable, since such
research could greatly improve human life.
Another factor to take into account is that good research is
not simply a matter of throwing money at it, which makes
it good. There needs to be talented people, with a true
love of learning, who want to seek out to know the world
more, who the state would support by such funding in
order to help them carry out their research. The state
doesn't have the power to make such people, but they
come naturally in the society and are created and gifted
with talents by God.
Not everyone has the same vocation and many people will
not be called to a vocation as a scholar or a researcher.
Hence, the state does not need to fund everything since

there will only be so many people who have the vocation
to do research.

Ideally, it is better for the society to support such people in
pursuing their vocations to benefit the world through
research without the need for state involvement, but if this
research they have been called to carry out is not possible
because the society will not support them, then the state is
right to step in and intervene to help it, so long as the
economic needs of the society are taken care of.

Lord, we pray that states will fund research as they ought
to do so and not as they shouldn't do so. We pray that you
help humanity to find the secrets of your creation and use
this knowledge to bring benefit to the world. We ask for
these things, if it is your will, in Jesus' name, Amen

XXVII: Expansion

Acquiring more territory can sometimes be beneficial to the state, because the resources or lands in the new territories can be used to help the state.

However, territorial expansion should occur within just means.

The only legitimate forms of territorial expansion are three sorts:

1) Where there exists territory never claimed or used by anyone previously

2) Where there exists territory that has been claimed or used by people, but the proper owners of the territory are willing to give or sell their territory without threat or compulsion.

3) Where there exists territory that has been claimed or used by people, but those people have since abandoned the territory or otherwise ceased to exist, and the land is left without a claimant.

Territory cannot be acquired through war or conquest. The original owners of the territory remain the owners of the territory until they either cease to exist or freely abandon their claim without threat.

Territory can be occupied during war, but this is not the same as having proper ownership over it. A state can occupy territory belonging to another state as a result of war and it can legitimately keep control of it until the threat to its own state is taken away, but it can never truly acquire it and make it its own territory without the free consent of the prior state.

The reasons for this are more fully discussed in my book

Territorial Disputes. But the key answer as to why this is this way is because natural law dictates that the only way a system of territory can work is if the right to hold authority over a territory is independent of actual control on the ground. Otherwise, states would not have a right to repel invaders who invade their states, since the moment the invaders took control over some territory, that territory would belong to the invaders since the right to hold authority over the territory was not independent of who controlled it. Similarly rebel armies, bandits or criminals who took over some land claimed by a state would then automatically become proper rulers of the land in their own right, since control equalled to rights to hold authority.

Furthermore, nature itself doesn't dictate a particular length of time at which right to own territory expires once some party other than the sovereign state has temporarily lost control over it. Therefore, the original state that held authority over territory remains the proper owner of that territory until it either ceases to exist or it voluntarily gives up its control over it.

It can be good for states to expand, but only if they do so by legitimate means.

Purchasing of land is a legitimate way of acquiring territory, but only if it is not accompanied by threats or violence to require the other side to agree to the deal.

Lord, we pray that states will expand as they ought to do so and not as they shouldn't do so. We pray that leaders will have a better understanding of natural law and apply its principles to politics. We ask for these things, if it is your will, in Jesus' name, Amen

XXVIII: Sporting Events

Many governments are willing to invest large amounts of
money and effort into hosting large sporting events.
There are several benefits that they can see coming from
such events, such as revenue from tourism, national
prestige, economic boosts that come from public
expenditure and even just the spirit of the event is seen to
be beneficial sometimes.

When these events lead to greater revenue and economic
benefit to the state, they can in fact be looked upon as a
kind of business investment.
Pure laissez-faire capitalism would dictate that the state
should stay out of the economic realm and simply just
provide the bare minimum needed to keep the system
going. Government investment into business would be
seen as interference in the market.
However, pure laissez-faire capitalism is an incorrect model
to understand how the system works best.
The freer a society is, the more it is able to accomplish and
the better it will function. It is better that companies
regulated themselves than for the government to do
regulation for them.
However, freedom can only be given when people can be
expected not to abuse it. Hence, since in most places,
companies will do abusive things without regulation, they
thus do not deserve to be given freedom and must be
placed under controls.
But freedom does not mean that the government should
not itself get involved in the economic life of the place.
The principle of subsidiarity dictates that lower levels

should be allowed to make decisions that their level is capable of handling. However, there may still be things that are simply too big for the lower levels to be able to handle.

Projects that require investment that go beyond what the private sector can reasonably afford and still make profits in the short-term may require the government to invest in them if in fact these projects are deemed as beneficial to the society.

Large sporting events could be one such example of this, depending on the circumstances. Sometimes the lower levels of society may handle everything needed to be financed in order to run such events.

A lot of countries when approaching these kinds of events seek to make their country's team as the best.

The tenth commandment teaches not to covet. When countries compare themselves with other countries, this can be a way of violating this commandment.

In China, just a quick scan through the news that appears on the internet each day and you can find loads and loads of stories that are basically just attempts to compare China with other countries. When other countries do worse than China, this can be cause for celebration. When other countries do better than China, then it means China must advance further.

China is not unique in this either. Many countries try to compare themselves with their neighbours or with other states in many fields and they take pride when they do better than other nations.

Donald Trump's America and Communist China both had something they share deeply in common: they are both strongly concerned with making their nation as number one in everything in the world.

All of this is a violation of the tenth commandment that teaches not to covet what other states have.

The commandment not to covet is not to say that one cannot want to have more in life. If you don't have a nice house, but you wished that your house was as nice as someone else's, this is not really what the commandment is about.

The commandment is concerned about people whose relations with others are affected by the way that they covet what rightfully belongs to the other, leading them to envy and grow jealous of others. It is concerned with people who compare themselves with other people because they want to be better than others.

The golden rule explains what this sin is. People would not like if their friends felt happy when they suffered misfortune and their friends enjoyed benefit, hence, if one does not wish for others to treat oneself this way, then one knows not to treat others this way either.

There is nothing wrong with a wish to have more, but there is something wrong with a wish to have than others, when this wish is because one wishes to surpass them and be greater than them. It is against charity to act like this. Hence, when engaged in these kinds of competitions, to try to be the best one can be has nothing wrong with it. But to seek to be better than others does have something wrong with it. People should not get upset when their team loses to the other team, but they should celebrate within the spirit of the sport itself for all who competed.

States that put on such events should still recognize the

system of priorities when spending money on them. Although economic benefits may come from such events, they should not be considered a higher priority than human life itself or the salvation of souls.

If the investment being put into such events could be used in other places where human life's survival needed it, then the state has no justifiable excuse to spend the investment on this.

In 2008, in the Beijing Olympics, the Chinese government spent a massive amount of money to hold what was called the most expensive Olympics ever. In order to impress the world with China, they built huge projects to hold the games, using large amounts of concrete and steel to build these structures with a lot of money.

In 2008, shortly before the games were held, China had a major earthquake in Sichuan. Thousands of children died when their schools that were built with a cheap construction budget collapsed and crushed or buried them.

China perhaps had enough money to hold both an elaborate Olympics and have better construction for the schools, hence to say that one came at the expense of the other is not really correct. However, the political will to put on a show for the world and impress the world with China's greatness was apparently much stronger than the political will to ensure that students were going to school in structurally-sound buildings.

The safety of those students should have been a higher priority than impressing the world, since the priority of human life trumps other considerations with the exception of salvation.

States should not be putting on these kinds of events like

this if they are not going to spend money in places that the survival of human life itself depends on it.

States should not seek to be the best or better than others. They should seek to serve God and to do what is right and what is beneficial to their citizens.
If investing in such events is determined to hold palpable benefits for the people that would make the investment worthwhile, then the state can spend such. But it should not attempt to do so because it wants to compare itself with other nations and be better than them. Nor should it attempt to do so if there are other things of higher priority that it is leaving neglected.

Lord, we pray that leaders will host sporting events or other big events as they ought to do so and not as they shouldn't do so. We pray that you help countries to stop comparing and envying other nations, but to seek to love God and other nations as they love their own. We ask for these things, if it is your will, in Jesus' name, Amen

XXIX: Racism

In Exodus, Moses told the people of Israel that the Lord
was slow to anger and abounding in steadfast love. He
would visit the iniquity of fathers upon their children to the
third and fourth generation, but he would show mercy to
those who loved Him to the thousandth generation.
Adam and Eve committed sin and they were punished with
death for it. Their children also died as well. We believe
that original sin came from Adam and Eve and that all of us
have inherited death and a broken nature from their first
sin.
I have sometimes thought about whether this thing that
Moses said about the third and fourth generation
inheriting the sins of the forefathers and the original sin of
Adam and Eve could be referring to the same thing?
When God cast Adam and Eve from the garden, what is
recorded doesn't actually have God saying anywhere that
'now all your descendants shall suffer these
consequences'. Actually, He is quite specific and He refers
first to the snake, then the woman and finally to the man.
And when He gives them punishments, He is talking to
them specifically. He tells the snake that he shall eat the
dust, he tells Eve that she shall have pain in childbearing
and he tells Adam that he shall work in the sweat of his
brow to make his bread. He doesn't say anywhere in the
text that their descendants will have to suffer these things
as well.
But the Christian doctrine of original sin is that all people
inherited the effects of their first sin. Paul wrote in the
New Testament that in Adam all men die (and in Christ all
men live).

God doesn't say to Adam and Eve that descendants will suffer for the sins of the fathers. But Moses, speaking on God's behalf, says this to the people of Israel.

The people of Israel had gone through the Passover and God had killed all of the firstborn of the land of Egypt with His angel. This would have certainly included children and newborn babies too. They were being punished not for their own sin, but for the sins of their parents.

David's newborn son that he has through adultery died because of David's sin.

Some people have difficulty with the idea of 'ancestral sin' because God is essentially holding people to account for sins that their ancestors did, which they are innocent for. In other words, the idea of it has God punishing the innocent who have committed no crime. Abraham pleaded with God over Sodom and said that God could not condemn the righteous with the wicked, and God agreed with Abraham and said that as long as some righteous remained in the city, He would not destroy it for their sake.

However, if we really think that 'ancestral sin' is a barbaric concept and incompatible with what we know about God, then how can we still believe in original sin? Original sin is essentially an ancestral sin that encompasses the entire human race.

All people suffer, are tempted and die, because of the actions of their first ancestor, which they themselves are innocent for. How many babies are there in history have died in infancy or children who have died in the womb as miscarriages? And yet this doctrine says that they would not have died if Adam had not eaten the fruit.

God cannot punish the innocent. The story of Sodom tells

us this. So how can any of this be reconciled to this?

I don't think of original sin as being a punishment, nor do I think of ancestral sin as this either. I will use an example to explain:

Suppose you had a rich man who had three children. He wasted all of his money on prostitutes and gambling, and in the end, he had no money left to bequeath to his children when he passed away. The children then ended up suffering because of their father's choices. One of them was unable to afford medicine and he ended living with a sickness that he could have otherwise avoided. One of them remembered the life he had lost before and was tempted to steal money and go into crime in order to get wealthy again quickly through dishonest means. The other one went to work and had to struggle in labour much of his life to make ends meet.
Now, these children suffered because of their father's actions. However, they didn't suffer because someone was punishing them, instead they were suffering because the inheritance that their father should have left to them was lost through their father's bad choices.

Adam inherited a paradise from God. He inherited a world where one could live forever without suffering and death. He lost this paradise for himself when he committed a sin and was cast out from it. Whether Eden was a place or a state of being or a perfect nature... whatever it was, Adam once had it, but he lost it by his sin.
When Adam had children, his children could not live in this paradise, because Adam could not pass it on them, since

he had already lost it.

God provided a world without death and suffering to all humanity. But the way it was meant to be transmitted was from Adam to his descendants. Adam lost that and therefore his descendants lost it too. God wasn't punishing Adam's children for what Adam had lost. But He was punishing Adam by letting his children suffer these consequences because of his sin.

I talked about this more in my book *Witchcraft* but in short, love requires that we are sensitive to one another. What this means is that it is possible for us to be helped or to be hurt by one another. If no matter what I do, you are still just as happy, then it is impossible for me to have a relationship with you. Only when it becomes the case that if I fail to love you that you suffer and your happiness depends on whether I love you, is it then possible for a true relationship to exist between persons. It becomes impossible for love to actually exist, because there is nothing I can truly do for you if you are equally happy no matter what I do.

If no matter what Adam did, his descendants still enjoyed eternal happiness in paradise, even though he lost it, it would be impossible for him to have a relationship with them. It would be impossible for him to really do anything for them, since they would be equally happy whether he tried to hurt them or to help them. Therefore, it had to be necessary that his descendants would suffer if Adam himself failed to obey God's law. Therefore, by the same logic, descendants of sinners thus need to suffer if their ancestors sin, because only when that becomes true is it possible to say that the ancestors are capable of loving their descendants. Only when it becomes possible not to love, is love ever capable of existing.

Therefore, ancestral sin makes sense. We all suffer things in life when other people sin and we ourselves are innocent. It is natural that we should suffer like this, because God designed us to be able to be helped or hurt by the actions of others. If what other people do can cause me to suffer, even when I am innocent, why should it not be the case that what my ancestors do cannot cause me to suffer, when I am innocent of what they did?
One of the punishments that God places upon sinners is that He makes it so that the people they care about will be among those who will suffer for what they did.
God visits the iniquity of the fathers upon the children, but this is not a punishment for the children. It is a consequence for the sin that the children are suffering themselves, but it is not a punishment.

But the Bible doesn't only talk about ancestral sin bringing consequences on descendants. It also speaks about 'ancestral blessings' where the descendants are blessed because the ancestor did something pleasing to God. Abraham pleased God, and His descendants were blessed because of it. David pleased God and God made promises to him that his descendants would rule the house of Israel forever. Noah blesses his three sons and it is often interpreted as meaning that the descendants of each of them would be blessed in this way. Israel similarly blessed each of his twelve sons in a different way and those blessings are also interpreted to mean that they extended to the descendants of these sons as well.

The concept of 'ancestral sins' or 'ancestral blessings' paves the way for racial divisions. This conclusion might seem surprising, but I will explain its logic:

If God blesses Abraham's descendants and gives them something that He doesn't grant to all the other nations of the world, it means that God is treating people differently on the basis of their race. God reveals Himself to the Israelites, but not to the Egyptians or Persians, not because of any merit or lack of merit, but because the Israelites had an ancestor that pleased God and received a promise from God, and the other nations did not come from that man. If God blesses the descendants of particular persons and that blessing is enjoyed by all the descendants of that person, regardless of their personal merit, but those who did not descend from that person do not receive that same blessing, then once those descendants multiply and become clans, tribes or nations, it essentially means that God is going to treat people differently and give a blessing to one racial group that He isn't equally giving to the other. Moses said that the Lord has mercy upon those who love Him to the thousandth generation. People are different races because they have different ancestries.
If God blesses the descendants of one person more than another, because that person pleased God more than the other who was more sinful, once those descendants multiply, they become a nation or race and the end result would mean that God is giving people of one race something better than the other, not because of their merits, but because of their race.

In the New testament, Jesus meets gentiles at several

points who want His help and He tells them that He cannot help them, because 'it is not right that the children's food should be given to the dogs'. Only once they showed their faith in Him was He willing to grant their requests. His primary mission was to the house of Israel, because they inherited the promises given to Abraham and his descendants. The people of Rome, the people of South America, the people of Japan, etc. didn't get to have the Son of God walk in their midst, preach to them and do miracles for them, because they didn't have Abraham as their ancestor; they belonged to a different race.

The Jews didn't deserve for God to be so close to them because of their own merit. But because they were born under a promise, God revealed Himself to them in ways that He did not show Himself to other peoples.

The idea that God visits punishments upon later generations and the idea that God does not punish the innocent do not have to be contradictory if they are understood in a particular way.

God gave paradise to Adam and Eve, and they had the power to pass this on to their descendants, but they lost it by their sin. The fact that their descendants after them were not born into paradise is not really because God is punishing them, but it is because their ancestors lost what they should have passed on as an inheritance and thus the descendants suffered as a consequence.

God blesses people with peace, prosperity and happiness, and God would allow for this blessing to be passed on to their children if they served Him, but when they sin against Him, this blessing is not able to be passed on and their descendants after them have to suffer war, poverty and cruelty instead, not because they had done something wrong, but rather because their ancestors lost what had been given to them and which they should have been able to pass on.

This is the only correct way that a concept of ancestral sin could be understood. God cannot punish people for things that their ancestors do, but people can suffer because of their ancestor's sins. Their ancestors either inherited something and lost it, or they themselves did something that had consequences that fell on their descendants.

Suppose if you had two brothers, both of whom had wives and children. They had a father who gave them equal amounts of wealth and materials and then sent them to two different islands. The one brother was abusive, taught his children a bad example and had many vices that his descendants after him acquired as a result. The other brother was good, taught his children a good example and had many virtues that his descendants after him acquired as a result.

Let us suppose that the children have offspring and eventually over many generations they turn into two different races. On the island that came from the bad brother, the society is filled with vices and it lives in poverty, warfare and constantly has troubles. On the island that came from the good brother, the society is filled with virtues and it develops much wealth, excels in learning and builds a great civilization.

When the people of the race that was prosperous cross the ocean to find their long-lost relatives on the other island, they will find that there is a great difference between them. They may even be led to believe that they possess some kind of natural racial superiority over the other, simply because it looks like their people have so much more than the other people.

They both started from the same place, but because of virtue and vice, one group became a race that was very prosperous and the other became a race that was very poor.

The prosperous race becomes greedy when they see the weaker race and they decide to colonize them, enslave them and take advantage of them, because they don't realize they are of the same family and they conclude to themselves that this is the natural way that things should be according to nature. In fact, they are of the same nature, equal in dignity to each other, but the vices and virtues passed on by so many generations leads to a wrong conclusion of a natural superiority that must exist.

They both were given equal gifts at the beginning. The father gave both of them the ability to become prosperous and strong, but one of them lost the opportunity that was given and the other took it and became blessed. The sins of one did have penalties passed on to his descendants, but it was not because God was punishing the descendants that they received these penalties. Rather the ancestor failed to pass on the blessings he had received and left his descendants without it.

God rewarded Abraham because of his faith by blessing his descendants. This blessing would mean that God would treat one race differently than another because of their ancestry.

However, this is not a punishment either. If God gave the blessing to Abraham's descendants as a reward to Abraham, it is not a punishment upon other people of other ancestry if He didn't give the same blessing to them as well.

If God had never blessed Abraham, these other nations would have still been without this blessing. The fact that He gave the blessing to one race apart from others, does not mean He is punishing the other races, but rather that He is rewarding one and not rewarding the other. If He hadn't rewarded the one, the other still may not have been rewarded at all.

Furthermore, the way that God blessed was not that this blessing was something that was to be exclusively enjoyed only by Abraham's descendants. Rather this blessing was to first come on this one race, and the other races of the world were going to be blessed through the blessing that had come upon this one race. Once Christ died for all people and the Word of God was proclaimed throughout the world, this blessing did then get extended to others from the Jews who had first inherited it.

Isaac inherited more from Abraham than Ishmael did or his other children did. And Isaac's seed received a blessing that was greater than the seed of Ishmael, although both were blessed. God had a different blessing that was given to Ishmael, although it was inferior to what was given to Isaac.

This is essentially racial discrimination, because over time once these groups split from each other and turn into different nations and racial groups over the course of many generations, the logic is that one race is blessed more than another because of the blessing that came upon their ancestor.

The people of Israel inherited the promises of Abraham, but other peoples did not. In the modern world if we had said that one racial group should get better treatment than another, we would call this racial discrimination. But the logic presented in the Old Testament on these things is essentially discriminating between people on the basis of ancestry, and thus it is discriminating between people on the basis of race.

God clearly does discriminate between races in the Old Testament. He does give a reward to one over another because of the ancestry of the person and not through their own merit. But this discrimination is not an evil or a negative thing.

If a person dies and he leaves his inheritance to his own children, rather than to other people, no one would think that this was an unjust form of discrimination. If a person left his inheritance, not just to his own immediate children, but to all his descendants after him, rather than to other people who did not descend from him, how is this morally any different from passing it on to simply his immediate children only?

But, if all of his descendants after him become a race separate from the descendants of other people, this would effectively mean that he is discriminating between one race over another. Abraham's blessing given by God and passed on to his descendants is essentially this, however.

During the time of the Atlantic slave trade, some people justified the enslavement of Africans under the belief that they descended from Canaan (the son of Ham, grandson of Noah). In the Genesis narrative, Canaan was cursed by Noah and made into a slave of his uncles Japheth and Shem. Some people historically interpreted that black people were from Canaan and therefore they fell under the same curse, which meant that they were bound for slavery.

Moses said that God had mercy upon the descendants of those who loved Him to the thousandth generation, but He would visit the sins of fathers onto their children to the 'third and fourth generation'. In other words, the ancestral blessing is something that goes on forever, but the ancestral curse has a time limit to it. Obviously, even if Canaan was the father of all Africans, there has been more than 'three or four generations' since the time of Canaan to the present, so these words from Moses do not seem like they quite fit this.

However, let us assume for the moment that the words from Moses and what happened to Adam and Eve's descendants are indeed the same thing. Adam and Eve's descendants have obviously continued for more than three or four generations as well, so that doesn't seem to work.

I have a solution for how this can be reconciled, however. Adam and Eve sinned, and so they suffered death, suffering and temptation as a result of their sin. This temptation then led them to sin more. Ultimately the decision for anyone to sin is from themselves and not even the devil can force anyone to sin, but the first sin made it easier for people to then commit further sins. It caused it so that it was hard to be good and easy to be bad.

Adam and Eve sinned, and their descendants sinned more because of the effects of the first sin that they inherited from Adam and Eve.

Now, let us suppose that these words of Moses are correct even for Adam and Eve. It would mean that the sin of Adam and Eve was only punished to the third and fourth generation. However, once the second, third and fourth generation began sinning themselves, the effects of the sins by these later generations would then in turn be visited upon their own descendants to the third and fourth generation. And the descendants of those people in turn would sin, and then that would be brought to their descendants, and so on.

Adam and Eve's first sin then in one sense only was visited to the third and fourth generation, but in another sense it caused a chain effect to take place where each succeeding generation then sinned afterwards and caused the punishment to continue on to their own descendants. Adam and Eve's sin caused their descendants to sin more easily, and then those descendants did sin, and thus cause their own descendants to sin more easily as well.

If this is the correct understanding, it would mean that if you ever were able to get three or four generations of people to exist that never gave into temptation and remained perfectly sinless, then the children that were born to them would be born without the taint of original sin. Perhaps if these people did sin but they made reparations for their sins in some sufficient fashion such that God did not visit their sins upon their descendants, the same effect would also occur.

I could point out here that the only people that the church believes to be born without original sin are Jesus, Mary and John the Baptist, and all of three of them were of the same extended family. Jesus and Mary had no original sin from their conception, while John the Baptist had no original sin at least from some time when he was in the womb. Elizabeth, the mother of John the Baptist, was the cousin of Mary. Mary's parents, Anne and Joachim, are both counted as saints by the church. John's father Zechariah committed the sin of disbelieving the message of the angel Gabriel, but Zechariah was punished on the spot for this and he repented of it.

Theologians will explain why it was necessary for Mary and Jesus to be born without original sin. But why was it theologically necessary for John the Baptist to be born without original sin?

John's baptism was not the sacramental baptism, but he baptized with water. And even if it was the sacramental baptism, the church teaches that a person does not need himself to be baptized in order to legitimately baptize another person. If an unbaptized person, still bound to original sin, uses water and the correct formula while having the intention of baptizing another person, then that baptism he gives is a true sacrament.

John's mission at the Jordan perhaps could have been done by someone who was born with original sin, just like how all the prophets of the Old Testament were born with original sin and yet were guided by the Spirit to speak God's words to the people.

Perhaps the reason why he was free from original sin though was not because of a theological necessity, but it has something to do with this idea I am invoking that original sin only gets transmitted to the third and fourth generation, and we all possess it because every generation since Adam and Eve have repeated their sins, but somehow this was broken in the ancestral family of Jesus and Mary. This is just speculative though and it could certainly be wrong.

If this model concerning how original sin and ancestral sin is correct, the same effect should actually happen anywhere in the world. If a family in the 21st century went three or four generations living holy lives without any consequences of their sins being carried over to the next generation, then at the end of the three or four generations, the next generation that is born would then be born without original sin, just as were Mary or John the Baptist.
I am speculating, but maybe this hasn't happened, because the holy families in history that had generation upon generation devoted so much to God ended up with the later generation becoming monks or nuns, and not having further progeny after that.

Keep in mind, being born without original sin doesn't mean that they would be born without suffering. Mary and John the Baptist both suffered in their lives, as did the Lord Jesus. But it would mean that the consequences for sins that came from ancestry wouldn't fall upon them. They would still suffer the effects of sins committed by other people, but not the ancestral sins.

If that is true, then the effects of Canaan's sin could only continue to all of his descendants if his descendants kept committing the same sin that earned this punishment upon their ancestor and thus carrying the consequences of the sin on to their own descendants. The sin of Canaan seems to be that he looked upon Noah's nakedness and thus failed to have the filial piety that he ought to have had for his grandfather. Moses says to honour your father and mother so that your days may be long in the land that the Lord will give to you. This commandment has a promise attached to it, unlike the other commandments.

The implication of the promise is that those who fail to honour father and mother will not live long in the land that God gives to them. Indeed, Jacob lied to his father and said he was Esau, following this he had to go away from the land promised to Abraham and live as a servant for several decades in exile in another land. Honour your father and mother and you will live freely in your own land. Fail to honour them and you will be a slave in a foreign land.

I wrote more about this in my book *Witchcraft*, however, putting it simply, nations are made strong or weak depending on how much people are following this commandment to honour and obey those that God has placed over them. The nations that colonize other nations are stronger because they have adhered to this commandment, while the nations that are colonized are weak because they have not adhered to it.

Following from that, perhaps it is true that people in Africa hadn't followed the fourth commandment and thus had made their nations and societies weaker, such that it became possible for them to be bullied by foreigners. And maybe there is a possibility that this failure is something that goes from generation to generation back to Canaan or some other ancestor they had.

Ham, Canaan's father, was considered to be the ancestor of Africans, and he had three other sons besides Canaan. The curse was only explicitly placed on Canaan, although maybe it was placed on Ham and Canaan was mentioned by Noah so that it was understood it was going to carry on to his sons?

In African history, there were strong states that appeared at various times, and I am not simply just referring to North Africa or Egypt by this. It may be true that African societies were weak and this was because they hadn't followed the fourth commandment, but that doesn't mean it was something that went on forever and that it encompassed all of them without exception from some ancient ancestor for all time... otherwise, how would one explain some of the stronger African kingdoms that existed at various times in history?

Furthermore, I should also point out regarding the Atlantic slave trade that it was a certain portion of African societies that was exported abroad as slaves. Many of the Africans that went into slavery were sold by other Africans to European traders who gave them European goods in exchange. There were trading forts that existed along the African coast for centuries during the age of colonialism. These forts existed in lands ruled by Africans who sometimes saw an advantage in the presence of the European traders.

The rulers of those lands were not the ones that were sent into slavery on plantations. It was the weaker members of their societies that were traded and sold into slavery. The rulers of those places were not at risk of being enslaved or ruled by the white man and it wasn't all Africans who were subject to this kind of racial oppression as was borne by those that got sent into the ships across the ocean.

It wasn't until the end of the 19th century that Europeans took over Africa and put an end to all of these African states, and then they only ruled it as colonies until the late 1950s to the mid 1970s, when all of these countries became independent one after another. The age when Europeans ruled all of Africa as colonies was actually short enough that it could have fit into a single human lifetime. Britain ruled Hong Kong and Singapore longer than it ruled Kenya.

When speaking of the entire group, the Amerindians in the Americas were far more oppressed as a whole than were the Africans, because the Amerindians had all of their land taken away from them and, in some places, they were enslaved in huge numbers, killed in huge numbers or at least reduced to a second-class status in the colonies.

The Africans, by contrast, were largely free and independent from the time of Columbus all the way to the end of the 19th century, at which point they became subject to domination for about 80 years, after which they regained their independence and ruled their own land again; the same has not happened to the Amerindians of the Americas who largely live as underprivileged minorities in countries run by the ancestors of Europeans.

Some of the Africans were enslaved by their own people and then sold to Europeans for tobacco, guns or manufactured goods, but most of them were not. Africans are actually not really the group that would fit the most if we were to say that there was some racial group in the world that was forever bound for slavery from ancestral sin, who was destined to be 'a slave of slaves', as Noah said regarding Canaan.

'Canaan' obviously was referring to the nation that the Israelites displaced by their invasion and genocide in the book of Joshua. A logical assumption in the narrative is that the descendants of Canaan were referring to these people. The Israelites destroyed the people of Canaan and took their lands for themselves. The Amerindians in the Americas received a treatment from their conquerors that had similarities with this conquest, although the Africans, on the other hand, only suffered those sorts of things to a much lesser degree.

Leaving this issue aside for a moment and returning to the main topic of this chapter: ancestral sin and ancestral blessing produces racial division.
If God is going to bless the ancestors of some people and not the ancestors of others, and if certain sins are going to be transmitted and repeated from generation to generation among certain groups but not among all groups, then yes, this will create the effect that some racial groups are going to be stronger, wealthier and more dominant than the others.

Christianity was largely concentrated in Europe for a very long period in history. God will bless those who serve Him and love Him. Perhaps white people have enjoyed so many benefits and privileges greater than other people because they had ancestors who loved and served Jesus Christ, while people of other nations did not know Jesus Christ and thus didn't receive the same blessings. Moses said that God has mercy for a thousand generations upon the descendants of those who love Him.
The people of Africa, Asia, the Americas, etc. largely didn't

know Jesus Christ or the Christian faith up until the past few centuries. The blessings that came upon the people of Europe perhaps didn't come upon them, and the end result is that we see white people are privileged in ways that other racial groups are not.

It is often easier for a white person to get a better job and a better education than a person who belongs to another racial group. They can make the same mistakes, commit the same sins and do the same evil things as people of other groups, and yet not receive the same severity in consequences for their actions.

A white drug dealer in Canada is treated far more leniently when caught by the authorities than a drug dealer in China. A person who doesn't try hard at school or who does poorly in work is still more likely to have a better future if he is a white person in America than if he was a black person in America who did the same thing.

If many of the white people in western society were placed in the same conditions as people in the slums in India were subjected, they would perhaps die; they wouldn't survive like the Indian slumdwellers do.

Social theorists try to explain this by saying that there is hidden racism or 'structural racism' that fills society that causes people to more greatly favour one racial group over another. What I am saying about ancestral sins and blessings doesn't negate this. The hidden social preferences that favour one group over another may be something that is caused by this spiritual reality regarding ancestral sins and blessings, but the ancestral sins and blessings could be doing more to cause one group to advance more than the other than simply through hidden preferences of people.

For thousands of years Europeans worshipped Jesus Christ
and to some degree, they obeyed His commands. If God
blesses the descendants of those who love Him, this is
perhaps an explanation as to why white people are so
privileged in the world.
Ancestral sins, however, could only be accounted for things
that happened in the previous three to four generations of
their families, not for all of time. If an entire nation
commits some kind of sin collectively and it occurs within a
time recent enough that the people who committed it
were within three to four generations of those currently
living, then yes it would mean that this nation would
collectively have this sin of their ancestor visited upon
them. And this might in turn weaken their own ability to
resist temptation and lead them to commit the same,
similar or perhaps even a worse sin. That in turn would
then lead to the effects being inherited by the future
generations after them.
Many nations of the world could be affected by such things
in invisible ways. This in turn could cause them to be less
privileged or oppressed than other nations.

If racism was the only factor that could explain why white
people had such dominance throughout the world, then it
has trouble explaining why it is that that even came about
in the first place.
If Europeans lived in Europe and Africans lived in Africa
and Amerindians lived in the Americas, etc. before any of
them had much contact with one another, racism doesn't
really explain why one group became stronger than the

other. Racism doesn't explain why one group developed the means to subdue the rest of the world, while the other parts of the world didn't achieve that kind of strength. Racism doesn't explain why Europe was capable, from a technological, economic or military perspective of subduing all these places around the world in the ages of colonialism and imperialism and creating a world where white people ended up on top. Racism doesn't explain why the other races were not strong enough to do the same thing. All that racism explains is how it is that races that didn't belong to the dominant group had trouble ascending or improving their position in a world after it was constructed and dominated by the dominant group. God's blessings last for a thousand generations and His punishments go to the third and fourth generation. If we considered as to what this means on a mass scale within a world where certain ethnic groups and nations worship Jesus Christ far more than others, this could explain why you would have such a big disparity growing over time.

In Africa itself, Ethiopia has continuously been a country with a large Christian population since ancient times. During the colonization of Africa, Ethiopia was the only place in Africa that successfully resisted European attempts to take over control, while the rest of the continent was carved up by different colonial powers.
It was only in the 1930s, when Mussolini sent his army in to invade Ethiopia that Ethiopia briefly lost its independence under Italian occupation, only to regain it at the end of World War II. If God had mercy on the Europeans to allow them to advance so much even though they didn't deserve it for the sake of ancestors they had

who worshipped Jesus Christ, then the same logic ought to apply for other parts of the world that worshipped Christ as well, outside of Europe. Ethiopia's history perhaps bears up this theory on this point.

A non-white nation that honoured God for long periods should become privileged as well to some degree if this theory is true.

If this idea is correct, however, there are some further interesting implications that could come from it.

Today, many people in the west have left behind the faith of their ancestors and no longer worship Christ. At the same time, the church in Africa has grown tremendously, and the foci of the church has moved away from Europe more and more towards other parts of the world. If these speculations I am making are true, then the Philippines should eventually become a powerful country in Asia. Africa and Latin America should become places of great wealth and power. What happened with Europe becoming a place of power, wealth and advancement, should eventually happen in these places as well, and the nations that have turned away from Christ and God sinfully may eventually become subservient to them as well. As Noah said to Canaan: 'a slave of slaves'.

This may take a very long before it is realized, however. And it is quite possible that these places will break faith long before they reach that point, as temptation wears them down.

In Biblical times, the Israelites looked with envy at the nations around them, since those nations seemed to have so much more than they did. The Israelites were not as rich or powerful as the Egyptians, the Babylonians, the Assyrians or any of these other great civilizations that surrounded them. However, they had God as their possession.

Although it took time, perhaps we could look at them today and consider. The Jews of the world today around the world are in a far more dominant, wealthier and more powerful position than the people of Egypt or Iraq.

In the Middle Ages, Europe was less advanced, politically weaker and poorer than the Islamic or Chinese empires. However, eventually they reached a point where they dominated not just these places, but the entire globe and erected a world according to their own values and ideas. Today, likewise, you see the Philippines is seemingly much weaker and poorer than Japan, Korea or China. You see Africa and Latin America filled with many impoverished people. Given time though, if what I am predicting is correct, they may share in the same fate that the Jews or the Europeans shared in and there will come a day when people will look at those places as places of great prosperity, power, advancement, wealth and culture.

Moses said in Deuteronomy that if the people of Israel loved the Lord and obeyed His commands, they would possess the gates of their enemies, people would borrow from them and they would not need to borrow from anyone, they would drive their enemies before them, etc. But if they did not love the Lord and did not obey His commands, then their enemies would take their lands, their crops would fail, they would be poor and in want, they would suffer many things, etc.

Does God want people to dominate, conquer or enslave other peoples?

No, he doesn't want this.

However, if He has mercy upon a people and lets them become stronger, more advanced and more gifted in many fields, they will have the ability to choose to use these blessings for good or for evil. If they choose to use them for evil, God is not pleased with this. However, the fact that they gained these blessings to begin with rather than remaining poor, weak or undeveloped is perhaps related to this idea of ancestral blessings and ancestral punishments. God blessed the Europeans with so many gifts. These gifts and blessings were perhaps because they and their ancestors served Him, while other parts of the world did not know Him. The Europeans who gained these blessings then had the choice to use it to help the world or to use it to harm the world. The ventures of colonialism included both help and harm, although the principal motivations of the colonialists were often selfish ones rather than holy ones.

Now, in the present time, they tend to be the parts of the world losing the faith, while the church spreads in the areas they once colonized. Perhaps if they had used their talents for good, rather than evil, they would have received even more blessings; perhaps the current waves of temptations leading people to apostasy in the west are itself a kind of divine punishment against them to let them fall into these temptations that lead them to collective apostasy, because of all the sins that their ancestors had committed which still have echoes down to this day.

This idea of ancestral sin and blessing doesn't negate the

idea that virtue makes a state strong either. Rather it works in conformity with it. The more virtue a state has, the freer its people can be and the greater strength it can reach. At the same time, the ancestors of people who loved God will also bring blessings upon the descendants and the ancestors of people who sinned will incur punishments upon their descendants.

A person can live a holy life and die a saint, while still having inherited original sin from his birth and having to go through suffering in life as a result of punishments that he inherited from his ancestors. Similarly, a nation can be virtuous and honour God now, thus allowing it to be freer, while also having to pay the consequences visited upon it by God for crimes of past times.

It may also be true that different kinds of blessings and different kinds of punishments will be incurred for different kinds of ways that people served God or sinned against Him.

When the Pope threatened Martin Luther with excommunication in 1520 (prior to his actual issuing the excommunication the following year), he spoke of the Germans in his letter as a nation that had inherited the Christian empire from the Greeks, and that they had done so well in getting rid of heretics before that point and had shed so much of their own blood fighting against the heretical Hussites in Bohemia.

Including the crusades against Islam, the crusades into Eastern Europe by the Teutonic knights, the crusade against the Hussites, the wars fought by Germans soldiers to serve the Holy Roman Emperor against Ottoman Turkish invasions, the wars fought by Germans on either side of the wars of religion… there is actually a very long history of Germans who took up arms to fight for (what they believed was) God's cause.

As long as what they did was in good conscience, God may bless them for what they did. Perhaps in later times of history, especially in the late 19th or 20th centuries when German military strength seemed so great, this could itself have been a blessing that they had gained from God. In other words, God had blessed their ancestors who loved Him enough to fight for His cause, and thus God blessed their skills at fighting wars. Their ancestors inherited this blessing as an undeserved mercy, and they then had the power to use it for good or for evil.

The Jews inherited the scriptures and the covenant with God because of their relation to Abraham. But they also had the power to use this for good or for evil. They had the power to use the scriptures to interpret them in such a way as to recognize that Jesus had come, or to interpret them in such a way as to abuse their true meaning and declare that Jesus was not the Messiah. They would not have had the revelation from God had it not been for the mercy upon them for the sake of Abraham, but it was up to them to use this gift for good or for evil.

Look at the amount of work that Italians, Spanish or other Europeans did in order to decorate their churches with art. It was from these nations that some of the greatest painters and artists also came from. God perhaps blessed their skill as a mercy upon their ancestors who had had such devotion to using art to honour God.

Many of the great European universities were originally

institutions created by the church for studying God. They wrestled over the meaning of scripture, they pursued a deeper knowledge of who God was and what His Word meant, and perhaps God blessed them so that modern science and advancement would come from them as well for the sake of what their ancestors had devoted to God. Seek God and His kingdom first and everything else will be added to you. Seek to understand God's Word first, and He will make you understand everything else too.

Every aspect is included in this. Cuisine, art, science, technology, military skill, navigation, institutions, wealth, power, etc. are all part of this. The people who had used their skills that God gave them to serve God in one way or another perhaps gained God's blessing upon themselves and upon their descendants so that their descendants would excel in these fields, even if they had long forgotten the faith that had motivated their ancestors to use these things to serve God.

It is like the story of the talents. The master rewards those who used the talents wisely by giving them more than what they had at the start. If nations use the skills and strengths they have been given to serve God, God will perhaps bless them to make them even better.

Once they have more, then they can use those things for good or for evil. God blesses their skill in art, and they use that skill to keep honouring Him or to use it to make images of things that are sinful. God blesses their knowledge of the world, and they can use that knowledge to serve His will or to do things that are wrong.

Trying to explain dominance of white people by invoking

racism is an insufficient explanation. White dominance contributed to the idea of racism, since people tried to explain why it was that white nations seemed so much more advanced and powerful than other parts of the world, and the idea that there was some kind of inherent superiority seemed to explain this in a way that some people may have been comfortable with.

Racism's advancement concurs with Christianity's decline. Europeans and westerners believed less and less in Christ, and they needed to explain their superiority over other races by invoking ideas of natural superiority on the basis of race in order to account for why they were so dominant. This racism then did create a world where those of other races had difficulty advancing in the system dominated by the dominant race, and racism can then explain why those races remained so far below.

However, why should it have been that white nations became dominant in the first place, why it wasn't ships from African nations that came to Europe and put down their symbols to declare England or France as New Zululand or New Kongo, is not just from racism, but it is from history and development. Why they achieved that level of history or development is perhaps partly explained by the fact that their ancestors had won God's mercy by serving Him.

All people are ultimately equal. If white nations became strong and powerful because they had served God for such a long time, then the same thing should also happen to nations composed of other races that do the same thing. And just as the whites were able to use the power and development they had achieved for good or for evil, the same would also be true of other nations that accomplished the same thing.

Serving God does not necessarily have to be an issue of serving God by name either. A nation that isn't Christian, but which followed God's laws as they are written in nature perhaps would also gain the same kinds of ancestral blessings as well that would carry on for generation to generation.

East Asian cultures, for example, have precepts in their traditional morality that have some correspondence to Christian teaching on the fourth commandment. Japan, like Ethiopia, was never colonized or ruled by foreigners until its defeat in World War Two.

Ancestral punishments have another issue of interest for them. Some nations issue apologies or pay reparations for things they have done wrong in the past. Many nations don't do this and refuse to ever admit any wrongdoing except in perhaps superficial ways, but some nations do this.

The purpose of issuing apologies and making reparations is not simply just to mend relations with other people, but it is also intended to mend a relationship with God.

If God only brings consequences for sins to the third and fourth generation, however, then that would mean that from the fifth generation and prior, those sins are no longer remembered and people do not need to repair the damage from them, since the consequences for those sins would no longer have any direct relation on those living in the present.

John Paul II apologized to the Greek Patriarch about the crusaders who attacked Constantinople in the Middle

Ages. However, the sins of those crusaders were well beyond the third and fourth generation from the present. He made this apology to mend the relationship with the Greek Orthodox church. But if what I write here is true, God would not have required this sin to be repaired any longer, because the consequences for the sin would no longer bear on the present.

Nations should do reparations for their sins, because doing such reparations may take away from the punishment that they deserve for what people had done in the past. If a nation truly repented and made reparations for all that it did, perhaps it could entirely escape from all the consequences that would have fallen upon it for its sins. However, these reparations do not need to be for every last thing that people have ever done. Rather it should be to the third and fourth generation prior to the present. For example, the United States should make reparations for the sins of its society against black people both in modern times and in the period before the civil rights movement of the 1960s, however, it shouldn't need to make reparations for slavery, since slavery is already past this mark of the 3rd and 4th generation for almost all people living in the United States today.

Japan and Germany should make apologies and reparations for crimes committed in World War II. Britain and France should not need to make apologies and reparations for crimes committed in the Opium Wars in China.

The Catholic church should apologize for abuse of minors by clerics in recent history. It should not need to apologize for what the Inquisition did to Galileo.

Now, they don't need to apologize and make reparations,

but that doesn't mean that they can't. However, simply observing that God does not remember the sins of people further than the 4th generation, the implication is that those sins even further in the past no longer need to be repaired.

What does the 3rd and 4th generation mean? Why this as opposed to some other marker? Indeed, why say 3rd and 4th as opposed to simply just '4th'?

I wonder if it perhaps could be something to do with what God says in Genesis when He declares that 120 years will be the life of a man. Indeed, the oldest people who have ever lived in the world in modern memory didn't get much further past 120 years. It seems like perhaps it is very difficult or maybe even impossible to get a person to live much further past that number.

A generation, in which one group of children essentially replaces the previous generation in its management of the society, could be about 30 to 40 years perhaps. Today it is longer, although in that time period, maybe this would be about the right amount. Three or four generations, with each one being between 30-40 years, comes out at about 120 years.

If no person on Earth is gong to live much longer than 120 years, then it means that the sins that happened prior to 120 years ago were not committed by any person alive today, nor was there any person alive today who was directly victimized by those sins.

Maybe this is a good rule for nations to follow. They should seek to make apologies and reparations for all things that were committed by their governments, their state institutions or their citizens for 120 years prior to the present. But for things even older than that, it is better perhaps just to leave them to history, count them as things that happened in the past and no longer recall them as crimes.

Ultimately God uses all the sins and crimes of the world to create something good in His divine Providence. There is no need to keep assigning blame and fault forever, since God will turn them all to good once the consequences have faded away.

I wonder if maybe some specific events in world history could be interpreted within this framework of 120 years as well. For example, the Covid-19 pandemic occurs almost exactly 120 years from the Boxer rebellion in China, when Chinese militias massacred Chinese Christian and foreign civilians, while foreign soldiers then invaded and plundered China, while forcing it to pay decades of reparations. These events left deep scars on China that contributed to the later chaos and struggles that China went through in the 20th century. The time in which the devil may accuse all of these nations for their crimes and call for punishments upon them for it, would have maybe expired from 2019-2021, according to this idea if 3-4 generations equals roughly 120 years. Maybe the things that the world and China felt in the Covid-19 pandemic was one final punishment upon China and many nations for what happened in those events in 1900.

The beginning of the Napoleonic wars in the 1790s roughly corresponds to 120 years prior to the beginning of World War I in the 20th century. The loss of most of the British colonial possessions in the 1950s and 60s corresponds roughly to the 120 year-mark since the First Opium War when Britain invaded China in order to open itself to trade, including trade in opium. Many people don't know it, but most of the Victoria Crosses that were awarded to soldiers of the British Empire up to the time of the Second World war were made from captured Chinese cannons in the First Opium War.

I don't know if these were punishments that came upon these nations after 3-4 generations, however, it seems possible to me to speculate.

I am not implying that God is going to punish nations exactly 120 years after they do certain things, but rather according to the words of Moses, He will only punish nations for things that occur perhaps within the past 120 years from the present, with the last opportunity for the devil to accuse the nation before God occurring at around the 120-year mark. The devil perhaps moves quickly when he knows that his time is short.

However, if what I have written is true, nations could free themselves from the consequences of their sins if they face up to their pasts, make apologies for it and do reparations on account of it.

China paid reparations for the Boxer rebellion for decades to other nations, although this was forced upon it and China later adopted a narrative of portraying the eight-nation alliance of that war as being villains, while itself was a victim. Maybe because it paid reparations for what it did that this itself lessened whatever punishments would later come upon it for what happened in that war.

Nations that admit to their faults truthfully, which do not whitewash them, apologize for them and make reparations for them, perhaps are able to avoid many calamities for themselves. They break the cycle of just going back and repeating the same kinds of sins again that will simply just leave more consequences to their descendants.

If this above theory is true, it will be interesting to see what should happen at certain points of time in the 21st century in front of us. The World Wars, for example, would have the last punishments for them falling from around 2034-2038 and 2057-2065. The world right now is still perhaps receiving punishments for the sins committed in those wars, but perhaps the devil may seek to make his last accusations before the clock runs out for when he may accuse us at those points.

Regarding 'racism' there is more to say on the topic here. In the Bible God distinguishes between people based on their ancestry and He gives blessings or punishments in relation to what their ancestors did. In the laws of Moses, God actually commands people to discriminate on the basis of race.
He commands them to massacre the Canaanites who live in the land of Canaan. He commands them to allow certain ethnic groups into the assembly of His people but not other ethnic groups.

Deuteronomy 23: [3] The Ammonite and the Moabite, even after the tenth generation shall not enter into the church of the Lord for ever: [4] Because they would not meet you with bread and water in the way, when you came out of Egypt: and because they hired against thee Balaam, the son of Beer, from Mesopotamia in Syria, to curse thee. [5] And the Lord thy God would not hear Balaam, and he turned his cursing into thy blessing, because he loved thee. [6] Thou shalt not make peace with them, neither shalt thou seek their prosperity all the days of thy life for ever. [7] Thou shalt not abhor the Edomite, because he is thy brother: nor the Egyptian, because thou wast a stranger in his land. [8] They that are born of them, in the third generation shall enter into the church of the Lord.

The Lord here says that even to the tenth generation this punishment falls upon the Ammonites and the Moabites. However, this perhaps could be explained in the same way as I explained the sin of Adam and Eve extending to all human beings by replication, even though the consequences shouldn't fall past the third and fourth generation.

This is true racial discrimination, however. If the church today passed a canon law that said that the descendants of some ethnic group couldn't take the Eucharist forever, because their ancestors had persecuted the church in their country, we would not hesitate to say that that was racial discrimination.

In fact, as I referenced earlier, slave owners in the American south justified slavery of blacks on account of what they supposed was the ancestral crime of Canaan,

who was punished with being a 'slave of slaves'.
However, that is exactly what Moses, under God's
direction, gave to the people of Israel in this part of his
laws.
As I mentioned, Moses also called for the annihilation of
certain nations too. He called for the Israelites to massacre
the Canaanites. Later in the first book of Samuel, Samuel
ordered Saul to exterminate all of the Amalekites on the
basis of what the ancestors of Amalekites had done to
Israel in the wilderness, and he curses Saul and declares
that the kingship will be taken away from him and given to
another after Saul neglects to fulfill this command to
exterminate. In the narrative, God does as his prophet
then predicts, by raising up David in Saul's place and
making him King of Israel.

These men were God's prophets acting at God's command
and these things were written in the Holy Scriptures
according to God's inspiration.
Obviously, it contradicts our modern values as they
concern racism or genocide.
How should we understand these things?

I already talked about the genocides earlier back, but
discussing simply the issue of discrimination on the basis
of race deserves more attention here.
Martin Luther King Junior said that he had a dream where
people would not be judged by the colour of their skin, but
by the content of their character. I think this sentence
should serve as a definition for what racism is: the
judgement of people according to their race or nationality,
as opposed to their actual merits.

Simply being a particular race doesn't make you a good or a bad person. All races were created by God, and all that God created was good.

Now, why is it wrong to judge people on the basis of their race or nationality, as opposed to their actual merits? The answer is because it is wrong to cast judgment on the basis of appearances and not on the basis of truth. Christ Himself told us not to judge like this.

John 7:24 Judge not according to the appearance, but judge just judgment.

If we think that someone is a criminal or they have some kind of vice because they belong to a particular race or ethnic group, then we are judging on appearances and not on the basis of truth. We would not like other people to judge us on the basis of appearances, therefore we should not do such to others as well.
However, this is not just true of race, it is true of all forms of judgment by appearances. I can't assume that because someone is homeless, for example, that the person is lazy, or has substance addiction or is a thief, etc. I can't assume that because someone didn't get to mass on Sunday that they didn't have a valid reason for why they couldn't be there. I can't assume that because an employee was late to work that this means that he doesn't take his job seriously. I can't assume that because someone forgot to call that this means he doesn't respect me.
We don't know what a person is intending and what they think in their hearts. We don't know why a person does a particular action or why he failed to do a particular thing.

The person who is homeless might be homeless because he lost all of his money through no fault of his own and now no one will give him a job. The person didn't get to mass on Sunday might have gotten a dispensation from the priest because of some necessary work he does. The person who was late to work might have had an emergency at home. The person who didn't return my call might have run out of power on his phone.

We tend to assume that we know what people are thinking and what people intend, but we don't know this. Most human judgments tend to be based on appearances, and yet that is exactly the kind of judgment that Christ teaches against.

Mind you, those judgments could be correct. Maybe the person is homeless because he became addicted to alcohol. Maybe the person who didn't go to mass on Sunday doesn't take the sabbath seriously. Maybe the person who was late to work had no valid excuse and wasn't a serious worker. Maybe the person who didn't call me back thinks I am not worth speaking with.

However, it is wrong to assume those things are true, when one doesn't actually know and can't actually see what a person thinks in their hearts. Even if they do turn out to be true, it is wrong to assume that they are true without actually knowing oneself.

It is wrong to assume that a person is responsible for a moral fault without being able to know what the person's intentions were or the whole circumstances that surrounded what a person chose to do. However, at the same time, it is almost impossible to carry out a system of justice and laws if one needs to know the intentions of the person in the heart in order to convict someone.

The law of Moses did not require that the judge knew what the person's intentions were. The law of Moses only required that there were at least two or three witnesses that could verify that a person carried out a particular action and that was enough to convict. This did not stop innocent people from being punished. It is certainly possible to get two or three false witnesses that give corresponding wrong testimony to convict someone. However, this was the standard that was adopted for legal cases.

In our modern legal system, we have a principle of 'innocent until proven guilty' and trials for serious crimes often involve a jury panel that needs to reach a unanimous agreement before a person can be convicted. Even though the principle behind this is that a person should not be convicted unless there is no reasonable doubt that they could be innocent, however, the reality in practice is that if this principle was truly followed literally, almost no one would ever be convicted. It is always reasonably possible for multiple witnesses to be collaborating together to wrongly testify against someone. It is always reasonably possible for the evidence supplied by the police or other agents to be fabricated with ill-intent. There is nothing 'unreasonable' about thinking that such things are capable of happening in a sinful world.

We assume that the evidence and the witnesses are true, but is there ever a way to make sure that there is no reasonable possibility that they could be false?

Moses didn't say that no one should be convicted until there is room for reasonable doubt, because in reality this principle doesn't work. Modern legal systems do not follow

this principle, even if they say they do; possibilities which
remain reasonable, a jury or a judge will discount or ignore
in order to sentence someone they think is most likely
guilty. A legal system that sincerely followed this principle
would end up convicting almost no one, and many people
who would harm society would be left to continue harming
it, since it would be impossible to punish them.
Moses gave a simple formula that had to be passed in
order to have sufficient evidence to convict someone in a
case. This formula could end up causing innocent to be
punished as well, but this was considered sufficient for
society to function.
Legal systems have to be like this. A legal system run by
fallible human beings will always result in some innocent
people being punished by the system. However, it is still
better to have the system in place than it is to have no
system and the world turning to a violent chaos.

Now, with regard to race and ethnicity, different groups of
people may have a tendency to engage in some behaviours
more than other groups. Muslims usually don't eat pork.
People in China are less likely to take time off at Christmas
than people in Germany. People in Afghanistan are less
likely to know how to drive a car than people in Texas.
People in Siberia are more likely going to be prepared for
cold weather than people in the Philippines.
These are simple examples that most people would agree
with. No one considers it racism or unfair discrimination to
assume that because someone belongs to one of these
groups, that they are more likely to engage in one of these
behaviours or that we can make these assumptions about

them in practice.

However, moral virtues and moral vices are similar to this. People don't all follow God's laws equally. Some are more virtuous; some are more sinful. Groups of people can also be more virtuous or more sinful as well collectively.

People in 1930s Germany were more likely to be making anti-Semitic statements than people who live in 21st century New York City. This isn't because being German made them intrinsically anti-Semitic, but it was because the culture and society around them acted as a strong temptation that pulled them collectively towards this kind of vice more than other places and times.

Culture and environment influences people. Being a particular racial or ethnic group doesn't make you a good or a bad person, but the culture and environment that this race or this ethnic group collectively lives within will cause the people living inside to be influenced in particular directions. With regards to moral evil, it will serve as a temptation to the group collectively and this will draw the group to collectively be likely to engage in a particular vice than other groups that didn't experience the same temptation in their own environments.

Some cultures value telling the truth more than others. Some cultures have greater respect for parents and elders than others. Some cultures have more deference for authority and respect for laws than others. Some cultures respect the rights of people to hold differences of opinion more than others. Some cultures respect human life and shun war more than others. Some cultures respect the institution of marriage more than others. Some cultures hold more shame on nudity than others. Some cultures are more patriarchal than others. Some cultures are more embracing of diversity than others. Some cultures value learning more than others.

Being a particular race or ethnic group doesn't make one have a different moral character, but the culture that being a member of such a group causes you to be influenced by will have an effect on your moral character and everything else about you, and this is something that can happen collectively to groups of people.

It may be true that people of a particular group tend to engage in a particular vice more than others do, but that still doesn't allow for people to assume moral faults for particular individuals on the basis of the group to which these individuals belong. That is because when people pass judgments on the basis of a person's ethnic or racial identity, since they assume that someone of such group is likely to have a particular fault, they are ultimately passing judgement by appearances and not in accordance with Truth. The judgement could be true; indeed, they may be right in thinking that certain groups are more likely to engage in certain vices than others, however, they can't know for a particular individual whether that person is guilty of a certain vice just because he belongs to such a group.

Titus 1: [12] One of them a prophet of their own, said, The Cretians are always liars, evil beasts, slothful bellies. [13] This testimony is true. Wherefore rebuke them sharply, that they may be sound in the faith

Paul wrote to Titus that people from Crete were lazy and they were liars. He was actually quoting a Cretan poet named Epimenides of Knossos, who lived many centuries before, and agreeing with those words.

This is undoubtedly what in our modern ideas we would refer to as a racial slur. He was describing an entire ethnic group of people as being liars, evil and slothful. However, this was written by Paul, a saint and apostle of Jesus Christ, and it was recorded in the New Testament of the Bible because it was inspired by the Holy Spirit. Thus, we can attribute what in our modern sensibilities would be a racial slur to the Holy Spirit of God.

I don't mean to say by this that the Holy Spirit is evil. Rather I mean to say that this behaviour is not a sin, otherwise it wouldn't be here. It is not Paul or the Holy Spirit I am faulting, but it is our modern sensibilities that are wrong, which see such behaviour in making such statements or general judgments over a group as necessarily evil.

Paul hasn't here made any comment on a particular individual. It doesn't say that he met a particular Cretan and assumed he was lazy and a liar because he was a Cretan. Paul rather just spoke of the collective group of Cretans and made this judgement about them, because this was true. It likely wasn't true of every last Cretan absolutely, but it was probably something that was commonly true of many Cretans in Paul's time period, otherwise, he wouldn't have spoken this and written it under the Spirit's inspiration.

When Moses ordered for the Canaanites to be destroyed, he listed the sins that they were guilty of in Leviticus 18 and 20. Was every last Canaanite guilty of those sins? Probably not, but as a society and as a whole, perhaps it was something that most of them were either guilty of doing, guilty of approving others of doing or guilty of at least keeping their silence about it. Thus, Moses ordered for them all to be destroyed, even though innocent people who did right would have been included among them. Moses gave laws that told people to discriminate on the basis of race in certain matters. This was not because being a particular race made one person more virtuous or sinful than another, but it was because those groups collectively had engaged in things that merited such measures to be blanket given to them.

Any system of justice will cause innocent people to be punished. Any legal system will be unfair to people within it. This is true with or without laws that discriminate on the basis of race.
Any legal system will have unfairness and injustice, because it is impossible to ever be sure whether the person being punished is truly guilty or not. However, those injustices and those unfair things have to be tolerated, because the alternative is not to have a legal system at all, since human beings don't have the ability to know what is in the heart of each person and run a legal system that is fully just and fair. Only God alone could do that, and He will do that at the final judgment.

It is not wrong to have laws that discriminate on the basis of race, ethnic identity, religious affiliation, national origin, etc. Our modern sensibilities reject this, but our modern sensibilities are not wholly based on the Truth.
Allow me to give some examples of when such forms of discrimination could perhaps make sense.
In the United States, people are free to own guns. Some

people use this freedom responsibly and either don't own guns or the guns they own are kept safely. Other people, however, use this freedom irresponsibly and the guns they own end up by used for murder either by themselves or other people.

Now, the rate of gun murder in the United States is not uniform all across the country, nor is it uniform across all racial and ethnic groups. Published statistics show vast differences in the per capita gun murder rates in different parts of the country. Black people and Hispanics are also much more likely to be victims of gun violence than white people, according to published statistics. This isn't because they are being killed by police, except in a minority of instances; in the vast majority of cases, they are being killed by criminals with guns.

While there are published statistics showing the racial background of the victims of gun violence in the United States, it is far more difficult to find statistics that show what percentage of the perpetrators of gun crimes belong to different races. This is perhaps because the sociologists and statisticians think it would be unethical to publish such information, as it could be used to degrade particular ethnic or racial groups. However, the fact they consider it unethical to publish such things is itself perhaps evidence that the information they have encountered is not producing a conclusion they want people to consider, which may mean that we can infer that a disproportionate number of those who kill with guns in the United States also belong to these minority groups.

Now, the people who want to end gun violence in the United States often call for more restrictions on gun ownership. This is a logical conclusion, since if people cannot handle their freedom responsibly, then more controls need to be given.

But, suppose that you discovered that the same result could be achieved by simply just restricting or taking away the right to own a firearm for certain parts of the country or for certain groups of people. If that was the case, then it would be better to restrict those groups or those regions, rather than to restrict everyone, since unequal freedoms is still better than no freedom for anyone.

For example, if you found that you could greatly reduce gun violence by making it illegal to have guns in urban centres of the United States, especially places like Chicago, Los Angeles, New York, Houston, Miami, etc., while you still allowed people in rural areas to have guns. Or if you removed the right to bearing arms to all the males in the United States, while females were still permitted to bear arms, and you found that this caused the gun murder rates to plummet, since the vast majority of those engaging in gun violence were male, while at the same time females have a greater need for a gun for personal protection than males. Or if you removed it from particular age groups, so that a person had to be at least 50 years old before they were allowed to bear arms, since the vast majority of those engaging in gun violence are under that age.

In the United States, maybe removing the right to bear arms to people below a certain income bracket might cause gun murder rates to drop sharply as well, since most gun violence tends to be done by those with below average income.

There are plenty of white people who engage in gun violence in the United States, and while statistics don't exist, it is a fair assumption that even if minority groups have disproportionately higher rates, the majority of gun murders in the United States are still probably done by white people, due to the fact that the majority of people in the country are white. Hence, while banning guns for minorities would dent gun violence, much of it would probably still remain.

Now, any attempt to do such a thing in the United States, however, would be met by considerable backlash by many people. People might engage in violence in response to such measures and thus they could create greater problems to the maintenance of social peace than what the measure was attempting to do. Thus, pragmatism would dictate not to use such a measure, unless the groups in question could be convinced to peacefully acquiesce to being treated unequally like this.

These measures are discriminatory, but they would be better to be done like this than to simply ban or restrict guns for everyone, since it is better to preserve freedom for those who will not abuse than it is to take away freedom from everyone. I suspect that the best measure of those I listed above would be letting different regions to determine whether or not they would allow their locale to let people bear arms and implement the second amendment. The urban centres of the US where there are the highest gun murder rates also tend to be the parts of the country where people are most opposed to gun ownership; many people who lived in those places would probably welcome it if they were allowed to restrict the second amendment rights for those who lived in their localities.

When particular groups are more likely to engage in

particular crimes than the rest of the population, it makes more sense to take away the freedoms for those groups, in order to stop the crime, than it does to take away the freedom uniformly for the whole population.

Israel occupies the West Bank, for example. Christians in the West Bank are far less likely to become suicide bombers than Muslims. If Israel decided to discriminate and allow people who were publicly confessed Christians to drive or walk through their check points freely, while all the Muslim Palestinians had to stop and be searched each day, this could be better than just making everyone have to be stopped and searched each day.

Drug traffic is far less likely to be crossing into the United States from Canada than it is from Mexico to the United States, as is illegal immigration. The United States guards one border much more than the other, not because just being Mexican makes you more likely to be a drug smuggler or a law-breaker than being Canadian, but because the patterns of behaviour among the collective whole of either group are different and merit a different response.

Gender also works like this as well. If one gender is more likely to engage in a crime than the other, then it is better to take away the rights of that one gender than it is to take it away from everyone.

According to statistics that are published, college-aged males are much more likely to engage in drunk driving in the United States than college-aged females and older people. If greater restriction was then placed on the rights to either enjoy alcohol or to drive cars on college-aged males, this would perhaps be better than placing the same restrictions on both males and females, or on the whole population. For example, if you changed the drinking age, so that American females could start drinking at 21, but males had to wait until some later age, or they couldn't get a license to drive a car until some point later in life, this would be better than if you just put the age later for everyone and restricted everyone.

There is nothing inherently wrong about states passing laws that discriminate between people on the basis of different categories.
If certain groups in a particular place are typically engaging in a particular harmful behaviour, there is nothing wrong with the state making laws that specifically target these groups in order to stop the behaviour.
More freedom is better than less freedom. But you cannot give freedom to whom it cannot be trusted. If a state finds that freedom on a particular issue can be trusted to a particular group without them generally abusing it, but the state finds that giving the same freedom to a different group will lead them to abuse it, why should the state take away freedom from all?
If the problem can be solved by taking a freedom away from a particular group of people, but the rest of society retains the freedom, then this is better than if freedom were taken away from all, since more freedom is better than less freedom. This would mean discrimination on the basis of the group to which you belonged, but it would not be wrong.

In some societies like the United States or South Africa,

racial segregation was widely used in order to separate different races from each other in society. Officially, this was based on an idea of 'separate but equal' where each race was to be treated equally, but would not occupy the same space as the other. So, they had segregated schools, segregated military units, segregated public facilities, etc. However, in reality the state did not treat them equally but gave much better attention to the dominant whites over the blacks and other races that were treated with segregation.

People who supported this system perhaps did so because they didn't like the idea of their children going to school with the children of the other races and didn't want to be near the people of the other races. In other words, they didn't want to be close and make friends with these people.

There is nothing wrong with making more friends with people of one's own race than with those of other races, but there is something wrong in rejecting friendship with people of other races because they are people of other races. All people should love one another. It is OK to give more love to those closer than to those that are distant, but to keep people away and reject friendship with them because they are distant is not good. This was essentially what segregation was meant to do.

Mixing races together in a school and introducing students to people who are different from them is something that assists an educational environment, rather than taking away from it. If there was truly an educational value in it, perhaps because one group of students was far advanced over the other even though they were the same age bracket, this wouldn't need a strict racial segregation to solve it. Merely doing an aptitude test of some sort and then dividing the students according to their ability into one school or another would be sufficient for this. The end result could still be a racially segregated environment, depending on the results of the test, but it would not need to be strictly so, since either race could still theoretically end up in the other school on the basis of the test.

If public swimming pools or buses somehow operated better when people of different races stayed away from each other, then there would be an argument for why such segregation was a good thing, but as it was, segregation didn't serve any such purpose other than enforcing a distance because some people didn't want to be close with those who were different from them.

Furthermore, when the state uses its own resources unfairly to help one group over the other, when the state had an obligation to help all of its citizens, this is also wrong. Segregation essentially was doing this in practice, even though if in principle it was claiming that the races were to be treated equally.

Discrimination is heresy in modern political thinking; there are people who would demand special training or education given to bring one to confess and repent of this heresy and the forfeiture of one's rights to good employment as well, like how heretics of past times had the rights of their property revoked and were publicly ostracized. But discrimination is not heresy in the eyes of God and our ephemeral society and its ideals will eventually die too and be replaced with something else, just as history will always prove.

Discrimination is a tool long used in statecraft and used even with God's inspiration in the Bible. It is not an evil thing, just as long as it is used correctly, like all things. It is because it has been used so abusively in the past that we count it as an evil thing.

Affirmative action measures used today and similar things that are done to advance the cause of coloured peoples over white people are themselves forms of racial discrimination, which the society largely accepts and justifies on the basis that they are designed to serve the oppressed rather than the oppressors.

Affirmative action and similar measures discriminate on the basis of race, but they are not called 'racist' or 'racial discrimination' because they are seen to be just by those who hold power and who maintain a narrative that they themselves are not engaged in racial discrimination.

Is there any essential difference from the perspective of principle in this to what happened before?

Whites used laws and other measures to discriminate against black people, on the grounds that they believed such measures were just as well. They also didn't think that what they were doing was something evil. They considered that black people had been responsible for a crime that their ancestor Canaan had committed and therefore that meant that they deserved to be treated like this.

When those arguing in favour of affirmative action justify it by saying that the ancestors of modern white people have engaged in things that produced inequality to black people living today and therefore it is right to discriminate in favour of the black person, the concept is actually little different ultimately from what was used before. It is invoking the concept of ancestral sin of a group of people to justify some kind of discriminatory measure against the descendants in the present.

In actuality, their adoption of a kind of discrimination on the basis of race, their adoption of a justifying narrative that invokes ancestral sin and a natural justice, their adoption of implicit beliefs that being white makes a person racist or racism is only a problem for white people, their adoption of beliefs that whites defending their own race against abuse or injustice is itself racist, their assumption that a particular white police officer is guilty of racism when he uses some kind of force against a black person because the officer is white, etc. ultimately is their own adoption of the kinds of tools that were once used in the past, which they considered to be wrong. In a certain way, they are ultimately vindicating that the racists of the past were correct, since they take the same sorts of tools and make them their own.

If anyone thinks I am writing this because I am saying that affirmative action is racist and should be dismantled, then the point I am making still hasn't become clear.

I am saying that affirmative action is racial discrimination, and I am also saying that racial discrimination is not necessarily wrong; it has a right usage and wrong usage, like all things.

There is nothing inherently wrong with racial discrimination. There is nothing wrong with judging that particular groups of people collectively are more likely than others to engage in certain behaviours or have certain traits. There is nothing wrong with using these tools in statecraft, but like all things, they must be used in the right way.

Affirmative action could be argued to be a good use of such tools, because it helps to serve the poor and oppressed in particular parts of the world. It gives an unfair advantage to those who are often born with less and have a harder time advancing, in order to help give them more opportunities to escape poverty and live a dignified life.

This is a key point where affirmative action is not the same as the racial discrimination of the past. Since affirmative action is using such tools to try to uplift people who are largely on the bottom, while the tools that were used in the past was used to try to push people down who were on the bottom.

Some people are upset about affirmative action today because it is in fact a form of racial discrimination, even if it is not meant to be oppressive.
After all, there are people who are in racial minorities who are doing quite well from a socio-economic perspective and they benefit from affirmative action, while there are also people in dominant racial groups who are doing poorly and they are hurt by affirmative action.
I think an easy way to solve this would simply just be rather than to use affirmative action to benefit a particular racial group, to creatively redesign and use the same measures in order to benefit those whose parents and grandparents fell below a certain income threshold or something like this; the end result in countries that use affirmative action

today would still be that a large body of the beneficiaries
of such a program would be part of the historically
oppressed groups, but it wouldn't be absolutely so.
I don't fault the people of today for using such tools, nor
do I necessarily fault people of the past for using such
tools. God granted power to the people of the past and
used them to serve a purpose. He gives power to those
who control society today to likewise serve a purpose. And
He will give power to those who control society in the
future to serve a purpose.

Moses used such tools at God's command. Paul makes
such judgements under the Spirit's inspiration.
There is nothing wrong with racial discrimination in itself, it
is just a question of how it is used.
God created all the races and everything God created was
good. Whether you are white, black, yellow, brown or red,
you should honour God who gave you your racial identity
and be proud of it as one of His children.
Every person that God created is beautiful, good and
wonderful in the way that they were created. Humanity is
God's handiwork. To say that someone that God created
was inherently ugly, evil or bad, is to insult God and this is
a sin.
God gives different gifts to different people, and perhaps
He gives different gifts to different races. One race might
be better in some things than another, but the other race
will also be better in different things than that race; and
together they can make something beautiful for God.
The same is true of other categories. God created the
different genders. He created the different ethnicities, the

different languages, the different characteristics that people have which group them into one group or another, and all that God made was something good.

Being a particular race doesn't cause anyone to have any particular moral fault. However, the cultures that different races or different groups contain may influence those who are part of that group collectively to be more likely to go into one particular sin or the other.

Recognizing those realities and discriminating between groups of people in a way that is meant to serve justice is not a sin. Discrimination is possible on certain levels, but people must still not judge others by appearances.

Moses decreed to discriminate people on the basis of race for entering the assembly, but not to do such discrimination in the conduct of criminal trials. If someone was accused of breaking the law, it did not matter who his father was or who his ancestors were, all that mattered was whether there were witnesses or not who could confirm that accusation against him. You could not assume that someone was guilty of something because they belonged to a particular group and those who do such are using the tools of racial discrimination in an unjust way.

A black man who was assumed guilty of a crime and hanged because he was black was an unjust use of such tools. A white person today when he is assumed to be a racist because he is white is also an unjust judgment.

A policeman cannot assume that a particular black man carrying a knife is the one who killed a victim because he is black and he is carrying a knife. Nor can a public who wasn't there at the scene that day assume that a particular police officer shot a particular unarmed black man because that officer was a racist acting under racism or disregard for human life and not under a legitimate reasonable belief in a potential threat, even if it turned out to be wrong. Even if it were true that the black people were more likely to engage in particular crimes because of the culture that influenced them, or even if it was true that the white people were more likely to be racist because of the culture that influenced them, one cannot assume that a particular individual is guilty of something just because they belonged to one group or the other.

One can judge that groups of people are more likely to engage in some behaviours than other groups. One can legitimately make laws to discriminate between people and give people different rights or privileges on such bases. But one cannot assume that a particular individual is guilty of any particular crime or vice because he belongs to a particular group, without first knowing evidence against him specifically, because that then becomes judgement by appearances, which the Lord teaches against and to which He himself fell victim.

The fourth commandment teaches to honour father and mother. We ought to love all people in the world, but we should put our own parents first ahead of others. God is more important than our parents and we owe Him everything, but what we owe to our parents is more than what we owe to the rest of the people of the world. Helping your siblings, your children and your relatives is also part of this, since we show our love for our parents and our ancestors by serving these other people who are closer to us in our own family. There is nothing wrong with helping your own family more than you help those outside your family. The New Testament itself teaches this and it says that whoever does not take care of his own family is worse than an unbeliever.

People who belong to the same ethnic group or the same race as us are often closer to us in family than those who belong to other ethnic groups or races. All the human race is one family that came from Adam, but we are closer or further from each other on the basis of which branch of the family that we came from.

God's law commands that special love should be given to one's parents over that of other people. This love for parents also means that one should treat one's own siblings and relatives with something more special than other people.

Now, extending this outwards, why would it be that a tribe of people who had shared family and ancestry should not also be obliged to treat members of their own tribe with a special love over that of people not belonging to their tribe? Or even further, why should it be that people who are of the same race and a shared ancestry should not do the same?

In modern ideas, this is considered to be racism once it is extended outwards to that point, however, morally speaking it is really no different from giving special attention to those who belong to one's own family, which the law of God in fact commands.

Giving better treatment to people of one race or another is not a sin from this perspective. The way that one honours one's own ancestors can be to give a special love to those who descend from those ancestors.

All of us come from the same ancestry, but we are more distant or close depending on our racial heritage and family background. We all have an obligation to love one another and deal justly with one another as members of the same family, but we have a duty to give such love in a special way to those who are closer to us in family than to those who are further away from us.

Acting as an individual and helping out people of your own race or your own ethnic group more than those who are outside, I think, has nothing wrong with it as well, since it is also a way of serving those who are closer to you in family than those who are farther away from you.
There is nothing wrong with individual people helping their own race before helping other races, just as there is nothing wrong with individuals helping those in their own family before helping those outside. If a Frenchman owns a company, and he wants to hire French people to work for him before he hires North Africans, because he wants to help those who are closer to him in the human family, there is nothing wrong with this, anymore than there is something wrong if he chose to hire his own near relatives over strangers. Nor is there anything wrong with a Chinese owner who preferred to hire Chinese or a black owner who preferred to hire blacks.
Acting as an individual, this has nothing wrong with it; acting as a government, however, is a different issue.
The government is acting on God's behalf for the common good of everyone and it can discriminate between groups, but it shouldn't do so on the basis that those who hold power in government want to help those who belong to the same group as they do, since they are acting as

stewards of God's authority over the world, who is equally the Father of all and not just the Father of the particular group that is holding the most power. There are races and ethnicities closer to you than other races and ethnicities, but there are no races and ethnicities closer to God than other races and ethnicities; He is equally the same Father of all of them.

Government acts in His place when it receives the mandate to govern, and it must work accordingly, which means it can't help out those who are closer to the people holding the office more than it does for others.

Be that as it may, quite a number of states in the world do this. All across the world, the group that holds power in the state tends to help others of their group the most. This often leads to conflicts, civil wars and ultimately may cause the group holding power to eventually lose it. God grants stewardship to those who serve in government and He can also take it away and give it others, when they abuse what they were given.

A government can legitimately discriminate between its citizens and non-citizens. If it is going to help its own people first before it helps other nations, there is nothing wrong in this, since that is it its duty. But it doesn't have a right to discriminate among the people that God has given it stewardship over, because the particular individuals holding the authority granted by God want to serve those who belong to their own group first.

There is much more that can be written about this issue, but I'll leave it here for now. In short, I repeat that discriminating between people on the basis of their group is not wrong in itself, but like all things it has a right use and a wrong use. I've tried to explain here what the difference is.

Lord, we pray for an end to unjust discrimination of people. We pray that states will enact laws that are just and not punish those who are innocent. We pray that people will use race and other categories to discriminate when it is appropriate to do so and not when it is inappropriate to do so. We ask for these things, if it is your will, in Jesus' name, Amen

Conclusion:

The church is not meant to run the state, but it is meant to teach and proclaim the gospel. However, all things in society, including those who run the state, are obligated to obey the gospel that is taught by the church.
If a society ever completely obeyed this gospel, politics would no longer be necessary.
For those reasons, I don't expect there to ever be a state or a government that obeys the gospel perfectly, for if there were, that place would already be a paradise and it would no longer need a government.
I believe that every state will inevitably violate the gospel, whether in small or great ways. Eventually these violations will lead to the destruction of every state in its own due time. Small violations, when left uncured, inevitably become big violations. Venial sins eventually turn into mortal sins when they are not done away with and they are instead repeated so many times.
People have to die because of sin, states must also come to die because of sin.
The paradox of power is that human sinfulness is what causes the need for states to exist, since sinful people cannot be left to live together in peace if they are not controlled, but at the same time human sinfulness is also the reason why every state eventually corrupts itself and is destroyed.
Christ had the solution to this paradox in the foundation of His own kingdom. Human kingdoms need to exist because of sin, and sin is also what destroys them. The kingdom of God is created by love, and love is what sustains it forever. Human kingdoms have the paradox that they must be

destroyed for the same reason that they exist, but Christ's
kingdom is sustained by the same thing that created it.
This is why His victory over the world and over all powers is
also inevitable.
All earthly kings will eventually cast down their crowns and
bow beneath His feet, all authorities and powers will be
brought down, all states will eventually have an end to
them, but His kingdom will outlive them all and continue
for eternity.

Lord, we pray that your kingdom will come in this world.
We pray that you help all people everywhere to love God,
love neighbour and to do your will in this world. We ask for
these things, if it is your will, in Jesus' name, Amen

All Glory to God